BY LOVE (

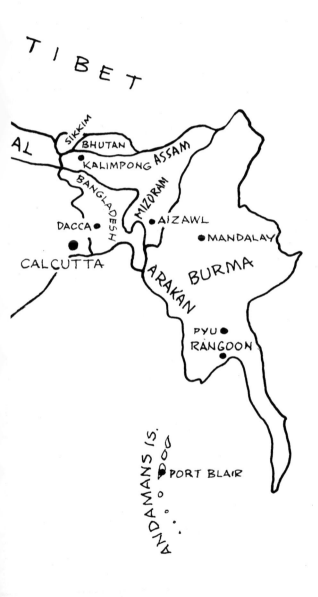

BY LOVE COMPELLED

The Salvation Army's One Hundred years in India and adjacent lands

Solveig Smith

Salvationist Publishing and Supplies, Ltd
117-121 Judd Street, London WC1H 9NN

©1981 The Salvation Army
First published 1981
ISBN 0 85412 385 7

Mrs Commissioner SOLVEIG SMITH
is a Salvation Army officer who has served in India, Burma,
Great Britain, Pakistan, Japan and Denmark from where she
retired with her husband, Commissioner Don Smith. She is
the author of several books including *In an Indian Garden,
East is East* and *Hasegawa of Japan.*

Made and printed by The Campfield Press, St Albans, England

CONTENTS

DATES of incidents and dates when work commenced, given in the text, follow a chronological order as far as possible. Hyphens after dates in the chapter headings indicate year from which the subject matter begins.

Preface

THE prevalent opinion that the West has no right to impose a foreign religion, synonymous with the western civilization, on an eastern country with an old culture is beyond dispute.

When Frederick de Lautour Tucker and his little band of three landed in Bombay 100 years ago, they did not come to offer a western way of life, they came to translate the love of God in service.

Gandhi, though not a Christian, had grasped the truth of the Christian gospel when he said, 'Love is the centre and soul of Christianity.' Love was the motivating power of the missionaries and the same divine love was born in the hearts of the converts who rose up to serve their own people.

India was the first country to which The Salvation Army directed its missionary endeavour and 100 years have now passed into history. Frederick Coutts, a retired General of The Salvation Army, affirms: 'History enables a community—whether an entire nation or a section of a nation—to place itself in relation to its own past, its present opportunities and its future prospects.'

In trying to sketch, within the limits of a prescribed number of words, a picture of the 100 years of the Army's activities in India and neighbouring countries, much, to my regret, has had to be omitted, but my hope is that it will give that third dimension so necessary to bring the present into the right focus.

The book would not have been written had it not been for my husband's help. From his wide knowledge of things Indian he has brought to life past happenings as well as correcting my manuscript. Thanks are also due to Lieut.-Colonel Walter Hull, the Literary Secretary, International Headquarters, for his encouragement, to Lieut.-Colonel Leslie Pull, Under Secretary for South Asia, for his co-operation, and to Lieut.-Colonel Cyril Barnes (R), the 'oracle' at the IHQ archives for his ever-ready answer to every question. Also to the many who have supplied material through correspondence.

S. S.

1

The 'great' invasion (1882)

'WHEN I think of India', wrote Jawaharlal Nehru, India's first prime minister, 'I think of broad fields dotted with innumerable small villages; of towns and cities I have visited; of the magic of the rainy season which pours life into the dry, parched-up land and converts it suddenly into a glistening expanse of beauty and greenery, of great rivers and flowing water; of the Khyber Pass in all its bleak surroundings; of the southern tip of India; of people, individually and in the mass; and above all, of the snow-capped Himalayas—for India stretches from the tropics right up to the temperate regions, from near the equator to the cold heart of Asia.'

If the map of the south Asian subcontinent were superimposed on one of Europe, it would stretch north to south from Norway across the Mediterranean and almost to the African coast, and east to west it would cover an area from a point well inside Russia to England. This subcontinent has an area of 1,600,000 square miles. Add to it the neighbouring countries of Burma and Sri Lanka, which are included in this survey of The Salvation Army's work over the last 100 years, and you will get an idea of the vastness of the area and the diversity of its peoples.

The diversity is immense. The tall fair-skinned Pathan in the north has little in common with the slighter-built, darker-hued Tamil of the south (we are now dealing with India as a whole before partition), the philosophically minded Bengali bears little resemblance to the industrious Sikh. They differ in appearance, in manner of dress and diet, in life-style and language, yet a common factor unites them, they are Indians with the same national heritage, with a civilization which goes back to the time when we in the northern regions lived in the Stone Age. In Mohenjo-daro in the Indus Valley and Harappa in Western Punjab are ruins of ancient cities, proofs of a highly developed civilization that is said to have existed over 5,000 years ago.

1

Down the ages India has been the target for invasions: the Persians, Greeks, Parthians, Bactrians, Scythians, Huns, Turks and Arabs, but never was there a more bizarre invasion than the one which took place on 19 September 1882. An army of four making its way to Bombay on the P & O SS *Ancona,* Major Frederick de Lautour Tucker, Captain Henry Bullard, Lieutenants Arthur Norman and Mary Ann Thompson. Other armies had come to conquer, this Army came to serve, but the English and vernacular newspapers had it that 'The Salvation Army was attacking India!'

When they started out from London there were six of them, but it was found necessary for Mrs Louisa Tucker to accompany one young woman-officer back to England for personal reasons and they disembarked at Port Said, Mrs Tucker sailing again for India on the next available ship.

The authorities in India, being unfamiliar with The Salvation Army's military jargon, visualized the landing of a formidable force which might cause communal riots resulting in violence and bloodshed, consequently the Bombay police were lined up on the quayside at Apollo Bunder for the Army's arrival.

The Salvation Army was still in its infancy. Founded by the Rev William Booth among the poor in the East End of London, England, The Christian Mission took the name of The Salvation Army in 1878. A quasi-military form was adopted in order to fight more effectually against the evils in the world. Its motto became 'Saved to serve', its motive to reveal God's love to man through service.

After the four had stepped ashore the superintendent of police approached them asking, 'When will the rest of your army land?' Major Tucker replied, 'We are the whole Army,' at which the police officer in evident amazement and, one may assume, with a grin, said, 'We were expecting you to arrive 1,000 strong!'

Major Tucker knew that strength lay not in numbers, and in high spirits he and his little band started marching down the crowded streets of Bombay. Carrying the Army banner he was followed by Captain Bullard playing the cornet, Lieutenant Norman beating the drum and Mary Thompson jingling a tambourine. No wonder they caused a stir! Never before had the proud Britons been seen on the streets of India in such a guise. Not only was the music a novelty, but the party was dressed in a blend of Indian-European dress. The men wore turbans with a red band on which *Muktifauj* (The Salvation Army) was inscribed, long yellow coats similar in cut to the Indian *achkhan* and white trousers. Mary Ann Thompson, brave woman, wore a yellow dress set off by a hat with the Salvation Army band of red ribbon. All four wore boots.

A procession with drum and trumpet was no unusual sight to the people of Bombay. Processions of all kinds, wedding, funeral and religious were part of the daily street scene. It was the contrast between the dress and the white skin which caused curiosity. If it had been Tucker's intention to arouse interest he certainly succeeded, but the 'uniform' had a more important aim. It was an attempt to identify the Salvation Army missionary officers with the people of India, the yellow colour being used by India's 'holy men'.

The Founder of The Salvation Army, when sending out his very first missionary force to India had instructed them:

> With the apostle, to become all things to all men, in order that you may win them to your Master. This must mean, if anything at all, that to the Indians you must be Indians.

'The Army did not spread abroad by the determination of its leaders,' wrote St John Ervine, 'it spread by the force of its own energy and strength.' General Frederick Coutts adds in *No Discharge in this War*: 'The notion of William Booth as a religious Alexander sighing for fresh worlds to conquer is as wide of the mark as can be. New shoots began to grow in unexpected places seemingly of their own accord. The wind blew where it listed.' And the wind of the Spirit blew also over India.

God used Frederick Tucker as His instrument to accomplish this. He was a man well acquainted with India and its people, belonging, as he did, to a distinguished family who for three generations had done outstanding service for the country. Frederick was born on 21 March 1853 at Monghyr, Bengal (now part of Bihar State), where his father held the position of commissioner in the Indian Civil Service. He was brought up in a religious atmosphere, but a real awakening of his own spiritual life came to him during a revival meeting led by Dr D. L. Moody, where he felt that God spoke to his soul and called him to service. He would have given up his planned career in the Civil Service then had it not been for the indignant protests of his family. Instead he tried to combine Christian witness with his official duties as assistant commissioner

3

and magistrate. It didn't please his superiors and he was told that his preaching on the streets of Dharmsala had to stop. But his interest in the Indian people lay deeper than administering justice as a magistrate, he wanted them to know Christ and His deliverance from sin. The idea of preaching Christianity to the Indian people as an Indian gospel had taken hold of him. Christ was a Man of the East, not of the West, he reasoned, then why interpret the Christ of Palestine to India in English fashion? The average missionary living under European conditions was regarded by the people as a sahib, one of the ruling classes, the preacher of a foreign faith, the faith of India's conquerors.

He had read about the new religious movement which had started in England—The Salvation Army—it had appealed to him and he had sent a donation. Now, with the receipt he received a copy of its paper, *The War Cry*. He read it with interest. An article by the Founder, William Booth, spoke directly to his own heart and he said, 'Here are the people I have been seeking,' and decided there and then to take leave of absence and travel to England to find out more about The Salvation Army.

His first encounter with William Booth was at Exeter Hall, London, where he heard him preach. So impressed was he that he went up to General Booth after the meeting offering himself for service in The Salvation Army. Hearing that it was Tucker's first contact with the Army, William Booth advised him to take a little more time before deciding. 'You have not seen enough of us to know what we are,' he said. 'Go among my people and find the dark side as well as the bright. Discover everything about us for yourself. Then come back to me, if you still want to be one of us, and I will then decide.'

Frederick Tucker's mind was already made up. Very soon after this incident he attended a meeting in Bristol led by Captain Isaac Unsworth. When the meeting was finished he went up to the Captain and said, 'I am going to be a soldier in your Army, so give me a badge to wear.' They found him a strip of red ribbon bearing the words 'The Salvation Army' which he tied round his hat. The following day, still wearing the hat with the red ribbon, he visited friends in London and told them he was going to resign his post in the Indian Civil Service and become a Salvation Army soldier, much to his friends' consternation.

His wife, Louisa, whom he had married a couple of years

previously, was also distressed. Although herself a keen Christian she felt no personal call to exchange her position as the wife of a well-to-do government official for that of a poor Salvationist. But, to her great credit, when she realized the earnestness of her husband's conviction she decided to follow suit and stand by him.

But let us go back to the newly-arrived party of pioneers, marching, singing and playing through the streets of Bombay. They made their way to a house in Tenth Lane, Khetwadi, which had been rented for them by a Mr Gladwin, who had been at the quayside to welcome them. Mr and Mrs Gladwin, former Methodists, threw in their lot with the pioneers and were given the rank of Captain and did valuable service in the Army helping to pioneer the work in Sri Lanka (then Ceylon).

The very next day the Army moved on to 'the attack' and missionary friends rallied round to help. A large tent, donated by Salvationists in England, was erected on the spacious *maidan* (open field) near Crawford Market in the centre of the city. The pioneers mounting 'war chariots' (converted bullock carts) struck up the sound of trumpet, drum and tambourine and made their way from Khetwadi via Dhobi Talao to the Esplanade. Huge crowds gathered for the meeting, the sides of the tent had to be rolled up to enable the vast congregation to hear the speakers. Major Tucker, speaking fluently in Hindustani, captured their attention at once. A young Marathi Christian translated the testimonies. Everyone was singing in Hindustani from a song book compiled by Tucker, the pioneers having learnt the songs on the voyage out.

It was a spectacular beginning, but trouble was brewing. The first to feel the heavy hand of the law was Lieutenant Norman; while playing the cornet a policeman stepped up and arrested him, taking him off to the lock-up. The following day he was let off with a fine of 20 rupees. The Governor of Bombay, Sir James Ferguson, fearing the equanimity of the State would be upset through religious riots, instructed the commissioner of police to summon Major Tucker. Taking Captain Bullard with him the two presented themselves before the commissioner of police who told them that processions were forbidden and if they wanted to hold meetings they must be confined to tents or halls. Tucker, as familiar with Indian criminal law as the commissioner, knew there was no such restriction and refused to comply, and to the commissioner's brusque warning, 'You won't go,' he calmly replied, 'We shall go,' adding, 'and we are prepared to suffer the consequences'. This was

5

the beginning of a confrontation between Government and the Army pioneers which lasted for many months.

Government officials may well have been concerned that the Salvationists, by their processions and open-air meetings and unusual tactics would stir up religious rioting and strife in a country where Muslims and Hindus lived uneasily together, but one suspects that the eccentric behaviour of the newly-arrived Britons was an embarrassment to the officials who considered it lowering the prestige of the white man.

During the following days meetings were held in the tent at Crawford Market and the Hindu Theatre in Grant Road. 'Never in the history of Indian missions had evangelistic meetings been attended by such throngs,' reported *The War Cry,* the Army's weekly newspaper. Special meetings were announced for the Esplanade Theatre on the Sunday and police permission to march to the hall was requested. It was refused, whereupon Tucker decided to put the matter to a test. The march was headed by Major Tucker carrying the Salvation Army flag inscribed with the words 'Blood and Fire' referring to the Blood of Christ and the fire of the Holy Spirit. Lieutenants Arthur Norman and Mary Thompson followed playing instruments.

When they reached the junction of five roads in Obelisk Road they were confronted by the deputy commissioner and the superintendent of police, supported by English and Indian constables mounted and on foot. The deputy commissioner, advancing in front of the intrepid three, called out in a commanding voice, 'In the name of Her Majesty, Queen of England and Empress of India, I order you to disperse.'

With as much authority in his voice, Tucker stepped forward, raised his hand and replied, 'In the name of His Majesty, King of kings and Lord of lords, I command you to stand aside.' Tucker and his two companions were taken to the police court charged with 'forming an assembly likely to lead to a breach of the peace'. They were told to find bail, which they refused to do, whereupon Tucker and Norman were placed in the European lock-up, while Mary Ann Thompson was taken to a room in the quarters of a married police officer above the court. Singing and praying could be heard from the lock-up throughout the evening and into the night.

6

In the meantime the fourth member of the pioneer party, Captain Bullard, was 'holding the fort' at the Esplanade Theatre where large crowds had gathered for the meeting. The audience consisted of European and Eurasian ladies and gentlemen, Parsees, Hindus, Muslims and various representatives of other sections of the Indian community. A Bombay newspaper gave a favourable report on the meeting commending Bullard on his earnestness.

The following morning the three prisoners were taken before the local magistrate who imposed a fine of 100 rupees. Tucker declined to pay. The magistrate then ordered the fine to be collected by the sale of the Salvationists' few belongings. The superintendent of police showed his sympathy with the Army by buying the goods for the said amount of money, paying the fine and returning the goods to Major Tucker, who was deeply moved by this generous and unexpected gesture.

Many felt sympathy with the pioneers. No less than 20 vernacular newspapers wrote in favour of the Army.

The Hindu Prakash, with the largest circulation in Bombay, wrote, 'This is a question of liberty of conscience. Why should it be granted to some, and denied to others?'

The Indian Mirror stated, 'If The Salvation Army can prove that Christianity is really the religion of the poor, that it can doff lavender-coloured breeches and Christy's patent helmets to put on the mendicants' ochre garb; that it can dance, shout and march with the ordinary proletarian poor human nature from the mill, the mine and the workshop; if The Salvation Army can prove that, it will have done service towards the future evangelization of India.'

The Lamp of Judaism, a local Jewish paper asked: 'Why should not the members of the new Christian sect have their processions in Bombay with music when Hindus are allowed their *Gunpati,* the Mohammedans their *taboot* and Bhanyas their marriage processions with great beating of tom-toms?'

In Calcutta the Brahmo Samaj, a reformed branch of Hinduism, staged a mass meeting. Its leader, Keshab Chandar Sen, sent a telegram to Major Tucker stating, 'One of the largest meetings ever convened in Calcutta was held in the town hall this evening to protest against unjust treatment of the Salvationists in Bombay. A memorial to the viceroy was adopted, asking for religious neutrality and equal protection for all.'

7

While the legal battle continued our brave soldiers wasted no time in spreading the gospel. Captain Bullard and Lieutenant Norman were sent off to Calcutta which was then the capital city of India. The 1,400-mile journey took three days by train. The hard and narrow wooden seats in the crowded third-class compartment were anything but comfortable, but the welcome which they received on arrival made up for any inconvenience. Several Europeans and a large number of Indians met them on Howrah Station. Needless to say, much of the enthusiasm shown was due to the previous mass meeting staged by Keshab Chandar Sen.

During the week's stay in the city Bullard and Norman were entertained by Dr Thoburn (later Bishop of the Methodist Church in India) and held their first meeting in the American Episcopal church in Dharmtala Street, later to be known as 'Thoburn Church'. Henry Bullard wrote, 'The great building was crowded and every bit of standing space in both the body of the church and gallery was filled. All classes of the community were represented. We conducted an ordinary salvation meeting and at the close a number of seekers came forward and knelt at the communion rail. We held similar meetings in the Duff College church and the Wesleyan church and a huge open-air gathering in Wellington Square in the centre of the city.'

At the end of the week the English daily, *The Statesman,* wrote in a leader:

> The Salvationists leave Calcutta today to return and assist in the great work in Bombay . . . the dread of hostilities between them and any class of natives due to utter ignorance . . . and the watchdog measures taken by the Bombay police were a ridiculous blunder. The Salvationists never argue or dispute, they attack no system of religion. . . . It becomes necessary to modify one's judgement respecting Salvationists' 'irreverence' when one sees it near enough. The apparent familiarity, the 'free and easiness' with which they address the Deity, appears to us to result from their extraordinary realization of His continuous presence. . . . The Salvationists, so it seems to us, in all their proceedings, never for a moment lay aside their consciousness that they are in the immediate presence of the Deity. They never quit it. They are as close to His feet while singing a song, beating the drum, or talking to the crowd, as when prostrate in prayer, and so without any ceremonial preparation they break out in prayer in the ordinary language of conversation and, with as little ceremony, break off and address the congregation.

Mrs Louisa Tucker, having boarded the first available ship for

India after seeing her charge safely back home, arrived in Bombay on 26 October to join her husband. A grand welcome meeting was arranged for Mrs Tucker, and the lively, expectant audience eagerly awaited her appearance. But Mrs Tucker did not turn up. Nor did the Major, nor did four other Salvationists. Where were they? The Indian *War Cry* breezily reports their whereabouts:

> Here we are once again, only this time there are six of us, establishing ourselves in the temporary headquarters provided for us by the paternal government in the Girgaum Police Court. While Captain and Mrs Gladwin and Lieutenant Norman were holding the fort at the Framji Cowasji Institute, we had a grand time at Girgaum with singing and marching round the large room which acted as our cell. The presence and power of the Lord filled our hearts with joy, and we consecrated ourselves afresh to His service, while He assured us, 'Behold, I have set before thee an open door and no man can shut it'.

This time when the Salvationists were brought before the magistrate Major Tucker presented a masterly defence and the accused were discharged, though this was to prove only a temporary respite from the over-zealous attentions of the law. But nothing could quell the fervour of the pioneers; no less than three meetings were held daily, one in the Hindi Theatre and two at the 'salvation tent' at Crawford Market. Men and women confirmed their belief in Christ as their Saviour and the first 'swearing in' of soldiers was planned. Soldiers of Christ who would fight against all evil. Among the converts was Walter Keil, a young telegraphist, by race a Burgher from Ceylon of mixed Dutch and Singhalese ancestry. With a crowd of miscreant friends he had gone, out of curiosity, to see The Salvation Army. At the close of the meeting Major Tucker had put his hand on the shoulder of the young Walter and asked, 'Where will you spend eternity?' It made the young man think, he realized the need for a purpose in life and decided to follow Jesus and serve Him in the Army. Within a few weeks, as Lieutenant Yesu Patham, Walter Keil was actively engaged in full-time service for God and the Army. He served faithfully for 41 years as an officer, mostly in south India and Ceylon, and received from the hand of General Bramwell Booth the *Order of the Founder,* a worthy recognition of a long life of self-sacrifice and devotion.

Major Tucker's vision was to see the whole of India kneeling at the feet of Jesus and he wanted without delay to spread the good news to other parts of India. He decided to visit a number of towns in northern India, places which were known to him and where he

9

knew the language. With his wife and Captains Bullard and Norman, who had recently returned from Calcutta, he set off for the north. They covered no less than 2,500 miles and wherever they went they were greeted cordially. Doubtless some of the interest shown was due to the nation-wide publicity given to the Army through the newspapers. In Allahabad great crowds thronged the meetings held in the Baptist church and the Methodist church. At Delhi they were received at the railway station by an influential Mohammedan prince, numerous Indian Christians and other well-wishers. The deputy commissioner allowed a procession and they were given the use of the town hall for a meeting to which many hundreds were unable to gain admission. In Lahore members of the Brahmo Samaj and Arya Samaj had arranged a torch-light procession. Meetings were held in the railway theatre, the Rang Mahal, and in the Montgomery Hall, at the time regarded as the finest auditorium in India—all overcrowded. At Lucknow, a city of mosques, they were allowed to march the streets playing and singing. In the city of Benares, sacred to Hindus, a large *shamiana* (open tent) was erected on the banks of the River Ganges, where meetings were held after they had marched through the crowds of Hindu devotees. Seemingly it was a highly successful tour, but in his heart Major Tucker was not satisfied, there was something missing. They were not getting at the heart of things—the great mass of the common people were still untouched by the gospel.

The turn of the year brought reinforcements, four officers arrived from England. Two of them, women officers, were sent directly to Calcutta. Major Tucker commenced a second extensive tour in the north while Captain Bullard returned to Calcutta. Here a temporary hall of palm leaves and strong poles was set up in the centre of the city opposite Wellington Square. Many sought Christ and a small corps was formed. Among the Indian Christians who helped was a group of educated, young Bengali women who, in their white saris, provided quite an attraction. Meetings were also held in the theatre and opera house, and one Sunday afternoon more than 3,000 crowded in to hear the Army in the marquee of the Wilson's Circus.

In January 1883 Captain William Gladwin, who had joined the pioneer party on its arrival in Bombay, was sent on a lone expedition to south India and Ceylon. He arrived in Colombo on 26 January and proclaimed the love of God for all mankind at Kahn clock tower, Pettah. When news got around the island that Captain Gladwin of The Salvation Army was visiting Kandy a young Singhalese Christian keenly anticipated meeting him. Arnolis Weerasooriya belonged to one of the leading families in southern Ceylon. In his boyhood his mother, a devoted Buddhist, used to take him to the *Pansala* (Buddhist temple) where his uncle was the chief priest. When his father embraced Christianity he was subjected to much persecution from the family, and his wife, taking the children with her, left him. But by his persistent love and patience he won them over and the family was united again. He was keen that his children should have a sound education, and Arnolis, who showed great promise as a student, was sent to Trinity College, Kandy. Here he completed his studies after which he accepted a post as teacher. Nominally he was a Christian, but it was while reading *From Death unto Life* by Haslam that light broke upon his soul and he became an active Christian testifying to the students of the college, by which many of them were brought into the same experience of a new birth. His fervent love for the Lord Jesus made him declare, 'If there is anyone who loves Jesus more than I do, let me sit at his feet and learn from him.'

When he saw Captain Gladwin dressed in the saffron garb of a fakir he exclaimed, 'Here is someone who loves Jesus better than I do. A white man has discarded his usual dress and adopted that of India for the love of Jesus to win the people of the East, whereas I, a son of the East, have discarded my native costume for that of a foreigner. How then can I say that I love Jesus equally well? I have found someone who loves Jesus better than I do.' His mind was made up, he, too, would join The Salvation Army. When he returned to his home and told his parents of his decision he was met with strong opposition. Eventually he got their consent and made his journey to Madras, where a few months earlier the Army had established a corps led by Captain Gladwin. Arnolis wrote to his father from Madras, 16 September 1883:

Bless the Lord, all the time He is with me. I have fully tried the Army and its modes of work. These modes have the touch of the apostles very much. I have signed the papers of the Army, and sworn allegiance to it. May God help me to stick to it till I die!

When Major Tucker, on a visit to Madras, met Weerasooriya he realized immediately that here was someone who possessed remarkable natural gifts which would make him extremely valuable for the salvation of India, that God had sent him the kind of man who would help to unlock India's heart for the Saviour.

From Bombay, where he was receiving training to become a Salvation Army officer, Weerasooriya wrote again to his father, 6 November 1883:

> God has put me just now where I ought to be. Whenever it is His good will and pleasure He will send me to Ceylon. I am just now closely attached to the Major of the Army. . . . I belong to Jesus. In this world I must fight and not rest. I have given myself up to the Lord with a solemn vow for life, and I mean, by the grace of God, to stick to it, come what may.

When Major Tucker returned to Bombay from his extensive tour in the country where he had met so much goodwill and had complete freedom of movement, he felt an irresistible compulsion to attempt street meetings again, as had been permitted in other cities. *The War Cry* reports:

> What a thrill now to march along, 40 strong, voices ringing out, drums and timbrels providing exuberant accompaniment, and even a Methodist parson to carry the flag!

In case anyone should be uncertain about the Army's right to march in the streets, Tucker made the case quite clear through the pages of *The War Cry*, explaining the Army's stand in regard to the authorities. He wrote:

> You are asking, 'Why then do you go out again in procession contrary to orders, after a case has been decided against you in the law courts?' Stop a minute! You are making a little mistake! We are not now forbidden to go out in procession. It is the singing of Christian songs and the preaching of Christian truths that is now forbidden. The holy name of Jesus is not to pass our lips in talk or song. The drunkard may reel through the streets bawling words unfit to reach the human ear; the beggars may sing from door to door asking for alms; the Mohammedans may chant their *kalma* (profession of faith) as they follow their dead to the grave at all hours of the day and night; the groans and lamentations of the mourner, the oaths and curses of the blasphemer, the shouts of the drivers, the wranglings of the money makers may fill the air with all the discordant echoes of Hell, while the sweet songs of salvation are to be choked at once—and this under a Christian government! Surely if under such circumstances we should consent to be silent, we might expect the very stones to cry shame upon us. No difficulty will daunt us, no opposition will withhold us from proclaiming through the length and breadth of India the exceeding riches of the love of God which is in Christ Jesus.

Tucker was to prove his words for on Sunday 18 February 1883 the Major, together with three officers and 18 soldiers, was arrested for singing and carrying a banner in the street. This fourth arrest proved to be the most sensational. A well-known barrister in Allahabad, Mr T. Lewis Ingram, when he heard what had happened, hurried to Bombay offering his services free of cost. Mr and Mrs Ingram proved to be lifelong supporters and friends of the Army, one of their daughters becoming an officer and as Ensign Helen Ingram was known for her literary work.

The trial and judgement occupied five days. At an early stage in the proceedings the charges against 14 of the 19 accused were withdrawn on the ground that they had been acting under the orders of Major Tucker. In defence Mr Ingram quoted a government resolution from a previous court case in south India:

> The public high streets in all towns are the property, not of any particular caste, but of the whole community, and every man, be his caste or religion what it may, has a right to the full use of them, provided that he does not obstruct or molest others in the use of them.

Nevertheless, Thursday 8 March, the magistrate passed sentence on the five accused for 'causing obstruction' and Major Tucker, as 'the head and fount of the whole offending', was sentenced to simple imprisonment for a month and the others to pay a fine of 25 rupees each, or simple imprisonment for a week. They chose the latter and the five of them were taken to Bombay jail. An appeal was entered and heard by the High Court after Tucker had been in prison for a fortnight. One of the judges said to Major Tucker, 'Well, Mr Tucker, we shall be prepared to release you if you promise not to do it again.' Tucker replied, 'My Lord, if I had a rope round my neck, and were going to be hanged the next minute, I would not make such a promise.'

The student of history can judge for himself whether the authorities were adhering to Queen Victoria's Proclamation which stated:

> We declare it to be our Royal Will and Pleasure that none be in anywise favoured, none molested nor disquieted by reason of their religious faith or observances, but that all alike enjoy the equal and impartial protection of the law, and we do strictly charge and enjoin all those who may be in authority under us that they abstain from all interference with the religious belief or worship of any of our subjects, on pain of our highest displeasure.

Major Tucker, however, was undaunted by his imprisonment, he records: 'It happened to be my 30th birthday, and I have ever since looked back upon it with unmingled joy and satisfaction. My stay in jail was a time of rich spiritual refreshment. I seemed to hear the Saviour saying, "Come ye apart into a desert place, and rest awhile." '

After the High Court's decision to reject the appeal, the police determined to take further proceedings against The Salvation Army, and Captain Bullard and two women officers were arrested, but public opinion from both high and low was so much with the Army, that it was considered wise not to press the charge and the three were promptly released.

In London General William Booth and his associates were thunderstruck by the news of the prison sentence, but on reflection their anxiety was somewhat alleviated, and the General wrote to Major Tucker, 'We suppose that the imprisonment will not be very irksome to the flesh and that it may be really beneficial to your health, compelling you to take a measure of rest.'

It is interesting to note that 30 years later The Salvation Army was requested by the Governor, Sir George Clarke (later Lord Sydenham), to open an industrial home for stranded Europeans and take over the management of a new workhouse to replace the old one for destitute Europeans attached to the prison where Major Tucker had served his sentence.

On the day of release, 8 April, a large crowd of Salvationists and others gathered outside the prison gate and gave Major Tucker a rousing salute. The *Bombay Gazette* describes the scene: 'Precisely at seven o'clock the outer door was set ajar, and Major Tucker passed out. "Amen!" was the first word he uttered on beholding his friends, and "Amen" was the loud response of the crowd. The Major and his comrades immediately adjourned to a piece of land in close proximity to the jail, and there they held a thanksgiving service, prayers being said and hymns sung. Afterwards they formed in procession and marched to the headquarters in Khetwadi, singing hymns *en route.* The police authorities did not interfere. Indeed, there was not need for their interference, there being no sign of hostility towards the Army on the part of the natives.'

In the evening a meeting was held at the Framjee Cowasjee Institute to celebrate the release. The hall was crowded with friends and sympathizers and interested onlookers. Addresses were delivered by Major and Mrs Tucker and their powerful speeches had a manifest influence on the audience. The proceedings were conducted with more decorum than usual. Major Tucker expressed his thanks to the superintendent of the jail for the kindness he had shown towards him during his incarceration.

Three days later, however, another arrest was made, this time four officers and six soldiers were summoned to the court. Major Tucker conducted their defence and an agreement was ultimately reached allowing The Salvation Army freedom to march with trumpet, timbrel and drum in all areas apart from strictly Muslim areas. Painful though these prosecutions must have been, they proved to be blessings in disguise, for sympathy for the Army and interest in the work was aroused throughout the whole of India and Ceylon. Tucker and his band of brave soldiers had won for the Army and all Christians the right to open-air witness.

Advertising Major Tucker's release from Prison:

Release of Major Tucker
Saturday 7 April
GREAT
DEMONSTRATION
Meet outside
HM House of Correction
Clare Road, Byculla
at 7.30 am

*   *   *   *   *

Framjee Cowasjee
Hall
In the evening at 7 pm
MAJOR TUCKER
will relate his
PRISON   EXPERIENCES

Tickets: 2 annas
Reserved seats: 1 rupee
Get your tickets early if you
wish to be present
GREAT CROWDS EXPECTED

2

Begging bowls and bare feet (1883-)

VARIOUS references have been made in the previous chapter to The Salvation Army's periodical *The War Cry*. Major Tucker believed in the importance of the written word and within three weeks of his arrival in Bombay he had the first issue of the Indian *War Cry* published in both the English and Gujarati languages, the date was 11 October 1882. Fifteen thousand copies were printed of the 1 November issue and sold in one week. 'Mrs Tucker is at present our champion *War Cry* seller having disposed of no less than 450 copies in a week, and this in the rainy season,' wrote Major Tucker.

Toward the end of 1883 a third party of officers arrived from England, four young women, among them Captain Selina Roffey who had come out to marry Captain Henry Bullard. The very first Salvation Army wedding in India created a great deal of interest and was by all accounts a unique event. The marriage ceremony was to take place in a hired theatre at 8 pm to coincide with the usual meeting time. The wedding party grouped themselves for the march in front of headquarters' building. Major Tucker led the procession carrying the flag, behind him Mrs Tucker and the bride, looking radiant in her khavi-coloured sari, then came the bridegroom playing the cornet followed by Captain Norman with the big drum and Mary Ann Thompson with the tambourine—a few helpers making up the rear, all in all about a dozen. Crowds followed the wedding procession and were quite willing to pay the admission fee of one rupee four annas. The congregation was as varied as could be seen anywhere—Hindus, Muslims, Parsees, English and American missionaries and friends, and Indian Christians. Major Tucker led the evening's event and lost no opportunity to preach to the unconverted. Army officers were not then licensed to conduct marriages in India so the actual ceremony was in the hands of the Rev George Bowen, a devoted missionary who spent his whole life among the poor in Bombay.

No wedding banquet followed, the expense of such was considered unthinkable. As no regular salary was given to officers in those days, a special grant for wedding expenses was bestowed amounting to four rupees—approximately 25 pence in today's reckoning! The bride and bridegroom went direct from the theatre to the railway station to go to their new appointment. Captain Bullard had been appointed Divisional Commander for South India, the division then comprising two corps—both in Madras city. They broke the journey at Kandala, a small 'semi-hill' station near Poona, where they spent a couple of days.

The Army had opened up work in Madras six months earlier. Captain Bullard had been sent to investigate the possibilities in April 1883 and two weeks later Captain Gladwin together with his wife and Captain Usher and Lieutenant Victoria Roberts, took over operations.

The 2 May issue of *The War Cry* reports:

> Grand opening last night, Memorial Hall packed, large crowds unable to get in; one man was eager to help but had no money so he gave a postal wrapper for a copy of *The War Cry* and put his pocket knife in the collection.

A week later:

> We have been but three nights in our own hall and 30 souls have come out seeking salvation. The hall is a large shop, but altogether too small. About 350 cram in and crowds go away disappointed.

In other big cities the Army was consolidating its work. In Calcutta land had been secured in Dharamtala Street and barracks been erected and dedicated Saturday 5 May 1883. The same month, 23 May, the *Bombay Gazette* featured the opening of barracks in Bombay:

> Salvationist demonstrations were held last Saturday evening in the vicinity of the Boribunder Railway Station, it being the occasion of the opening of the newly-erected 'barracks'. As prelude to the inaugural ceremony, a procession with band by special licence, but with no colours, was formed at the tent opposite the market. Headed by Major Tucker, and followed by a large and motley crowd, the Salvationists marched singing along the Esplanade crossroads and into the Cruickshank Road. On entering the latter thoroughfare, the band struck up an accompaniment to the singing which was maintained till the barracks was reached.

17

The barracks was a very simple structure measuring 70 by 40 feet, consisting of a tiled roof supported by posts and surrounded with boarding, and adjoined the wall of the GIP (Great Indian Peninsular Railway). It was calculated to accommodate 800 to 900 people. Private Nelson, an Armenian convert, had the entire responsibility for its construction and thereby saved the Army money in that the total cost was only 800 rupees, about a quarter of the sum any other contractor wanted for the job. No wonder Nelson was appointed 'Barracks Master' and soon after sent to Poona to look for land on which to build barracks there.

Three days later Major Tucker went up to inspect his find. From Poona railway station they got into a springless bullock-cart to take them up Parvarti hill from which they viewed the land and Tucker was shown the site the Barracks Master thought suitable. Another trip in the bullock-cart to the owner of the property and after a bit of haggling an agreement was reached. Twelve days afterwards, 23 June, the corps was opened.

On this day officers and soldiers came up from Bombay. They held a great open-air meeting in front of the railway station on arrival, after which they marched with music to the hospital. Here they dispersed for rations and at 5.30 a 'Great Opening Meeting' was held at the new barracks in Rasta Ki Pet, near No 7 Chauki. The barracks was packed and many unable to get in. The shed was given the name 'The Salvation Army Circus'. Captain Norman was put in charge assisted by Brother Mahajan, a Marathi Lieutenant. The following month, July, came reports of a cadet training centre being opened: 'Cadets Donaldson and Cartney, our two first lads from Madras have gone to Poona where they will be properly trained for salvation officers.' 'Our Brahmin convert from Madras, who has been saved now over two months, has been promoted cadet and has proceeded to Poona to be trained as an officer.'

During the first 18 months more than 2,000 persons had publicly professed conversion, but few had actually joined the ranks. Crowds attended the meetings in the cities but few soldiers had been made and those mostly from nominal Christians. Major Tucker was not satisfied. Ninety per cent of India's millions lived in the villages and they were as yet untouched by the gospel. How could the non-Christian people of the country be won for Christ? He thought of General William Booth's advice, 'Get into their skin'. He thought of the early Jesuit missionaries, Frances Xavier and Beschi, the result of whose work was still to be seen in the large number of Christians in south India.

Cut off from all support, Beschi adopted a native name and dress, mastered the Tamil language, wrote numerous religious books and 'accomplished single-handed results which have perhaps never been surpassed for magnitude'. 'If a few Jesuits, alone and unaided, by the simple adoption of Indian customs, could secure such successes,' thought Tucker, 'what a grand future lies before The Salvation Army!'

The pseudo-Indian dress was discarded, the women adopted the sari as their every day dress, coloured khavi with a red border and red blouse, later a blue sari and white blouse was accepted as unofficial uniform. The men wore a red uniform jacket and khavi-coloured *dhoti* wrapped round like a sarong. In Gujerat, to conform to local custom, the *dhoti* was of a thinner muslin cloth wrapped between the legs. Turban with *Muktifauj* inscribed on a red band and shoulder-cloth, both khavi coloured, completed the outfit. From wearing boots they now walked barefooted, which must have been hardship indeed, but those early missionary officers found nothing too hard, no sacrifice too great if it would win someone for Jesus. Dr Sprague Oram, who joined the forces in Bombay, wrote to *All the World*: Even when tramping along on a burning road, with sharp stones and thorns like darning needles sticking into you, I look up and not down, and the pain and the dreariness go away, and I am happy—supremely happy.'

A former acquaintance of Major Tucker said to him on one occasion, 'It may be all very well for you to go about barefooted, living under trees and eating the common food of the coolies, but surely you don't expect your workers to do the same. How do they manage?' Tucker was able to point to his two companions who stood close by, who with the same eagerness as their leader, and all the other pioneers had accepted the life of self-sacrifice and delighted in it.

Major Tucker was by no means alone in his desire to become completely at one with the poor of India; they vied with each other in thinking out new plans, so as to win them for Christ. Staff Captain Paynter, one of the pioneers, took the Indian name, Jai Bhai (Brother Victory) and it was not long before the rest followed suit. The simple villagers would find it so much easier to approach a 'Jai Bhai' or 'Prem Das' than Captains Mackertich or Hawthorn.

Major Tucker took the name Fakir Singh—the Lion of Fakirs—Singh being used as a family name in north India. By this name he became known throughout India and Ceylon, and when in England for the first international congress, it was as Fakir Singh he was introduced. A name so eminently suitable for him. Adopting Indian names, Indian dress and life-style our pioneers turned their full attention on reaching the people in the villages.

The question was where to start? The country had been mapped out and divided up amongst the existing missionary organizations. These regions they regarded as their own reserves and any newcomers were looked upon as invaders in their territory. It did not matter whether the existing mission had insufficient workers to cover the field or inadequate funds to work it, they did not want any intruders. This created a problem, especially as the need was so great and yet the workers so few.

Taking Arnolis Weerasooriya with him Major Tucker set out, in March 1884, to find some rural area where they could commence the work. First they sought the guidance of the Holy Spirit in a half-night of prayer. The first district that came to Tucker's mind was the Punjab as he was familiar with this part of the country and knew the language, but personal preference was not allowed to interfere, they would go where they were guided.

On their way north they made a halt in Ahmedabad, the main town of Gujarat, where they intended to spend a couple of days. While they were there a telegram reached them recalling Major Tucker to Bombay on urgent business and Weerasooriya was left behind. He accepted an invitation to a Christian village called Ranipur, a little north of Ahmedabad. Here he conducted meetings telling the people of his own conversion, how as a nominal Christian God had showed him the need of repentance and a new birth, and of the great joy that had flooded his heart when he realized fully that he was now a true child of God. His message took such hold of the people that a revival broke out. Major Tucker was urged to return quickly and many wonderful conversions took place during the days that followed.

But there were also many people who would not accept this message. One village in particular refused them hospitality. Weary and footsore, after having walked for miles over the burning sand, the two of them settled down in the shade of a tree to rest. Tucker, exhausted, fell asleep. Some of the village folk passed by where they were resting. Seeing the sahib asleep they came nearer. It amazed them to see him barefooted knowing what hardship that entailed and they bent down to feel if the soles of his feet were hard like theirs. When they saw that the soft skin was full of sores and blisters they turned reproachfully to one another saying, 'This man has sacrificed for us and we have turned him away without food and shelter.' They waited till the sahib woke up, seating themselves at a respectful distance. Unaware of what had taken place, Tucker began to read his Bible when he woke up and seeing the men's interest invited them to come nearer. They started asking questions and Tucker was ready with the answers, telling them why they had come—to explain to them the love of God as revealed in Christ Jesus.

The villagers invited them back to their village where they were given food and drink. Later, in the evening, when the moon shone bright, the whole village gathered and listened to the story of Jesus—how God had sent His Son into the world that we might be saved through Him—and many sought deliverance from sin and found salvation. Referring to this incident later Tucker would say, 'I preached my best sermon with my feet!'

It was especially among the weaver community that the Army gained converts. They were the artisans of the villages, intelligent and hardworking, but earning very little from their skilled labour. Among the weavers (called *dhers*) was a folklore which was translated by one of the early pioneers, Staff Captain Henry Burfoot (Dayasagar):

> There shall be light in the heavens,
> incarnated in the generation of Abram,
> he shall be called the Great Son,
> this is the voice of prophecy . . .
> Verily, on that day the drum shall be beaten,
> and flags float in the wind,
> then shall the *dhers* be saved,
> around the earth I must go,
> and gathering into one the eighteen castes,
> I shall be called the Spotless One.

All the World 1884 relates the experience of some of the officers who were working among the *dhers*. After the people had heard their message they were told that whilst they believed they were holy men, they could not be received as the messengers of the Deliverer, because they lacked the drum and the flag! It did not take our officers long to produce the missing items and hundreds of *dhers* followed the flag and worshipped the Spotless One, Jesus Christ. After seven months no less than 1,213 converts were registered and 40 of these were made Salvation Army officers. 'Only about 14 per cent of those who have professed salvation have fallen away. This percentage, so small, is truly marvellous considering they are new to Christianity, that nearly all are unable to read, that many of them live in villages where no regular meetings are yet held, and that they are subjected to persecution so bitter as to be scarcely credible. There are over 70 soldiers in Anand and the corps is growing. The lasses in command of the work now use a camel for travelling from one village to another.'

Despite the most rigid economy, finances were so low at this time that Major Tucker had no other choice but to vacate rented property. His intention from the very beginning had been that the Army in India should be self-supporting, believing that 'no mission could be considered safe which depended upon foreign countries for its support'. Conditions of officership were modelled on Christ's words to His disciples in the Gospel of Matthew. Without money, food, change of clothes or bedding, officers entirely trusted the villagers for hospitality. Usually they managed to get two meals a day, sometimes only one. Where the people were friendly and wished to hear about Jesus, they would stop for some time. But when this was not the case they passed on to other villages.

These conditions may to a Westerner seem unreasonably severe, but the people of India would understand. The begging bowl was the accepted thing to the Hindu *sadhu* and Buddhist priest who daily went from door to door, and people would gladly give a share of their meagre rations, thereby hoping to receive a blessing. Tucker wrote at that time:

> We are often reduced to the greatest straits for want of money. Having made a donation of boots, socks, shirts, cooking utensils, etc, to the Army, we now rejoice only in two pieces of cloth, one for the loins, the other for the shoulder, and a pair of drawers, with one blanket for the night. If we are much more pressed I think we can manage to donate the blanket, the topcloth and the drawers, confining ourselves to a cloth round the waist. Perhaps you will cry out against us for going too far; but really we can't help ourselves. We have to screw up £300 to £400 to pay our debts, besides paying our current printing and other expenses here. Yet how glad we are of our poverty! What lessons it has taught us which nothing else could have done.

Major Tucker decided to cut expenses by moving his headquarters and the training home to some caves situated in the Bay of Bombay, the Kaneri Caves on Salsette Island, while two officers were sent off to Darjeeling to collect funds for the 'war chest'. The caves are said to have been the site of a Buddhist monastery in ancient times. The island was thickly populated and therefore thought to be good training ground for the cadets. The hardship of being cave-dwellers was doubtless offset by the warm, balmy air of the bay, and their stay lasted only a month and a half, when it was discovered that the caves were private property belonging to a Parsee. The 'squatters' were politely asked to leave. The training home was then transferred to Gujarat and headquarters returned to Bombay.

Four Gujarati women entered the training home, the first Indian women who were publicly accepted as cadets. From the very commencement of Army activities in India, as elsewhere, women stood side by side with men Salvationists and fearlessly preached the gospel. The 'Army Mother', Catherine Booth, wife of the Founder had set the example: 'If indeed there is in Jesus Christ "neither male nor female" but in all touching His Kingdom they are one, who shall dare thrust woman out of the church's operations or presume to put any candle which God has lighted under a bushel?' Both William and Catherine Booth affirmed the right of women to share with men in proclaiming the truths of God.

It was no small achievement for Gujarati women, being used to a sheltered life and by nature reticent, to accept the responsibility of Salvation Army officership with the ensuing poverty and hardship. But having received Christ as their Saviour, their love for Him compelled them to give themselves in service for others. A report of one of the meetings at the commencement of their training gives evidence of their utter devotion:

After singing 'We will follow Thee to Calvary' they related their experiences, after which each was presented with the Army regulation dress, a fakir-coloured sari, which is worn everywhere as a public confession of Christ. It was further explained to them what officership really meant; how the world would hate them, how they must be ready for prison, or even death. But there was no wavering, these women were in real earnest; their tearful eyes spoke for them as they knelt down and consecrated themselves to God for the salvation of a dying world.

It was not long after this that Gulab Bai (Sister Rose), one of the cadets, was called to stand the test. She, together with Captain

Chakarvarti (a Bengali officer), two sergeants and four women soldiers were arrested and received prison sentences for marching in the streets of Ahmedabad. The Captain was sentenced to two months, the cadet to 21 days, the others to 12 days. The magistrate threatened a six-month sentence if they continued their marches. Only Indian Salvationists were prosecuted, the magistrate hoping thereby to frighten them so that they would leave *Muktifauj* and no Salvationists would be left in Gujarat. He was mistaken, for after the prosecution more people joined Ranipur Corps.

Cadet Gulab Bai was one of the first to join The Salvation Army when it arrived in Gujarat, because of it she had to face severe persecution and was beaten several times by angry relatives. Yet, in spite of this and her prison sentence, she remained faithful, and later, with the rank of Adjutant, she was put in charge of a group of villages. The bravery of Indian Salvationists must not be underestimated, for theirs was the difficult task of acting in opposition of their own family, in a country where family ties are strong and the only source of security.

The work in Gujarat prospered and many corps were established, but the Irish-Presbyterian mission, which looked upon Gujarat as its territory, was displeased and contested the Army's right to work in the area. In fact, no church council had given The Salvation Army any particular district in which to work, but for Tucker there were no borders, Christ's injunction 'Go ye therefore, and teach all nations', meant all nations.

Bishop Thoburn of the American Methodist Episcopalian Mission held the same viewpoint and stated both publicly and in mission conferences:

> If India is to be won, and its teeming millions are to be savingly converted to God these geographical limitations cannot be maintained. The inability to find men and money to properly deal with the large and diverse population, makes it impolitic, if not absurd, to protest against the presence of The Salvation Army, as if our efforts were directed to an opposition purpose.

After some time the misunderstandings were cleared and for many years the mission people and Salvationists have worked side by side for the people of Gujarat. When in 1908 Commissioner Booth-Tucker (Fakir Singh) came to the district the series of meetings began in the Presbyterian church.

3

The pearl of the ocean (1885-)

IN Ceylon the work commenced by Captain William Gladwin was showing promise and it was only natural that Weerasooriya, being Singhalese, should want to preach the good tidings of God's love to his own people. He made the journey to the island—the pearl of the ocean—at the beginning of January 1885, Major Tucker following soon after. The very first village they visited together, Talampitiya, was unfriendly and refused them hospitality and it was necessary for them to seek shelter in a cave for the night. Next morning when they left the cave they saw the footprints of a leopard which had prowled round their sleeping place and they thanked God for His protecting care.

When the people of the adjoining village, Hewadiwilla, heard of their whereabouts they invited Tucker and Weerasooriya to come and preach to them and here they witnessed the same wonderful scenes that had taken place in Gujarat. There was a great outpouring of the Holy Spirit and the work spread rapidly to the surrounding villages. When news of these happenings reached Talampitiya, where they previously had been turned away, an earnest invitation was sent, pleading with them to come back, and here, too, many conversions took place.

From Moratuwa, a densely populated district some 15 miles south of Colombo, Christian friends sent an invitation asking them to come and hold meetings. The inhabitants were nearly all carpenters or fishermen, as they are today, a century later. Quite a number of them were Christians but the majority were Buddhists. They were all fairly well off, their homes strongly built, each with a little plot of land where coconut, jack-fruit and bread-fruit trees flourished and supplemented their earnings. The moist climate, tempered with the soft sea breeze from the Indian Ocean, made it the home of a healthy, vigorous race. Similar villages lie along the coastline from Colombo to Galle, one of which, close to Galle, was the ancestral home of the Weerasooriyas.

During the commencement of the campaign, Tucker and Weerasooriya took up residence in a hut made with palm leaves which also served as their headquarters and as a meeting hall. The benches consisted of planks sawn from the trunks of palm trees. 'With a tambourine for a pillow, and nothing softer than the plank for a bed, we became such experts that we could balance ourselves on the narrowest of them,' wrote Major Tucker.

Fortunately, they were not to suffer this for long. After a few weeks they transferred their headquarters and quarters to another palm-leaf hut situated in a grove of coconut palms by the seashore. Quite an idyllic place where, after the heat of the day and the meetings were over, the two men would refresh themselves by a dip in the blue waters of the ocean.

They were greatly encouraged by the results of the campaign. Captain Weerasooriya wrote:

> About three weeks ago we commenced to enlist soldiers here. Hallelujah! As we look at these three weeks we feel sure of winning Ceylon soon. More than 100 Buddhists saved and testifying. Only the other day the village headman said that there was indeed very little room for the devil now in the village. This headman is fully saved. One who sells *appas* (a kind of bread) in the village is in a rage, and has once or twice disturbed our meeting. The reason being that six thieves, who have been in the habit of stealing areca nut and selling it to him at a cheap rate, to his disappointment, did not make the appearance with the stolen goods as usual before dawn. On inquiry, he found that the whole gang had got saved the previous night at our meeting!

It would be wrong to suppose that conversions were easily made and progress achieved without opposition. In Galle, Weerasooriya was knocked down on the street one day and kicked and beaten, but instead of striking back, or even defending himself, he kissed the hand of his persecutor and, kneeling down in the road, prayed that God would forgive and save his enemies.

Pavastina was a young girl who, together with her mother, was converted in one of the meetings. She was engaged to a Buddhist but felt now she could not marry him. When the young man was told that the engagement would be broken off unless he too became a Christian, he became so infuriated that he waylaid Pavastina on her way home from a meeting and stabbed her in eight different places. Her cries were heard and people came to her rescue and the young man fled. Seeing her mother weeping Pavastina said,

26

'Mother, don't cry, he has not stabbed my soul, it is only the body.' After making a good recovery the young girl became a Salvation Army officer and later married an officer and rendered excellent service for God in the Army in Ceylon.

Many other incidents of quiet heroism could be told, of gladly sharing in the 'sufferings of Christ'. Weerasooriya was often heard saying, 'The Cross is the attraction. The cross, inflicted by men, was taken over by God and made the manifestation of love and the instrument of salvation.'

Few Salvation Army officers nowadays have so vast a field of labour as Major Tucker had; the whole of the Indian sub-continent and Ceylon was his 'battleground'. The few officers under his command were frequently transferred from place to place to meet current demands. There was a crying need for more workers. A corps was opened in Lahore in 1883, but had to be closed down for lack of personnel. The Major himself was constantly on the move.

In August 1885 he again visited the north and at this time made history by preaching in the Sikh's 'holy of holies', the Golden Temple in Amritsar. The Punjab was where years earlier he had held the position of assistant commissioner, now he came in the garb of a fakir with a sack for his bedding and a small tin trunk for his papers and other belongings, which he jokingly called his headquarters. He reached the city at night and made his way to the temple wondering what the Lord would arrange for him. Walking through the 'Hall Darwaza' a fellow-traveller recognizing him enquired if he had anywhere to stay for the night. Finding that he had not, he volunteered to take Tucker to the *Dharamsala* belonging to the Golden Temple where pilgrims usually stay. He was kindly received and a *rasai* (quilt) was spread out for him on which to sleep. A soldier in the Sikh regiment brought him a bowl of sweetened milk and early the following morning showed him round the *Darbar Sahib*, as the Golden Temple is called. After returning to the *Dharamsala,* with the characteristic courtesy of the Sikhs, Major Tucker was given permission to address the many pilgrims and visitors gathered there and later a meeting was arranged in the *Guru ki bagh,* a garden attached to the temple. Here a friendly crowd had gathered. Major Tucker was shown a place on the edge of an empty water tank where he sat down with crossed legs, Indian fashion, and taught the people. The meeting lasted for more than two hours and Tucker reckoned there could not have been less than 800 Sikhs hearing the gospel message that day. It was indeed one of the most remarkable events that had yet occurred in the Salvation Army's history in India.

The first international congress of The Salvation Army was held in London in 1886. Major Tucker with Indian delegates were invited but were warned not to plead for reinforcements or financial aid for the work in India as the resources of the Army in England were already taxed to the limit. Converts from Hinduism, Islam and Buddhism made up the party. Their presence and witness made such an impression upon the congress audiences, in particular Weerasooriya's fervent testimony, that many offered for missionary service. The General relented and it was decided to send out a party of 40.

Major Tucker saw it necessary to formulate a memorandum to prepare the officers for the sort of life they would be entering and the sacrifices they would be called upon to make. The following is a slightly abbreviated version:

MEMORANDUM FOR VOLUNTEERS FOR INDIAN SERVICE

Whilst it is most gladdening to find so many ready to go 'anywhere with Jesus', including to India, Ceylon or Burmah, it is especially important in connection with such a task that none should go to these lands who have not fully weighed the cost, tested, so far as they can, their fitness for the work, and resolved to offer not merely in the sense of being willing to go 'anywhere' **but in the sense of wishing to live and die for the particular race to which they are sent.**

Spiritual need—Remember that you are likely to be absolutely alone, it may be for months together, so far as English officers are concerned. No officers' meetings to go to, except very rarely. Your life, especially if in a village, will be far more closely watched than it would be in an English one, by a people whose ideas of religion make them far more particular than English villagers as to all the acts and words of a professed teacher of religion.

Remember that in the study of a language and of a people whose ideas are all entirely different from the English, you will have such a task as you never had in your own country, a task to be stuck to and worked out alone.

Remember that the difficulty of making soldiers must needs be far greater there than that of making them in a so-called Christian land.

Remember that the weariness and sickness of the body, which you are sure to feel more in India than here, are always used by the devil to pull you down, and that just at the very times when your fellow-soldiers will need most help to keep them going.

Remember that your influence, as an officer from another land, must needs be very great. You must be a model officer or a curse to the work.

Language—Next to spiritual qualifications, the great need is, of course, a knowledge of the language of the people. There is no question at all about its being a very heavy task, and unless you set your heart upon it, contrive how to get on from step to step, and keep steadily at it hour after hour, and month after month, you will be only a burden in India.

Native dress and living—The dress you will wear will somewhat depend upon the place to which you are sent. But you must make up your mind to leave entirely and forever behind you all your English dress and habits. It is extremely important that you should take with you as little as possible in the way of luggage. All that you can possibly do without should be left behind. Men and women must use a thick cotton umbrella, on account of the sun. Except in rare cases, officers will be barefooted, like all the rest of the people.

Quarters—The sort of house you may have to live in may be about 16 ft by 10 ft, with mud walls, tiled or thatched roof, lattice or wire windows; no fireplace or chimney—fires not being needed, except for cooking, which is usually done on the verandah, or behind the house. In the villages the men must expect to have no furniture at all, except some mats, and must learn to sit on the ground like a tailor. Women and married officers will have a bed, table and chair. You will have for your food such pots and vessels only as are used by Indians. You will have to learn to cook just as they do, and to wash your clothes at the stream with them.

Food—This will, of course, vary with the part of country you serve in. In a Gujarati village it consists of rice, peas, vegetables, fruit, unleavened bread, and milk. . . . In most parts of Ceylon fish is abundant, and is freely eaten. In the large towns ordinary European food can be obtained, but should be avoided as much as possible, except in cases of sickness, loss of appetite, etc. When travelling, or first entering a place, you will have to beg your food from door to door, in order to get on a friendly footing with the people. Always bear in mind that it is not intended you should ever lose your strength and health, on which the success of the Army will so much depend. It will be your duty immediately to inform headquarters if you are not getting enough to keep up your strength, as otherwise you may become ill and occasion enormous loss and expense that timely care would have saved. There being no sanitary arrangement in the villages, the water is often bad, and should be boiled before drinking. The only drink, in many villages, other than plain water, is milk, but by a little contrivance tea can usually be obtained.

29

A strange people—Nothing is harder to explain, and nothing more important to remember, than that you go to people whose ideas and life are altogether different from all you have ever known. The Indian people are intensely religious. It will be useless to talk to them, as you have done to English crowds, about having 'neglected God and turned a deaf ear to His call,' etc. You must not only learn their language, but learn about them at the same time—to find out what are their thoughts and feelings, and so know how to win them for their Saviour Jesus Christ.

A life work—All this must convince anyone that it is useless to go to India with any idea of permanently returning. We would not think of sending anyone out who we did not feel sure would be willing to make it a life work. There is, therefore, no promise or plan for bringing back any officer at set times. The Indian staff are ready to show all care and kindness, and would not wish to keep in India anyone whose ill health would render them useless there, whilst they might live and do good service in Australia or elsewhere; but they must be left to form their own judgement in each case, and we wish all who go to look upon India as their adopted country, and to expect, as a matter of course, to die there sooner or later.

Undeterred by the severity of the terms and promised hardship the chosen 40 set out in high hopes of winning India* for Christ. The SS *Clan Ogilvie* was chartered for the party, third-class passages being of very moderate rates. The days on the voyage were spent attending lectures, band practices and language lessons. In the meetings great concern for the salvation of India was expressed through the prayers and testimonies of the prospective missionaries. Lectures on India were given daily by Commissioner Tucker, who had been promoted to that rank, while Weerasooriya was now a Colonel and appointed second in command. They were then aged 32 and 28 respectively. In spite of his youth and being comparatively new to the Army, Weerasooriya proved himself worthy of the confidence placed in him. His officers, of whatever nationality, respected and loved him.

The party of 40, the first big group of missionary officers, arrived in Colombo 19 September 1886, exactly four years after the four pioneers landed in Bombay, to the very date. Officers and soldiers of Colombo Corps were at the landing jetty to give them a rousing welcome, after which all fell in for a grand march through the town to the Army hall where a meeting was held the same night. The hall was packed out with many unable to get in. The spirit of the meeting was one of joy and thankfulness and every testimony

*British India included Ceylon.

gave expression of a sincere love for the people they had come to serve.

Moratuwa was the next place to be visited. From the railway station a march was formed with band and banners which swept through the streets. A triumphal arch was erected outside the hall and many sought salvation in the meetings. More than 80 seekers were registered during the first month of their arrival.

The many conversions to Christ began to worry the Buddhist priests and as a countermeasure they launched a Buddhist Salvation Army, using Army songs and staging showy processions with dancing and drums headed by elephants bedecked with garlands. At first they attracted large crowds but their enthusiasm and desire to emulate the Army spirit soon wavered. It was doomed to fail from the beginning, their doctrine being a direct contradiction of the Christian faith in a living God and the gift of salvation. In Buddhism there is no Redeemer; the Buddha, Gautema Siddhatta's last words before he died were, 'Decay is inherent in all things, work out your own salvation.'

Having seen the new missionary officers well settled in Ceylon, Tucker and Weerasooriya left for Madras where Major Bullard was now divisional commander. Soon after their arrival Commissioner Tucker received a letter from the well-known China missionary, C. T. Studd, with a cheque for £5,000, a welcome gift indeed! A telegram was despatched to General William Booth with a request for further reinforcement of officers since money was now available to meet expenses. The General, keenly interested in India, promptly assented to the request and Weerasooriya was sent off to England to assist in their selection and in making the necessary arrangements for bringing them to India.

Included in one of the first parties of reinforcements was Henry Burfoot. When leaving England in December 1886 he took with him nothing more than four books, his Bible and three volumes of Catherine Booth's writings, and the Indian clothes he wore on the voyage. Of the 44 years he spent in India, the first 12 were spent among the poorest villagers in Gujarat. Taking the name of Dayasagar—Ocean of Mercy—he lived like them and married a Gujarati convert from Ahmedabad. He mastered Gujarati as well as other Indian languages, became Editor of *Jangi Pokar* the Gujarati *War Cry,* and for years contributed religious articles to secular papers, a mission which was carried on by a later scholar, Brigadier Dana Das (H. Pimm Smith).

Mrs Louisa Tucker shared with her husband his deep religious convictions and earnest desire to win India for Christ. In public meetings she addressed the congregations with great zeal. A Bramo Samaj paper wrote about Mrs Tucker:

> To say that Mrs Tucker was eloquent would not be to say what she really is. She is deliberate, she is forcible, she speaks in tones which seem surcharged with conviction and feeling. She has not unoften been seen bursting into tears when she makes an appeal to her hearers. . . . She is so frail, so thin, that it is a wonder how she can speak with such energy. Mrs Tucker could, if she and her worthy husband chose, become the wife of a judge and commissioner and occupy the highest places that are given to the official aristocracy of the land. But she has chosen now to walk as a mendicant in the company of lowly mendicants singing and glorifying her Saviour.

But the austerity of the fakir life-style, and the fact that she was 18 years senior to her husband, had its effect and she was often unable, for health reasons, to accompany him on his tours. She would then do her part in Bombay visiting the prisoners in jail, caring for the sick and selling copies of *The War Cry*. In February 1887 she contracted cholera and died. Her last words were, 'Jesus is present, I am ready!' News of her death reached Commissioner Tucker while he was on his way home from the south, but as funerals in the tropics take place promptly after death, he could not reach Bombay in time. The Indian *War Cry* reports the funeral:

> The remains of Mrs Tucker were carried to their last resting place in Sewrie Cemetery. We met at Marine Lines and had a consecrating time around the coffin. We sang on our knees the glorious and bright experience of our departed sister:
>
> > *I will love Thee in life, I will love Thee in death,*
> > *And praise Thee as long as Thou lendest me breath;*
> > *And say, when the death-dew lies cold on my brow:*
> > *If ever I loved Thee, my Jesus, 'tis now.*

When General Booth was informed of Mrs Tucker's promotion to Glory (the Army's description of the death of Salvationists), he sent Commissioner Tucker a cable expressing his sympathy and requesting him to come to England to take charge of the new party of officers now being selected for India.

Eighteen hundred and eighty seven was the year of Queen Victoria's Golden Jubilee and The Salvation Army celebrated it by sending 50 officers to India. This was the second big group of officers to be sent out, others followed at intervals, such as the Wedding Fifty (1888), the Memorial Fifty (1890), the Founder's Memorial Party (1913), the Scandinavian Party (1914), the Calypso Party (1921), and the Bramwell Booth 70th Birthday Party (1926).

It was found advantageous to send officers in large parties under the leadership of someone experienced in Indian conditions, using the voyage as a time of preparation. Being together the officers found strength in each other's friendship and the more diffident were encouraged by the confidence of others. Also the large parties helped to attract the interest and attention of the people to whom they were sent, thereby gaining more immediate results.

A dedication and farewell meeting for the Jubilee Fifty was held at Exeter Hall, 29 June 1887. 'While others have been celebrating Her Majesty's Jubilee in various ways and making costly offerings', said Commissioner Fakir Singh, 'I am certain no one has chosen a more blessed and glorious way than The Salvation Army for permanently blessing the part of the British dominion where more than three-fourths of our fellow subjects live. It is less than five years since we landed in Bombay, only four strong. Who would have thought that in so short a time we should have been able to bring out such reinforcements? What has God wrought? To Him alone be all the glory!' He also reminded the congregation that although he was very thankful to have 185 officers, as he would have when the present contingent reached its destination, yet what were they amongst the 250,000,000 people of India?

When the Jubilee Fifty landed in Bombay, 28 August, another letter from C. T. Studd was received with a further cheque, for £1,000, which was used towards the purchase of a building adjoining Victoria Terminus Railway Station in the centre of Bombay, which was known for years as 'India's great Salvation centre'.

4

'So send I you' (1887-)

AT first it was intended to divide the 50 new missionary officers between the Tamils in the south and the Mahrattas in western India, but General Booth finally decided that the whole party should make a concentrated attack on the Tamil country and promised further reinforcements for the Maharashstra.

The same year (1887) a large contingent was sent out from Australia and a smaller party from Canada and Sweden. Two Indian converts, Staff-Captains Chuckerbutty and Narain Das, visited Sweden in August 1887 and brought the need of India before the Swedish people. (The Salvation Army had then been in operation five years in Sweden.) Chuckerbutty was a converted Brahmin from Burdwas; at the age of 23 he was once about to take his life, when he came into contact with Major Tucker who showed him the way to a new life in Christ. Narain Das was studying law when he first met Tucker in Amritsar. Dissatisfied with his traditional religion his eyes were opened to the glory of God through the Lord Jesus. These two Indian visitors stirred the Swedish people by their testimonies.

At the same time William Booth sent out a call for 'Missionaries to the millions' through *The War Cry*. No less than 40 offered for service from Sweden out of which seven were sent to India. They landed in Bombay 5 February 1888. When the ship cast anchor they stood barefooted on the sundrenched deck, Carl Boivie (later Lieut.-Colonel) made a bundle of his European clothes and dropped them into the sea. His first prayer when he stepped ashore was 'So help me God', and assurance came to him in the words, 'The very hairs of your head are all numbered'. Anna Pettersson was another officer who as Mrs Costly was to spend 50 years in India. She wrote home from Bombay, 'We are working among the poorest of the poor. It is hard for the flesh but so much more wonderful for the soul'.

34

To accommodate some of the newcomers a temporary camp was set up in Coimbatore where several rows of mud huts were erected. Here the officers were preparing themselves for the great tasks ahead, trying to acquire some knowledge of the Indian way of life and language. A hall was erected and a training home for Tamil cadets was established. One of the officers wrote a description of the place in a letter home:

> It is a lot of little mud huts built in a square, white outside and in, with a dining room in the middle, which is built of palm leaves. Two or three sleep in each room. I shall never forget the first night lying down to sleep on the floor. We have no furniture, only a mat and a blanket. But I felt my Saviour had nowhere to lay His head, and though my body was on the floor, I felt His arms were round me, and the next morning I was as much at home as in London.

Among the early pioneers, to mention but a few, were Alfred Hipsey, Arthur Blowers, William Stevens, Joseph Pothecary, Edgar Hoe, Lottie McIlwraith (better known as Anbai), Clara Case, Elizabeth Geikie (Puramai), who became Mrs Stevens, and Mary Tomlinson (Mithri), who became Mrs Blowers. Henry Mapp joined the pioneers in Bombay where he was born of English parents. He discarded his status as a sahib and became a Christian *sadhu*. After years of service in India and elsewhere he was appointed Chief of the Staff at International Headquarters. Catherine Booth's charge—'to prove by self-denial their love for Christ'—was faithfully carried out by these pioneers.

One other officer, Captain William Johnston (Jaya Kodi), who pioneered the work in Travancore, was with his wife and children at the Coimbatore centre. He reported:

> Last week we turned out for a week among the villages. We started every morning about five, walking on until the sun became too hot, then taking up our abode under some trees near a village. Here the people came to us in crowds and we told them of salvation from sin. The people gave us food, and received us with all kindness. Few had ever heard of salvation.

With the increased number of officers it was thought the time was ripe to make a concentrated attack on the many large cities in south India, the stronghold of Hinduism. Officers were despatched to Tanjore, Negapatam, Kumbakonan and Trichinopoly. They would go first to the caste people and try to win them for Christ. The men officers adopted the custom of hair-style (the front half of the head clean shaved and the rest long) and caste marks used by Hindus, painting the Army colours—the yellow, red and blue—across their forehead to denote that they were Salvation Army *sanyasis* (religious devotees committed under oath to a life of ascetism and self-abnegation). They found it a talking point! To any enquirer of what the colours stood for the reply would be, 'The red is the symbol of the Blood of Christ which was shed on Calvary to save mankind. The yellow signifies the fire of the Holy Spirit which cleanses us from sin, and the blue stands for purity, which should be the hallmark of every Salvationist.' Not very many high-caste Indians were won and those who accepted Christ suffered severe persecution, but those who did become converted and stood up to the persecution, such as Narayana Muthiah, Yesu Dasen, Yesu Chandra and others, became a great strength to the Army.

After some time Commissioner Tucker came to the same conclusion as he had done previously in Bombay, 'that it was to the 60 millions of the depressed castes that our mission lay'.

Women officers, bravely toiling in India, could look back to their training period in London under Emma Booth, the second daughter of William and Catherine Booth. At the age of 19 she had been made principal of the first training home for women and sometimes had under her care as many as 300 cadets in a session. Commissioner Tucker, when selecting women candidates for India had had to rely entirely on her judgement. He had come to admire her keen mind and deep concern for her charges. Soon his admiration grew into love, a love which was reciprocated, and when he asked her to be his wife she readily agreed. The wedding was set for 10 April 1888.

As Salvationists all the world over, so did Emma and Frederick avow:

> We have not sought this marriage for the sake of our own happiness and interests only, although we believe these will be furthered thereby.

For them the union was to further the interests of India. Even the wedding was to be an occasion for attracting more candidates for India and to finance their journey. Hence an entrance fee of five shillings was charged, while seats for sixpence were reserved for Salvationists unable to pay more. The Congress Hall at Clapton, seating 5,000, was packed to the doors, many unable to get in. General William Booth presided, his wife Catherine at his side. The bride, in her neat navy blue uniform relieved by a white sash, looked radiant; the bridegroom was dressed in the yellow robes of an Indian fakir and was barefooted. The General commented on the fact that here were two who, when his days were over, 'would go forward to seek to spread divine love and brotherhood of mankind'.

In his speech the bridegroom likened their union to the two great rivers which meet at Allahabad (the City of God), where Hindu pilgrims flock to get their sins washed away. 'So I trust it may be that the Lord has united the two streams of our lives—that at this place we may be able to found a spiritual city of God, so that our united streams may be the means of salvation to millions of people— especially to that country which God has so peculiarly laid upon our hearts.' After the wedding it was announced that Commissioner Tucker's name was changed to Booth-Tucker by deed poll and that Emma was given the rank of Consul.

Amidst all the pressure and strain of the last days before leaving England, the bride took time to reveal a few of her inner feelings to the Editor of *All the World*:

> No one could be more surprised than myself when the call came for the new work. Knitting stockings and carrying gruel to old people seemed to me, as a child, the very most I should ever dare to do! Then I began to have a great love and tenderness for the children; and when I first had 25 lasses in my training home I felt the responsibility was crushing! But all through, even from those early days, I have had what I may almost call a passion for woman. I saw, I felt, I grasped what a woman could do, if she only had the chance and was fitted for it. That has been in all these years my guiding thought, and in taking up this new responsibility I do not feel I am having a change of work—it is only a mighty continuation of the same.

> It's curious, in looking back, to notice that India always had a special place in my heart. As a child, I could draw the map of India better than any other, and of all my happy training home work, the very happiest always seemed to be, when I was preparing my girls for India. My going is the clincher to all that I have ever striven to teach my lasses. I go to do what I have always taught them to do. In a letter I received a few days ago, I noticed the sentence, 'The women of India need a champion.' I yearn to inspire and lift them up, my lifework, therefore, will still be to reach and serve woman.

Mrs Booth-Tucker did to the very last, up to her tragic death, inspire and encourage women in their common cause. But it was not to be in India. 'God moves in a mysterious way, His wonders to perform.' Her time in India was to be only a matter of months, as we will see later. Eight wonderful years of devoted service she gave to the United States of America when, on 21 October 1903, after a very successful campaign, the train in which she was travelling was hurled off the line and Emma Booth-Tucker was 'promoted to Glory'.

But back to the time of our narrative. The weeks following the wedding were spent in selecting and training new recruits. During Commissioner Booth-Tucker's absence from India, Colonel Weerasooriya had been left in sole charge of the work and proved himself a very competent leader. Then came a telegram to say that the Colonel had died of cholera.

The last business which had engaged Colonel Weerasooriya's attention was characteristic of the man—thoughtfulness for others. He had gone to Mount Abu in search of a home of rest for missionary officers working in Gujarat. Great strain had been put on the officers during a cholera epidemic, and the hot season with temperatures soaring over the 100 mark was well on its way. Homes of rest had already been rented in Ootacamund in the Nilgiri Hills and Khandala on the Western Ghats.

Returning to Ahmedabad he visited an officer who had been stricken with cholera, which was then raging in the city. It was doubtless whilst at this officer's bedside that he caught the deadly malady. It was not the first time that he had fearlessly exposed himself to the infection. In the previous year he had helped to nurse another officer through a similar attack. But this time he was tired out with an exhausting journey in the hottest season of the year, and hence became an easy prey to the dreaded disease. He was able to continue his journey to Bombay, and it was not until he had arrived there that the cholera developed its fatal symptoms. The doctor was sent for, and every effort made to save his life, but in vain.

An officer, who at the risk of her own life, nursed the Colonel to the end, sent this moving account of his last hours to Booth-Tucker:

I feel that my best and truest friend, next to God, has left me. I can imagine a little of what you must feel by my own grief. Yet he died like a soldier, with no sign of fear; and amid the most terrible agony his face lit up with such a strange brightness, as he said with a smile, 'It's nice to

38

be saved!' As the dreary hours of night wore on, and our hopes grew fainter, we learned how much we loved him. As time wore on he spoke of trust being trust, and when one of us began to sing softly his old favourite hymn, 'Blessèd Lord, in Thee is refuge', he joined in singing the chorus, both in English and Singhalese, over and over, 'I will trust Thee! All my life Thou shalt control.' After a little while he passed calmly away. Next day, at 4 pm crowds thronged the Esplanade—rows and rows of carriages. With band playing, we marched him to the cemetery, and gave him a proper Army funeral, over 200 comrades and friends followed him to the grave.

General William Booth wrote from London:

Beloved Comrades!
God has allowed a heavy blow to fall in your midst, in the removal of our beloved brother, Colonel Weerasooriya, to Heaven. A man of wisdom, energy and love has fallen, a man on whom I had built many high hopes, and whom you revered and loved has left us. He has gone up to his inheritance, and joined the hosts of Heaven, and martyrs, who, having followed the Lamb on earth, are now with Him crowned and rejoicing in the Heavenly City—my faith grasps the promise that even this will be made to work together for the furtherance of the War.

Your path is plain before you, and that is to go straight on in the work with renewed energy, to give yourselves to the task of carrying it forward. You can ever reckon on the prayers and co-operation of
Your affectionate General
William Booth

It was indeed a severe blow for Booth-Tucker, not only had he lost a trusted officer, but also a dear friend. Thus in the midst of rejoicing came sorrow, and he had to leave his new bride and hasten back to India. With him travelled Major Lampart (taking the name Ajeet Singh) who, at a few days' notice, was given orders to leave for India and was appointed chief secretary. Major Musa Bhai, who had accompanied Booth-Tucker to England, together with four other Indian officers, was sent to Canada where Commissioner Coombe had promised 20 more officers for India. The 20 were picked from over 300 volunteers. Commissioner Coombe's own son gave his life for India. Salvationists in America, Australia, France, Switzerland and Scandinavia and other countries volunteered for service. The salvation of India was on everyone's heart all round the Army world.

Fifty officers having been selected, the 'Wedding Party' started out for India in the autumn of 1888. They travelled across the

Continent to Genoa, stopping for meetings in Paris. Their exuberant joy and enthusiasm created curiosity in trains and refreshment rooms and surprise when they were seen kneeling to pray before leaving. They arrived at Genoa at midnight singing 'Victory for me' and 'No, we never will give in', their fervour having in no way lessened by the lateness of the hour. Launches took them to the SS *Dominico Balduino,* moored in the harbour and ready to sail at daybreak.

The ship became a floating training home during the three weeks' voyage as with the previous large party. The Army had taken full possession of the lower deck's third-class accommodation. Mrs Booth-Tucker was now known as Commissioner Rahiman—the merciful or the compassionate one—her presence acted as an inspiration to all on board. The days went quickly, every hour being occupied with language lessons, lectures, band practices and meetings. At night passengers turned up to listen to the singing and speaking. So impressed were the ship's captain and his crew that they attended the welcome meeting in Bombay and even invited the party to come back and hold another meeting on board 'for all the crew seem to have joined the Army!'

Commissioner Rahiman won the hearts of the Indian people from the very start, as with her husband she travelled the length and breadth of India and Ceylon. A busy programme of meetings was planned for the cooler months starting in October. Wherever they went she had a word of encouragement to the women officers.

*   *   *

When Janet Unwin heard that three of her companions at the London training home had been chosen for service in India, she pleaded with 'Miss Emma', now known as the Consul, to let her go as well. 'The Wedding Party' was leaving in three days, could she be ready? She could.

On board the SS *Dominico Balduino* was another officer, John Russell, who found in Janet a kindred spirit and two years later John and Janet (now Manohar and Veera Bai) were married in Bombay in the Bori Bunder Hall.

They were among the very first to 'invade' the villages of Maharashstra, the western state of which Bombay is the capital. They made their home in Sirur, a large village surrounded by barren hills in an area where lack of rain causes scarcity and frequent famine. Similar to other officers their one-room mud hut was both home and office. Their one box constituted their only worldly possession and served as table, desk, wardrobe and stores. There was no furniture. They slept on straw mats on the hard earth floor at night. Later wooden rope-strung cots and mosquito nets were provided on health grounds, William Booth having urged Booth-Tucker to modify the extreme fakir existence.

Today there is a small brick-built Army hall in Sirur, the gospel is still being preached 90 years after that brave beginning. John Russell's service in India was cut short by typhus fever. He was promoted to Glory in Madras in 1904 at the age of 38 leaving a young widow with six children, the youngest, Leslie John, but two months old. Twenty-one years later Leslie returned to India to continue the work of his father, taking his Indian name Manohar. The last 10 of Colonel Leslie J. Russell's 33 years in the sub-continent were spent in western India as international auditor in Poona and financial secretary in Bombay. With his wife, Nellie, he made a pilgrimage to Sirur, the village where his parents had pioneered the work.

Another pioneer in Maharashstra was Catherine Bannister (Yuddha Bai), daughter of a London solicitor. With a group of other women pioneer officers she led a march, singing with great enthusiasm what they believed to be the Marathi words of, 'Come, O come with me where love is beaming'. The language teacher, whose prowess they had depended upon, had mistakenly rendered it: 'Come, O come with me, and see my husband'! Yuddha Bai vowed she would master the language and not depend on others' translation. With her feet in a bucket of water to avoid mosquito bites and prevent ants and other insects from running up her legs she would spend hours learning the difficult Sanskrit-based Marathi language. Her contribution to the Marathi song book is a lasting wealth to Marathi Salvationists. The names of Colonel Yuddha Bai and Brigadier Shanti Bai (her sister) will always be honoured in the Maharashstra.

Colonel Van de Werken (Dayali) and Lieut.-Colonel Gugelmann (Sundri) from Holland, who subsequently took charge of the Marathi Territory and helped to consolidate the work before they moved on to Indonesia, have left on record some of their experiences:

We had some remarkable encounters when it came to billets in our travels round the territory. We decided in one place to sleep in the open front of the quarters, so our camp beds were placed there after the meeting and we said good night to the people. But lo! they did not think of moving and, as one of our Indian officers said, 'they want to see the last of you'. We at last went to bed with the whole village looking on in dead silence.

Once our train stopped at a wayside station. The station-master came up to my window and asked, 'Will you send me a Bible?' 'Are you a Christian?' I responded. 'No, I am not. I must wait till my parents are dead, I could not grieve them by turning Christian, but I want a Bible for my son and daughter, I do not want them to grow up without a knowledge of that Book.'

5

A change of leadership (1889-)

'ONLY those who fully understand the desperate nature of the battle that has had to be fought, can duly estimate the extent of the victory God has granted to us in our Indian "War",' declared Commissioner Fakir Singh at the beginning of 1889.

To say that our advance has been more solid, as well as more rapid, than in any previous 12 months, expresses but poorly the things we have seen and heard and for which we give praise to God alone.

We have now a devoted band of 170 officers gathered from all parts of the world; round them are clustered more than 100 Indian officers and cadets, who have caught from them the real Army spirit. Our officers are very largely supported by funds collected in India. We have almost doubled the number of our corps at which meetings are daily held. Last year we had but 30, now we have 56. Marathi work has just been commenced with Bombay as the centre. During the past year we have erected substantial barracks at Gamri and Samarkha (Gujarat), Moratuwa Mulla (Ceylon) with two larger and more expensive ones at Coimbatore (south India) and Ambala (Punjab).

In Ceylon we have now 33 European officers and 47 national officers under the leadership of Major Jai Bhai (Paynter). The prison-gate work has proved a decided success and receives a monthly grant of Rs50 from the Ceylon Government. Every facility is afforded to our officers in the way of visiting the prisons, and meetings inside the jails are regularly held. A large number of criminals have professed conversion. At Galle and Jaffna, the two extreme points of the island, powerful work has commenced. Meetings have also been started among the Tamil coolies on some of the estates, we have now 19 corps on the island.

In Bombay we have also started a prison-gate brigade, which has already captured several desperate characters among the criminals. There are now four corps, a prison-gate brigade, and two training homes working. Besides headquarters staff there are now in the city 46 European and seven Indian officers.

In Gujarat during the past year work here was put to a painful and unexpected test by a virulent and prolonged epidemic of cholera, during which three officers and several soldiers received their promotion to the Heavenly rank. We have now 13 corps and 45 officers in Gujarat.

The Tamil country: The energy and push of The Salvation Army, together with its lively meetings, have been a great attraction to the Tamils of south India, among whom we have now gained a firm foothold. The entire work has been placed under the management of a Tamil Major. During the past year the corps have increased from five to 15.

Calcutta: Here we have an interesting work, which gives promise of soon developing into an important district. Among the Bengalees we have many warm-hearted friends and supporters, and in Calcutta itself we have established a corps which has fought bravely on amid many difficulties.

Ambala: The opening of the Punjab will form an interesting chapter in the future history of our Indian warfare. Already, through Staff-Captain Mrs Bulman's earnest efforts, a number have sought salvation. She has secured a piece of land at Ambala City and built upon it a large and substantial barracks, which is now nearly completed.

The Paper War: The circulation of our English *War Cry* with a circulation of 2,750 takes a leading place. We are issuing 1,845 vernacular papers every week published in four different tongues—Singhalese, Tamil, Gujarati, Marathi. An auxiliary worker in Kandy has been sending copies of *All the World* to all the influential people he could think of, beginning with the Governor of Ceylon.

In England the deterioration of Catherine Booth's health was giving cause for grave anxiety and her daughter Emma felt it her duty to be by the side of her mother and nurse her during the short remaining time allotted to her. So with sad heart she said goodbye to her husband to whom she had been married only a year and to the country which had won her affection, and returned to England in April 1889.

Commissioner Booth-Tucker had occasion to visit England five months later, but only for a short while. Another party of officers was to be selected, known as the 'Self-Denial Twenty'. The 20 were assembled together in eight days and 'scarcely one of them knew before that time that they were destined for the distant East. When 'wired' (sent a telegram) in many cases the immediate reply was 'Anywhere for Jesus'. Among them was Captain Clara Case, who at the beginning of the Self-Denial week had been impressing upon her cadets the importance of personal self-denial.

Afterwards, kneeling in prayer, she felt how insignificant her own offering had been and said to God, 'How can I give Thee something that will really prove my love to Thee?' Two days later a telegram arrived—she had received the Lord's answer—it was the call to India. She responded at once. The following Monday, 30 September, she farewelled from the Congress Hall, Clapton with the 19 others. It was another occasion for rejoicing and bringing the need of India to the fore.

The Congress Hall presented a scene of oriental splendour and was crowded to the doors. Hundreds of cadets were massed on the platform, carrying flags and wearing *chadars* (shawls) and turbans, the latter of all kinds of delicate hues. Mrs Bramwell Booth, Mrs Commissioner Railton, the Foreign Secretary, and various staff officers did honour to the occasion by donning oriental robes, and on the platform floor in front, were four little children sitting cross-legged with bare feet. Major Jai Bhai and his party of Indians helped to complete a very striking picture.

Again Commissioner Booth-Tucker had to leave his wife. Catherine Booth was gradually getting weaker and in her sufferings she found comfort in her daughter's love and care. In his speech at the farewell meeting the Commissioner said: 'I am about to leave my precious wife behind, but I have sometimes noticed that God's sweetest sweets have to be taken with the bitterest bitters.'

The voyage out was again spent in language study, orientation classes and meetings; this party distinguished itself by turning up at the ship's fancy-dress ball dressed in Indian uniforms and conducting a vigorous salvation meeting!

On arrival in Colombo, the party took part in a short campaign conducted by Commissioner Booth-Tucker, after which they were sent to their various appointments. Clara Case was given the name Nurani (Shining Light), which she truly lived up to. With two other young missionary officers—like herself ignorant of the language and customs of the country—she was sent in charge of the corps at Palamcottah near Tinnevelly. Fortunately for them an Indian translator accompanied.

The 'girls' soon settled down in the little mud hut and made light of the inconveniences. The same mats they slept on at night they sat on at meals eating rice and curry with their fingers—'nature's forks' Nurani called them. A tiny palm-leaf shed served as a bathing place, where with a coconut shell they douched themselves. In these conditions Nurani wrote, 'Our Heavenly Father cared for His children, who were carefree and supremely happy.'

But it was not every officer who could accept the hardship with as intrepid a spirit as Clara Case. Another officer wrote:

> Oh, the agonizing prayers, the silent, bitter tears, the daily struggle against the weakness of the flesh, and often the inability to express rightly and forcibly those vital truths on which the salvation of souls depends.

Indian women usually live a protected life within the family circle and at the time of our narrative few engaged in public work. Some women had excelled themselves by their courage and fearlessness, but they were the exceptions rather than the rule. Booth-Tucker felt at this juncture that a training home for women should be established and Staff-Captain Nurani was chosen for the job. She was duly appointed to open a training garrison in Madras—and to find the cadets! Even though she knew, as yet, little of India, she knew God's power and the value of prayer. Within six months the first session began with 10 Indian and two Anglo-Indian women. House-to-house visiting was part of their training. One day when two of the cadets went out for their usual three hours selling copies of *The War Cry* and visiting they were specially urged to seek God's guidance.

As they were walking towards the sea they noticed some women sitting out-doors and asked them if they wished to hear songs about God. They were invited to enter the house. As they entered they noticed some evil-looking men coming out, but being inexperienced they had no idea that they had come to a house of ill fame. They sang their songs about God and spoke of deliverance from sin. After this one woman sought shelter at the training home, which led to Staff-Captain Nurani arranging for the first rescue home to be opened in Madras. The Haven, The Salvation Army's oldest social home in India, is still meeting a great need. Under its roof are 80 or more women and children who need protection. The 'family system', by which each woman takes under her wing two or three little ones, ensures that every child receives love and care.

In a powerful article in the Indian *War Cry,* Nurani appealed for candidates for officership for the second session. She called for 'women with hearts brave and tender, bold enough to rise up and, breaking through conventionalities and customs, castes and prejudice, cry "My country needs me!"—You say you are only an unpolished simple girl, but in the hand of God you shall become a saviour, a deliverer of your countrymen and women—if only you are willing to risk all, even to sealing your testimony with your blood. Would it be very hard to die for your country's salvation? Is it too hard to live for it?' Twenty women accepted the challenge.

Often Nurani and her cadets were persecuted and roughly treated. On one occasion the police summoned a group, including Captain Sukh Singh (Arthur Blowers), to appear in court. Fines were imposed. Nurani did not want the Indian girl-cadets to go to prison and missionary officers were willing to pay the fine. The cadets, however, would not hear of it, they insisted on going to prison 'as our European sisters have done'. Sukh Singh, who together with another British officer was thrust into a cell next to the women-cadets, was greatly cheered hearing them sing, 'No, we never, never, never will give in!'

Happily the cadets were released before their time, due to 'Mother Nurani's prayers', they said. Their courage was a living testimony, and when later they again held open-air meetings on the beach the fishermen and women said, 'We believe in your religion, because you are not afraid to go to prison and suffer for it.'

Nurani and her women-cadets were the forerunners of dedicated and dauntless women, too numerous to mention—Indian, Singhalese, Burmese, Pakistani women who, together with their sisters from western lands, have given their lives for the salvation of the people of South Asia.

*   *   *

Catherine Booth, affectionately known by Salvationists the world over as the 'Army Mother' was promoted to Glory on 4 October 1890. A 'Memorial Party' numbering 64 officers left for India a few weeks after the funeral. Mrs Booth-Tucker was returning to India together with her husband and her sister Lucy. They landed in Colombo on Christmas Day 1890. The day following their arrival, 150 officers gathered in council and the same evening saw the opening of the finest barracks in Ceylon, situated on the main road on Slave Island in Colombo. In Kandy, Commissioner Rahiman (Mrs Booth-Tucker) gave the address in the spacious Audience Hall of the Kandy kings. But she was far from well, the long anxious months of nursing her mother had taken their toll. Other important engagements followed but Commissioner Rahiman became too ill to participate and it was arranged for her to go by ship to Bombay and rest there, while the others continued the scheduled tour.

Lucy Booth, now known as Colonel Ruhani (the pious or soulful one), took her sister's place and laid the foundation stone of the barracks in Moratuwa 1. 'Great meetings followed, first in Madras occupying Victoria Hall, "the finest building in the place", preceded by a large open-air gathering on the Maidan (Esplanade) and an imposing march led by the Memorial Brass Band and comprising a war chariot, mounted marshals, and about 120 officers, besides soldiers and a vast crowd of interested onlookers.'

Meetings in Poona followed, where the Lord Harris Theatre was crowded. Arriving in Bombay they found an important assembly of influential people gathered in the Framji Cowasji Institute to consider William Booth's social scheme for India presented by Commissioner Booth-Tucker. This scheme, called 'Darkest India',was to be an extension of William Booth's social venture in Britain named 'Darkest England'. Booth-Tucker was not to see the launching of that scheme, but he had already laid the foundation and years later did much to expand it.

Mrs Booth-Tucker's health did not improve and there was grave concern for her, so much so that the doctor advised an immediate return to England to a temperate climate. That the day of departure from India in January 1891 was a sad day for Commissioner and Mrs Booth-Tucker one can well imagine, but their faith in God was unshakable. They continued giving of their best, first in England, the Commissioner as Foreign Secretary, and later as leaders of Salvation Army work in America.

Colonel Ruhani (Lucy Booth) took over the leadership of the ever-expanding work in India and Ceylon. In October 1894 she married a distinguished Swedish officer, Emanuel Hellberg. A graduate of Uppsala University he became the Army's first Chief Secretary for Sweden, later being transferred to the Foreign Office in London from where he went out to India. Here he took the name of Raj Singh, married Colonel Ruhani and as her devoted chief secretary gave valuable service. Colonel and Mrs Booth-Hellberg left India in 1896 and the reins were handed over to Colonel Henry Bullard (Jai Singh) who was designated 'travelling Commissioner'.

One of the advances made at this juncture was the establishing of Army work in the Bhil country, the Panch Mahals. The Bhils are a tribe of people inhabiting the dense jungles and rocky Vindhya and Satpura mountain ranges of the western part of central India, remnants of the aborigines of India who were driven to the hills at the time of the Aryan invasion. The men wear only a simple loincloth and carry bows and arrows for protection against wild beasts in the jungle. The women are amply clothed and cover their arms and ankles with brightly polished brass bangles. Fear of the devil and evil spirits is the main tenet of their religion. Former incursions into this region had been made by the earliest pioneers, Captain F. Grundy (Ishwar Das) and the Armenian convert, Captain Mackertich, but it was not until 1891 that the Swedish Ensign Carl Winge (Jang Bahadur) was appointed to establish work among the Bhils.

It was a formidable task; the people were suspicious of any intruder and Winge being a white man, they immediately assumed him to be sent by government and distrusted him accordingly. In a village called Ablod, Winge applied to the headman for the use of a temporary hut while he erected his own. The headman refused, but a local priest, seeing the fakir-coloured clothes of the stranger, interceded and a hut was made available. Incidently the priest became one of the first converts and entered the ranks of The Salvation Army.

Having previously obtained a government permit to cut wood in the jungle, Winge now turned to the local people to assist him in felling trees. Everyone refused to help, hoping thereby to drive him from the district. Nothing daunted, Winge took his axe and went out to the jungle alone. When he came back with his newly-cut poles the Bhils gazed at him with amazement, for the trees he had felled were liquor-producing Mohwah trees which it was unlawful to cut down. When they saw that this white sahib was undismayed by their refusal to help him and humble enough to cut down trees with his own hands their distrust changed to admiration. The fact that he fearlessly cut down government protected trees also raised him in their estimation as a great man. They were, of course, unaware he was acting in ignorance of the law.

When the hut was completed two Gujarati women-officers were appointed to Ablod while Ensign Winge went to another village to prepare for further advances. Soon after arrival these two brave women went out, Bible in hand, to tell the people about Jesus.

Many conversions followed. Later, a hall was built with timber cut in the jungle and bricks for foundations taken from the ruins of an ancient Bhil city. This, the Salvation Temple in Ablod, will go down in Army history as the first place for Christian worship erected for the Bhils.

Eighteen years later Brigadier Hunter (Bahadur) reported: 'We have 40 Bhil officers, one holding the position of sectional officer, 45 corps, 100 outposts where the gospel of Christ is preached every week.'

Commissioner Booth-Tucker's youngest daughter, Muriel (now a retired Colonel), was once stationed at Dohad, the divisional centre, working among the Bhils.

Today the Panch Mahal Division represents a vital Salvation Army force of indigenous workers, a far cry from the early days when, in order to disarm suspicion and obtain an entrance among the Bhils, the men-officers, imitating the people, let their hair grow down over their shoulders and wore earrings and carried bows and arrows and the women-officers wore brass anklets similar to those worn by Bhil women.

Major and Mrs Carl Winge were later transferred to Muktipur Farm Colony where in the adjacent cemetery are five little graves in a row. Erland Richter recalls words spoken by Mrs General Booth in *I Missionärens Spår* (In the Steps of the Missionary): 'I am reminded of a conversation I had with a Swedish officer-wife who had just come home from India. I knew that she had buried seven children in India. I knew that she had striven for the salvation of India's people without self-pity or complaint, and when I suggested it may be better if she and her husband were given an appointment elsewhere, the mother (who was Mrs Winge) said quietly, "The Lord gave and the Lord took and I would not feel it right to leave dear India." '

It has been erroneously thought that Carl Winge lies buried in Dohad. Swedish records bear witness to his return to Sweden in 1921, being promoted to Glory in 1923 while on tour in his own country lecturing on India, and being buried in Södertalje, Sweden. The supposed grave of Carl Winge in Dohad is of another Swedish officer, Gustav Lager, and herein is another story of heroic fortitude.

Gustav Lager married Marie Naess, a Norwegian officer, in Anand. After the wedding the couple took up their appointment to work among the Bhils. Only a few days later the husband became the victim of a fever from which he died and Marie was left a widow. On her husband's grave these words are inscribed:

> *He gave his life for the salvation of the Bhils.*
> *He did not regret the sacrifice.*
> *God's grace was sufficient for each day. Hallelujah!*

Mrs Marie Lager spent all the remaining years of her life in service for the Indian people, for the most part in northern India, now Pakistan, and died a few months before she was to have retired. Her grave in Lahore cemetery bears the same words as those of her husband's in Dohad, the word India substituting the word Bhils.

6

'Plead the cause of the poor' (1891-)

WILLIAM BOOTH, 'the apostle of the poor', was not only concerned about his own people, his compassion encircled all God's children and reached out to the poor of India. His 'Darkest England Scheme' had just been launched and had met with success, he now wanted to investigate the possibility of applying the same principles to help India.

Arriving in India in December 1891 he was received with great courtesy wherever he went. The Viceroy and governors and other leaders of the people vied with each other in the cordiality of their reception.

Madras had seldom witnessed a more exciting spectacle than when William Booth arrived. In and around Egmore Station thousands of people assembled and the railway authorities found it necessary to close the entrances to the station platform, the station-master's office and other offices. Gaily coloured flags and Chinese lanterns enlivened the scene and in the centre of the platform a *shamianah* (open tent) with a pink canopy was erected.

Alighting from the train General Booth was met by the *Dewan* (Prime Minister) Bahadur Ragunatha Rao on behalf of the Indian community in general, and the Reverend Satthianadhan on behalf of the Indian Christian community. The General was conducted to the *shamianah* where he was garlanded, sprinkled with rose water and showered with flowers. Following these preliminaries, addresses were presented to him. William Booth received similar enthusiastic welcomes wherever he went. A fascinating account of the Founder's meetings in Samarkha, in the heart of Gujarat, is given in Booth-Tucker's *Muktifauj* of which the following is but the barest outline.

A dense mass of people had gathered on the extensive grounds through which the police were trying to keep clear a space for the march which was on its way. Even the trees were alive with spectators. First came the trumpeters with nine foot long Indian trumpets producing ear-splitting wails, followed by a long line of Salvation Army soldiers, then a crowd of prancing Bhils armed with bows and arrows. Twenty-five camels came next, looking disdainfully down at the cheering crowd, then a brass band with more soldiers and cadets, whilst a splendid elephant, whose massive proportion and grave demeanour added much to the dignity of the scene, brought up the rear. They marched round the ground and made a halt in front of the grandstand. The camels were made to kneel, the solemn elephant looked on in silence, the irrepressible trumpeters were quieted, and by vigorous waving of a white flag some approach to silence was secured while the General addressed the vast crowd.

During the afternoon the General addressed some 1,500 caste people who were greatly impressed by the message. It was estimated that about 10,000 Hindus and 2,500 Salvationists were gathered in the grounds on that day. The evening meeting was the crowning point, men and women surged to the front to kneel and seek God's forgiveness, determined to live a new life, and in the Hallelujah wind-up that followed it seemed, to quote Booth-Tucker, 'as if earth had got somewhat mixed up with the skies, and the multitude on earth mingled with the multitude round the throne'.

When William Booth returned to India four years later, in December 1895, he was able to present some definite plans for the uplift of the depressed classes of India.

Meanwhile, Booth-Tucker, who was always one step ahead, had already launched out on one scheme—to place 'The Landless Man upon the Manless Land', as he called it. Ninety per cent of the people of India were estimated at that time to be living in the villages. The great majority—the lower castes and the casteless—living outside the main village, working for next to nothing on the landlords' fields. To give land to these landless farm labourers Booth-Tucker obtained from government 557 acres of land in Gujarat, 15 miles from Ahmedabad. At the beginning things were not too promising, the site was situated just outside the zone of the western monsoon with the result that constant droughts made it difficult for the colonists to keep going. The problem, however, was gradually overcome by the sinking of wells, and what before had been wasteland covered with shrubs and thorny bushes inhabited by wild pigs and snakes, became fertile fields supplying a

53

livelihood and a raised standard of living for the hardworking settlers. The land colony was called Muktipur, 'Place of Salvation', and it became indeed a place of salvation for many. At the first light of dawn a trumpet would sound, calling the settlers for prayer before setting out for the fields. At noon it sounded for siesta and when it was time to lay down tools at the end of the day the welcome sound was again heard across the fields. The first manager was Major Naran Prag, a Gujarati officer, followed by the Swedish Major Carl Winge, who pioneered the work among the Bhils.

To develop the land reform scheme William Booth enlisted the help of another Swedish officer. Colonel Herman Lagercrantz was at the time chief secretary in Sweden and on one of William Booth's visits to the country they discussed the Swedish croft system (small scale farming). 'This would be something for India,' exclaimed the Founder enthusiastically and gripped by this new idea asked Herman Lagercrantz to go to India to implement the scheme.

Herman Lagercrantz had joined The Salvation Army soon after its commencement in Sweden. His father, one-time Governor of Lapland and Northern Sweden, wanted his son to take up a military career. It was as a military officer he attended a revival meeting in Stockholm, led by the English Lord Radstock, which resulted in his life taking a different direction, and meeting The Salvation Army soon after he decided to join it.

Colonel Lagercrantz took up William Booth's challenge with eagerness and at the beginning of the century he and his wife sailed for the East. In India the Colonel travelled extensively and contacted government officials and Indian landowners soliciting their help. Unfortunately his service on the sub-continent was cut short by a severe attack of typhoid fever and he and his wife had to return to Sweden. On medical grounds it became necessary to terminate active service in the Army and he returned to the quiet of the Swedish countryside on his estate Wirsbo.

Later Herman Lagercrantz was appointed Swedish Ambassador in Washington, USA, and subsequently in Copenhagen, Denmark. Throughout his life he remained a true Salvationist.

Soon after Muktipur Land Colony was founded a boys' boarding school and dispensary were added to the establishment, Captain Slater was appointed the first dispenser. The present dispenser, Brigadier Ashirvad Kalidas, is a link with the past. His father, Kalidas Vira, was converted in 1898 at one of Booth-Tucker's meetings held under the shade of a large banyan tree on the outskirts of Vishrampura, near Pedlad. Kalidas was born into a Brahmin family. Brahmins belong to the priesthood and as such will conduct marriages and offer worship according to Hindu ritual. As a young teenager Kalidas Vira used to accompany his father on his rounds in the neighbouring district, assisting him in his priestly duties and collecting fees from the people.

The day young Kalidas came back from Booth-Tucker's meeting his appearance had changed—his *shikka* (the topknot of Hindus) and *janoi* (sacred neck thread) were missing. One look at his son was sufficient to make the father furious, for no Brahmin could ever perform his religious duties without these tokens. The family threatened, pleaded and cajoled, but all without effect. At last his father appealed to his sense of duty by saying that if he refused to take part in the Hindu rituals their influence and income would be ruined and the family would starve. Regretfully Kalidas refused and begged his parents to accept Jesus as their Saviour and put their trust in Him.

After some months, being impressed by the change in their son, the parents too became Christians. In 1899 Kalidas Vira entered the training garrison at Gamdi and became an officer. During his 42 years of active service in The Salvation Army he won many for Christ through his singing and preaching. Blessed with a good voice and a love for music and poetry he would compose his own songs. He also started what is known as *gayantolis*, a group of singers singing Indian *bhajans* (songs). These singing brigades have played an important part all over Gujarat. In the early days it was the custom for a group of corps to arrange large annual gatherings known as *'melas'. Gayantolis* from the various corps would take part in the large open-air gatherings during the day and at night gather under a large *pandal* (tent) and sing their own songs, sometimes well into the night or early morning, drawing large crowds.

* * *

Previous to William Booth's second visit in December 1895-January 1896 Booth-Tucker, as Foreign Secretary, came to India to prepare the way for the launching of the social scheme for the uplift of the depressed classes. Before leaving England he had been granted an interview at the India Office with the Earl of Onslow, Under-Secretary of State for India, who had received him kindly and promised that the India scheme would receive the careful consideration of the government.

Again, as in 1891, Booth-Tucker was at the rostrum in the Framji Cowasjee Institute, Bombay. Reminding his audience of the previous meeting, he spoke of changes that had taken place since then, urging the government and philanthropists to do something for the poor and distressed. He advised the well-to-do and officials of the government to found a company to support the scheme, assuring them that if such a company was formed, according to the suggestions which would be made by the General of The Salvation Army, competent managers and supervisors for the working of the scheme would be forthcoming.

In the meanwhile, he informed them that some schemes were already in operation, one in Gujarat (Muktipur), where the government had given land for the settling of landless peasants, and another in Ceylon, where in 1888 work among prisoners had been commenced. The Army had erected a prison-gate home on land given free of charge by the government and where now a farm was operating and a large number of criminals were being helped into honourable employment. He also mentioned that the Army had opened 'rescue homes' for unfortunate women at Parel in Bombay and similar homes were established in Madras, Calcutta and Colombo.

William Booth spent eight weeks in India and Ceylon, seeing for himself the need of the people and presenting their case before the leaders of the land. His scheme was listened to with interest and won general support. The eventual outcome materialized in village banks where poor farmers could borrow money at low interest; hospitals and clinics where free treatment was given to those unable to pay; leprosy hospitals; settlements for people in conflict with the law; land colonies for landless peasants; industrial and village schools; educational centres and hostels; homes for women and children and help given in times of famine and plague.

Two days before the General's visit to south India a terrible cholera epidemic spread all over south Travancore and thousands of people died. To bring the General in the midst of this predicament was a great problem for those responsible for his welfare. Booth-Tucker and others advised the General to cancel the visit but he would have none of it and said, 'Cholera or no cholera, I am going there. I will not disappoint my people who are waiting to hear me.'

After William Booth's return to England he wrote:

> From what I have seen and heard with my own eyes and ears, as well as from what I have heard from the lips of my dear officers, I am of the opinion that nowhere on the face of the earth is there such a call for sacrificial service, and nowhere is there such opportunity for the reaping of immense results, as is to be found on the hills and plains and jungles of Hindustan.

> Some of our comrades have laid their lives down in the conflict and others are toiling today under that burning sun, who have proved themselves as true heroes and heroines as any the world has ever known, as truly deserving to be canonized as any whose names have ever been entered on the roll of the saints.

> But what of the future? That is my anxiety. The opportunities are so vast and the responsibilities connected with them so serious, that I am fairly staggered by looking them in the face. Some of the things I want to be emphasized are:

> 1. Maintain every advantage already gained, secure and train the converts already made.
> 2. Improve the training of officers.
> 3. Pay a thousand, nay ten thousand, times more attention to the children.
> 4. Keep on supplying barracks in those villages where we have a reasonable number of soldiers.
> 5. Establishment of corps in all large cities.
> 6. Working out a new Indian social scheme, which is destined to become a very great boon to the poor of this land.

You will see I have come back more than ever interested in India. I am deeply in love with it and were I a young man beginning life afresh, I would without hesitation say, 'Send me to India'.

During the General's visit the decision was made to divide India and Ceylon into four territories, so as to give better oversight to the rapidly expanding work.

Northern Territory, consisting of the North-West Provinces, the Punjab and the neighbouring areas under the command of Colonel Ishwar Das (Grundy).

Central India Territory, consisting of Gujarat, the Bhil and Naik country with the Mahratta District and adjacent parts under Colonel Jai Bhai (Paynter).

Southern India Territory, embracing the whole of the southern part of India, under Colonel Musa Bhai.

Ceylon, under the command of Brigadier Nurani (Clara Case).

In one of the Founder's concluding meetings in Bombay, he announced the appointment of Major Jai Singh (Henry Bullard) as travelling secretary in India, with the rank of Colonel. His duties were to include the editing of *The War Cry*, supervision of the social work, the farm colony and naval and military work, visiting all branches of the work and reporting to the Foreign Secretary at International Headquarters, London. No mean task!

Consideration was also given to the matter of length of service for missionary officers as up to this time no one was given promise of homeland leave. 'We are instructed to consider the offers of those who are willing to volunteer for a term of years instead of for life, as originally was required of officers.' At first the term became 10 years, later reduced to seven. It remained seven years right up to 1953, with six months' leave between each term. When air travel became the norm it was gradually reduced until in 1970 the term was set at four years with four months' leave.

7

Turning to Travancore and the Telugus (1892-)

THE first division in south India, formed in 1892, was the Cape Comorin Division, taking its name from the southernmost point in India where the waters of the Arabian Sea and the Indian Ocean meet. Its headquarters was situated about 10 miles from the cape, in Nagercoil, in the state of Travancore. Ruled by a maharaja, the state has a coastline of 175 miles and an estimated population of six million. Two languages are spoken, Malayalam in the north and Tamil in the south. The charm of its landscape lies in its variety, the peaks of the Western Ghats, rising to nearly 9,000 feet and stretching down the whole of the west coast of India, terminate in the Nagercoil region, a lush and fertile rice-growing area.

Although the country is rich in natural resources, poverty is the plight of a great part of the population. For centuries the community has been caste-ridden and the poor despised and virtually slaves of the higher castes. The caste system is the core of Hinduism which declares that man is born into a particular caste because of his deeds in a previous life and therefore must accept his condition without protest, performing the duties befitting to it.

The low-caste people were not allowed to enter the Hindu temples, so they worshipped the power of nature and also devils. They believed in witchcraft, and at every important festival devil dancing was a main item and sacrifices of animals were offered to please the gods. They were not allowed inside the market places neither were they to walk down streets of high-caste villages, in case their shadow should fall upon a high-caste and so defile him.

Gandhi agitated against the idea of untouchability, 'No one shall be regarded as an untouchable by reason of his birth,' he asserted. By precept and by act he did much to raise their status in the

59

community and secured for them at least a constitutional recognition of their rights to social equality. He gave them a new name, calling them *Harijan*—children of God. But in practical terms the Christian Church and The Salvation Army in particular, with its mission to the poorest in society, have given to the depressed classes a new vision of themselves in the community, a purpose in life and a new freedom in Christ Jesus.

In the early part of the century the caste system still penetrated every aspect of living and early converts to Christianity suffered severe hardship and were often persecuted by high-caste people who were afraid of losing their hold over them.

The work in the state of Travancore, where caste distinction is very strong, was commenced by Staff Captain Jeya Kodi (William Johnston). It so happened that Johnston was convalescing on a coffee estate belonging to Charles Cox, a former missionary who had turned planter. Having heard of the hard conditions the Salvationists were enduring he wrote to Booth-Tucker inviting anyone in need of a rest to come to his estate, Black Rock, situated 3,000 feet above the humid heat of the plains. While Johnston was recuperating he commenced holding meetings for the coolies who at the time were employed during the harvest season. A number of them were converted and witnessed to their new faith when returning to their own villages. The son of Charles Cox, coming home from his English public school, also joined the Salvationists and became an officer. His life on earth was sadly cut short, when as a young Staff-Captain he died of cholera.

Captain Yesu Patham Keil (later Lieut.-Colonel) was sent to follow up the newly-commenced work at Black Rock and surrounding villages. It was tough going at first and officers and new converts alike met with strong opposition. Major Yesu Ratnam (William Stevens, later Lieut.-Commissioner), the newly-appointed Divisional Commander of Cape Comorin Division, was walking down a village street after a night's meeting together with Subadar Gnanathesiger, a Hindu convert, when they were attacked and left severely beaten on the roadside. Following this incident they were both put in prison on a charge of causing a 'breach of the peace' and not released until three days later. Army halls were burned down, homes and paddy fields destroyed, yet the testimony of the newly converted was, 'The devil can burn our homes and paddy, but he cannot burn our souls.'

At a time when opposition was particularly severe four national officers, much concerned about winning souls for Christ, went to a solitary place on a hill outside Nagercoil called Medicine Hill. Here they fasted and prayed night and day. One of them, Major Deva Sundaram, suddenly cried out to the others, 'I see a great army in red coats like a shoal of fish in the sea—tens of thousands! I believe God will give us these souls for our labours'.

Leaving the others praying, Deva Sundaram went that evening down to the village of Attakulam at the foot of the hill and the whole village responded to his preaching and accepted Christ as Saviour. It was the beginning of a great revival, and such has been the steady progress over the years in this heavily populated area, corps have sprung up in such large numbers, 93 corps and societies in all, that standing today at one hall other corps halls can be seen across the fields in the near distance. It has since been divided into two divisions: Cape North and Cape South.

When celebrating special occasions 'pilgrimages' have been made to Medicine Hill to commemorate the first spiritual revival and to seek new power and inspiration. Officers have gathered for a day of prayer and exhortation on the mountainside, after which great open-air gatherings were held in the villages at the foot of the hill where the revival of early days had started.

Many officers, compelled by divine love, have devoted their lives in building up God's Kingdom in this part of India. Two former divisional commanders, Brigadier James Richardson (Yuddha Prakash) and Brigadier Robert McKay (Bharosa), lie buried in the small cemetery on the outskirts of Nagercoil, their lives having been formed in the same pattern to an extraordinary degree. Both were Scotsmen, the former from Greenock, the latter from Paisley. James Richardson came out to India in the year 1900 and was promoted to Glory from Nagercoil after 27 years of devoted service. It was he who, while home on furlough in Scotland, influenced the young Robert McKay to offer for missionary service. Robert followed in the older man's footsteps and after 31 years in India, filling the same position as his mentor was laid to rest by his side.

Another Caledonian, who gave her all for India, was Brigadier Margaret Leed, who came to the country in 1920. Her Indian name was Jivoli, which means Life-light. A more suitable name could not have been given her for she was always so full of life, spreading

61

light wherever she went. As a divisional commander she would cycle round the division covering many miles heedless of the burning sun. Brigadier S. A. Paul, a Tamil officer, wrote of her:

> Of all missionary officers known to me it was Jivoli Ammal who exerted the greatest spiritual influence on our young people. Although appointed as the territorial young people's secretary just three years before she was to reach the age of retirement, she went about her work with a zeal and stamina which put to shame persons many years younger.

Not wanting to leave her adopted country she spent her years of retirement in Coonoor in the Nilgiris, still serving the people she loved. Her life was abruptly cut short in 1972 by an intruder into her lonely bungalow. It could have happened anywhere in the world, but only a Christian like Jivoli could say before she died, 'Forgive him, Lord, for he knew not what he did.'

Of the many outstanding officers from south India, Nayarana Muthiah, probably more than any other, yielded an influence which was felt throughout the whole of India. Born and brought up in a high-caste Hindu home at Palamcottah, in the Tirunelveli district, he was proud of his heritage and kept rigidly to Hindu practices throughout his early youth. When The Salvation Army came to his town he looked at them with scorn and made them a target of harassment, pelting them with stones and mud. But all that changed. Later, as an officer in The Salvation Army he averred, 'It was not an eloquent sermon that changed my life, but a simple testimony from an Indian officer which brought me to the feet of Christ.' Muthiah had to suffer much for his faith. His family tried, by methods fair and foul, to bring him back to the Hindu fold. Three times they tried to kidnap him and once they succeeded. He renounced all rights to property which he would have inherited, signing it over to his sister, leaving himself penniless. He suffered imprisonment for the offence of preaching Christ at a street corner in Madras, but through it all he remained faithful.

Muthiah tells of an incident which more than anything proved to him the power of God's love in the life of His children. He was sent to the railway station in Madras to meet a group of famine children from Gujarat in the care of a couple of women-officers:

> I approached the carriage which our people occupied. As I made to enter, the stench was overpowering, and I turned away involuntarily,

sickened by the smell and the terrible spectacle of those poor starved children. Then I looked at the officers—delicate women—who had travelled three days and nights over the hot plains of India in this filthy atmosphere, tending the suffering children of my people, and my heart cried out: 'Here is the love of God!'

Muthiah came to know much personal sorrow. His wife, Yuddha Dasie, and two of his sons died in a cholera epidemic in Madras in 1905. One little mite asked, 'How do little children go to Heaven, Mummy, does Jesus fetch them?' Jesus had indeed gone before to prepare a place for His little ones. An eight-year-old daughter died in Anand from burns and another died in Bareilly. His own sorrow helped him to share the burdens of others and his sympathy gave strength to fellow-sufferers.

The one-time caste Hindu toured Australia and New Zealand for 16 months, and made two visits to England, the last as a member of the first High Council for the election of the Army's international leader. He was the first Indian officer to attain the position of territorial commander with Commissioner's rank, in April 1929. Loved by Salvationists all over India, where his capable leadership had brought advancement in great measure, he entered retirement in 1938 after more than 48 years of full-time service in the Army.

It is a befitting memorial to this outstanding Indian officer that today the territorial headquarters for the South-Eastern Indian Territory is situated in the Tiruneveli district where Commissioner Muthiah was born. Transferred in May 1979 from what used to be the old divisional headquarters in Nagercoil, it now occupies a modern building with spacious accommodation for offices, quarters and meeting hall.

Previous to this, in October 1970, Southern India Territory was divided into two territories: The South-Western Territory with headquarters in Trivandrum comprising the entire Malayalam-speaking area, geographically known as Kerala State since 1956, where Lieut.-Colonel James Kennedy was appointed territorial commander. The South-Eastern Territory with headquarters in Nagercoil comprising the southern district of the state of Tamil Nadu where Lieut.-Colonel V. J. Chelliah was appointed territorial commander.

*   *   *

During the last decade of the 19th century the word 'boom'

became a popular word on many lips. In Australia and America they spoke of 'gold booms', in Canada of 'land booms', in Africa of 'diamond booms', so why not a 'soul boom' suggested the intrepid pioneers? and they embarked on a unique method of evangelization and called it 'boom marches'. It had already been tried in Gujarat where 100 officers with horses, camels, flags, drums and brass band had 'swept the country', and thousands had accepted the Christian message.

Now Major Yesu Ratnam (William Stevens) decided to try the same tactics in Travancore. He called his officers together in May 1892, explaining how to carry out a 'boom march' and urged them to prepare by prayer. So keenly did three of his officers feel the importance of this new venture that they went into the woods and spent three days in prayer and fasting.

All available officers gathered in Nagercoil on the eve of the great event, among them were Sukh Singh (Arthur Blowers), Yesu Patham (Keil) and Deva Sundaram. Springless carts were loaded with bags of rice, bunches of bananas, cooking vessels and musical instruments. 'Scouts', in the form of experienced officers, had been sent out beforehand to various villages informing the headmen that The Salvation Army intended to send a party of Salvationists with music, flags and drums, asking whether they would be willing to receive them. Curiosity prompted many to welcome the white 'fakirs' and their *chelas,* but in most cases curiosity changed to genuine interest and concern as they heard, for the first time, the message of salvation through Jesus Christ. Where converts were made, an officer was left behind in the village to teach and care for the new in the faith, while the remaining party went on to the next village. During the campaign no less than 2,000 sought salvation, whole villages joined the Army and temples and idols were handed over to the officers.

Major Yesu Ratnam (Stevens) wrote in 1896:

Our work here is one of the most, if not the most remarkable that the Army possesses. Five years ago we had less than 100 Salvationists in this area, while today we have 4,503. Villages that five years ago had no Christians are now entirely Salvation Army. Commencing with a revival that I have seen nothing in soul-saving work to equal, it has not suffered any serious relapse. The work is entirely confined to the villages, many of which are small.

We have at present 26 day schools and one boarding school for officers' children. Some of the officers are very capable, devoted men and women. At the present time there are only two European officers in the division out of a total of 140.

The phenomenon of The Salvation Army's rapid growth in this part of India prompted *The Travancore Times* to write:

> Starting in Travancore in 1889 in a somewhat unobtrusive manner and confining its efforts at first to a few small villages near Cape Comorin, it was not until 1892 that the Army came prominently before the notice of the Travancore public. In this year, within a few weeks, some 2,000 people belonging to the villages of Agateespuram and Tovalataluqs renounced their old faith and practices, accepting that of The Salvation Army, freely handing over their old temples to be pulled down to make room for schools, or barracks, as their places of worship are called. The whole movement was so sudden, so unexpected, and the Army so little understood that some appeared to fear a revolution, and attempts were made to misrepresent things to government. The trial, however, gave the Army an opportunity of publicly explaining its methods and objects and doubtless removed much misunderstanding.
>
> A visit made by General William Booth, the Founder, at the end of 1895 and the explanations he was enabled to make of the object and work of the Army in this and other lands, aroused considerable interest and elicited much sympathy, which was further increased when, the following year, in response to the appeals of many converts, a medical work was established in a room in the headquarters, which proved so successful that in 1897 a small hospital was erected. This branch was considerably extended in 1900 by the erection of a number of new buildings and the commencement of a medical class for training of medical officers competent to take charge of village dispensaries, the whole being conducted by Dr Turner.

There are those who quite rightly query the value of mass conversions. Commissioner Howard, Foreign Secretary at the time, had this answer:

> Whilst I regard it as a victory in the name of Jesus to win hundreds of people from idolatry, who put themselves under the influence and instruction of The Salvation Army, it is only a preliminary to other stages of progress. We do not at once enter their names on the roll as Salvation Army soldiers; they become, as the result of this step, simply adherents of the Army. Our officers, from this happy starting point seek, by patient instruction, to bring each one to understand the nature of salvation, and lead all to claim permanently that grace by which we are saved.

In 1899 Travancore became a separate territory with headquarters in Nagercoil, having up to that time been administrated from Madras. Brigadier Yesu Ratnam (Stevens) was appointed territorial commander, succeeded by Colonel Sukh Singh (Arthur Blowers). In 1905 Colonel Nurani (Clara Case) took over the command and for 12 years worked ceaselessly for its improvement. When again Colonel Yesu Ratnam became the leader of the South India Territory, it had become the largest in the sub-continent with 818 officers, 61 cadets, 2,686 local officers and 114 teachers.

Ratnapuram is a village close to Nagercoil called after Yesu Ratnam, a permanent memorial to his work in south India, where Salvationists settled after his purchasing the land to free them from oppressive landlords. A thriving corps is still operating today where the villagers worship the living God, bearing witness to the saving and keeping grace of our Lord.

From the south the work of The Salvation Army spread north to the Malayalam-speaking people in what is now called Kerala State. The history of the Christian Church in this part of the country goes back many centuries, some maintaining that the Apostle Thomas came to Malabar in AD 52. Though no actual evidence is found to prove this claim, the church in existence today bears the name of MarThoma, also called the Syrian Church. It is, however, a well-established fact that Francis Xavier, the Jesuit missionary, landed at Goa in 1542 and spent seven years in India. His most successful work was among the Malayalam-speaking people. But through the centuries the Church had made little or no impact on the people of the depressed classes, and seeing their need Salvation Army leaders looked for a suitable person to pioneer among the people in north Travancore. Yesudasen, a man with initiative and drive, was chosen. Born a Brahmin from Trichur in the Cochin State, he had taken the name Yesudasen (Servant of Jesus) at the time of his conversion in Bombay, where he had come under the influence of Colonel Yuddha Bai (Catherine Bannister). He was trained as a Salvation Army officer in Bombay and appointed to south India. With his wife, an efficient and refined officer from Ceylon, he was sent to Mavelikara, where he rented a house and set up the first divisional headquarters in the Malayalee area. The year was 1896. Preaching the gospel in the villages, Yesudasen would ask for shelter for the night in the huts of the low-caste people. At first they distrusted him, knowing he was high caste, but soon their fear turned to trust when they understood that here was a friend who showed them the love of God by his concern for them. Yesudasen fought for the rights of the depressed classes and won for them the right to enter the village markets and freedom to worship on Sundays.

Two of Colonel Yesudasen's children became officers, both with distinguished careers, the late Mrs Commissioner Nurani Gnanaseelan, and Colonel Donald Sanjivi. The grandchildren of the one-time Brahmin, converted in Bombay, Mrs Captain Priya Hardman and Sergeant-Major Edwin Sanjivi, are spreading the good news in Canada today.

'Meanwhile the word of God continued to spread and grow' (Acts 12:24, *GNB*).

* * *

Advances were also made elsewhere. Staff-Captain Abdul Aziz, a Moslem convert, was sent to reconnoitre and commence work in the Telugu country north of Madras in 1895. The Telugus are a strong, hard-working people, modest in manner, very religious, and hold tenaciously to their caste. Their language is soft and melodious, called by some 'the Italian of the East'.

The Indian *War Cry* gives a vivid description of the background against which the pioneers worked:

20 July 1895, *A Call for Volunteers!*
Not for a foreign land, but for the Telugu country. Will all Telugu speaking officers, who are ready to join the attacking party, please communicate with headquarters at once.
31 August. The Staff-Captain is full of faith and has fixed upon a very suitable field and is now going in heart and soul to try and prepare officers. The Cape (south India) comes to his help and sends him a couple for a start.
14 September. The lads and lasses in the training home are real 'Blood and fire' cadets—three of us are going out next week in three directions to get some more candidates. Please pray for the Telugu Division.

Then it seems that a boarding school has been opened, for *The War Cry* of 12 October reports:

Staff-Captain Abdul Aziz has already quite a number of children in his boarding school which is superintended by his wife. He sallies forth shortly to set his first division going, to be followed by a second at a brief interval.

67

Of them it can truly be said, 'Faith, mighty faith . . . laughs at impossibilities and cries: "It shall be done!" ' Despite the dire poverty of the people, they supported the officers and gave to the best of their ability, as later reports show:

> In a little village of circular, thatched, mud huts, the people, not satisfied with giving the officers only a rent-free quarters, and cooking their food, have given a piece of land to build a barracks on, and a calf towards expenses.

The Army certainly made rapid progress and Sukh Singh (Arthur Blowers) could report after four years:

> We have now 29 corps, 70 officers, 6 day schools, and a soldiery nearing 2,000 strong.

Every operation was not as successful as in Travancore and the Telugu country. The same year, 1895, officers were sent to open work in the Central Provinces. A headquarters was established in Lucknow. Nagpur was once a centre of Army activities. The Army also worked in the Native State of Jodhpur in Rajputana. Other places could be mentioned where for some reason the work was closed down and no Salvation Army is found today.

In Bangalore, where formerly the Army had a flourishing silk farm and corps which was subsequently closed down, territory has been reclaimed and a corps reopened in 1979. A retired officer, Brigadier P. Emmanuel, visiting his nurse daughter living in Bangalore, gathered Salvationists and friends together for meetings whenever he went there. It became a regular feature with meetings held every Sunday, an officer from Madras taking turns with the corps secretary of Vepery Corps conducting the meetings until a permanent officer was appointed. The corps has now 180 soldiers on its roll.

8

Famine and plague (1895-)

THE pioneers went to India with General Booth's strict instruction to work solely among the Indian people, but it soon became apparent that there were needs to be met elsewhere. An ability to change established policies in order to meet a particular need must be counted as a strength rather than a weakness, for rigidity never makes for progress. This William Booth knew better than anyone. A statement in *The War Cry,* May 1895, reads:

> We ought here to call our readers' attention to the fact that work amongst the European population in India is now a recognized part of our operations here, having its own administration, and will no longer be dependent on whether officers can be spared from the Indian work. Our efforts are devoted almost exclusively to seeking the salvation of India's millions, and our dress and our methods are subservient to this end. Nevertheless, in order to reach the scattered civil population, and large number of British troops, some attention is given to the formation of civil, naval and military branches of our international naval and military league, and some officers are set apart exclusively for this work, who wear the ordinary English dress, and devote all their energies to these classes. It is very much needed, for in north India alone there are upwards of 50,000 British troops out of which very few profess to being Christians.

Bombay had the distinction, not only of having the first Salvation Army corps on the continent of Asia, but also of having the first corps in connection with the recently-formed civil, naval and military union. Very soon other branches sprang up in towns as far flung as Colombo in Ceylon, Dalhousie and Umballa in the north, Trimulgherry in the south, Cawnpore and Bareilly in the United Provinces, Nusseerabad in Rajastan, Calcutta, Poona and Kirkee. Branches were established in 18 of the largest military centres. Homes were opened with accommodation for servicemen on leave.

In Poona a commodious bungalow was requisitioned and in

Delhi property was acquired in the centre of the city on Connaught Circus. In Calcutta suitable premises were found in Sudder Street, where the red shield sign is still seen and draws travellers from all over the world. These places met a great need for the British soldiers of that day, deprived as they were of their families. For many it became a 'home away from home' in a rough and tumble existence. The civil, naval and military corps were run on the same lines as any other Salvation Army corps. Salvation meetings were held regularly and for many of the servicemen it came to mean a new life in Christ. Some joined the ranks of The Salvation Army as officers, donning the Indian dress of *pagri* and *dhoti* and fought for the King of kings in winning the Indian people for His Kingdom.

In the English-language Indian *War Cry* a full page was for many years given over to navy and military league activities. Reports came from remote places such as Bhamo in Burma where a leaguer was stationed and giving testimony to his faith. *The War Cry* brought cheer and moral support to those stationed in isolated places and contacts were kept up.

Bareilly reports:

> We leaguers of Bareilly Corps do indeed feel that a great and serious loss is ours in the promotion to Glory of our late Commanding Officer, Adjutant McAlonan. When he and his wife came there were no Christians among the leaguers and now we are about 30 strong.

From Bombay 1914:

> A naval and military home situated in one of the finest parts of the city has been opened (opposite the famous Taj Mahal Hotel). It is exceedingly popular, not only with the men, but with both the naval and military authorities. When the flagship is in harbour the admiral prefers his own staff to be located there. During King George V's visit to Bombay the flagship in harbour signalled ashore: 'Men wanting a clean place and good food should go to The Salvation Army.'

The home has been the spiritual birthplace of many servicemen.

The Red Shield Hotel, which the place is now called, is still a centre of great activity and attracts many tourists. The Officer-in-Charge, Major Annette Vardy from Canada, finds time not only to see to the guests' physical needs, but gives a listening ear to any in trouble.

*   *   *

70

Only those who have lived in tropical countries depending on the monsoon rain can fully appreciate the anxiety of the people when the rains fail, the despair that creeps over the land as the time of the rains approaches and passes without its life-giving water. The earth is parched and cracked, crops withered, trees stripped of all foliage with which to feed the cattle—and for many it means starvation and death.

In 1896 India was devastated by famine. Failure of successive monsoons brought about the worst drought in 200 years. An area of 475,000 square miles with a population of 60 millions was affected. Six million people were placed on government relief and 25 million dollars were spent in relief measures. Despite all this, the death toll was tremendous. *Muhtaj khana* (poor houses) were set up by the government at various points. The forest of the North West Provinces and Oudh was thrown open by order of the lieutenant-governor, so that the starving people could search for edible roots and leaves to appease their hunger. Husks of grain, usually given to cattle, found a ready sale in the bazaar for human consumption.

The Salvation Army set up numerous depots, some for the distribution of grain, some for the sale of grain at a cheap rate, 25 per cent lower than cost price. Sixty tons of grain were distributed free in addition to which 63 tons were sold at the cheap rate making a total of 123 tons for the month, distributed at 41 depots. One thousand, six hundred and twenty persons were given employment at 27 relief works, sinking wells, building sun-dried brick halls, digging tanks (ponds), levelling land, and constructing roads.

Colonel Balwant (Joshua Spooner) made an appeal for 'memorial wells' to be sunk in remembrance of those who had died, to help prevent future famines. The scheme was advertised in the Bombay press and many wells were dug as a result.

The devoted service of three generations of the Spooner family in India must be mentioned here. The Colonel's son, Adjutant Joshua Spooner, died at the age of 33 and is buried in Panchgani, western India. His grand-daughter, Major Margaret Spooner, served with distinction for 24 years as a nursing sister at various Salvation Army hospitals.

The famine was followed by epidemics of smallpox and cholera. At the Anand Training Garrison in Gujarat seven cadets died in one night. Colonel Henry Bullard, who at this time was in charge of relief operations, said many years afterwards, 'The daily scenes of misery and death haunt me still'.

Gena and Frances Smith, daughters of pioneer officers, were at the time of the plague stationed as officers at the Naval and Military Corps in Poona. Gena was 21 years of age and Frances was only 17. Being officially appointed by the city magistrate to assist in the search for the dead and the dying, they set out separately each day, accompanied by naval and military leaguers. The epidemic was spread rapidly by those already infected and hidden away in the houses. The people, held by age-old traditions, would not allow men to enter the women's quarters, so Gena and Frances entered the homes while the soldiers remained outside. 'They found sick men and women hidden away in mud hovels where neither light nor air could reach them, and corpses concealed beneath the paving of temples.'

'I would sooner face a battery of 100 guns blazing away together,' said one soldier to his comrade. 'How these girls manage to live through it passes me!' Nothing but the compelling love of God could have enabled them.

The British commander-in-chief wrote afterwards to William Booth expressing his appreciation of the work done by these two brave young women-officers.

The younger of them, Frances Smith, having escaped the ravages of plague and cholera, died later of smallpox. Gena became the wife of Harry Andrews, who pioneered The Salvation Army's medical work in India, and worked faithfully by his side for many years.

The most distressing feature of the famine and plague was the thousands of infants and young children who were left orphaned. With the aid of a famine fund more than 1,000 children were gathered in and placed in Salvation Army famine homes in different parts of India. 'They looked a heart-breaking spectacle,' said one officer, 'some were partially covered by a few rags, others were entirely naked, their faces pinched, their eyes hollow and their bones almost protruding through their skin, like so many skeletons gazing at you with half-frightened, half-wolfish eyes, holding out little bony, emaciated hands to you in mute entreaty.' At first they were difficult to manage, some were too far gone and died, but the many who recovered eventually adjusted to life in the homes because of the love and care of the officers.

The next thing which had to be considered was their education. The name 'famine homes' was replaced by schools so as to remove, as far as possible, thoughts of the hideous past. One such was the Girls' Industrial School of Satara, near Poona. Similar schools were established in many parts of India where the children were given education and taught a craft: embroidery, weaving and carpet making. Some were trained as primary teachers for the newly-established village schools. Quite a number became Salvation Army officers. Children of these officers themselves became officers and are with us today. Jeya Prakash and Teji Bai were brother and sister, born in Cambay, Gujarat. When the famine and plague swept through their part of the country they lost both parents and came under the Army's care. Jeya Prakash was sent south, Teji Bai north. Jeya was educated in the Salvation Army boys' boarding school in Madavaram near Madras. He became an officer and took the name of Nayarana suggested by his friend Nayarana Muthiah (later Commissioner). A marriage was arranged between Jeya and Chena Devakaruna, daughter of an Ensign. These are the parents of Colonel Nayarana J. Samuel, present Territorial Commander of the Madras and Andhra Territory. His son, Captain Devakaruna Rao, is a fourth-generation officer.

Jeya's sister, Teji Bai, who was sent north was also educated at an Army boarding school, married an officer (the late Brigadier Failbus) and their daughter is Mrs Colonel Alice, wife of a recent territorial commander of Pakistan, Colonel Gulzar Masih (R). The cousins, Colonel N. J. Samuel and Mrs Colonel Gulzar Masih, have never met, but still feel the bond of family and a strong loyalty to The Salvation Army.

Although the government was doing much to assist the cause of education, the poorer classes were neglected. The caste system dictated that if low or non-caste children attended, the high-caste children would remain at home. This meant there was no means by which our soldiers' children, belonging to the under-privileged classes, could obtain even the most rudimentary education. To remedy this The Salvation Army started day schools in many villages, where not only our soldiers' children, but other village children were taught. In the North India Territory 28 such schools were established by 1899.

Headquarters, situated at Bareilly in the United Provinces comprised a Salvation Army complex, consisting of headquarters' building, girls' industrial school, training home and staff quarters. By force of circumstances in the early years of the Army in India the training homes for officers were also industrial homes, it being found impossible to keep the cadets fully occupied on mental work as many of them were illiterate. The industries also helped to finance the places. Two such homes existed in north India at the turn of the century, one at Bareilly and one at Gurdaspur in the Punjab. The former was first erected during the famine, giving employment to the needy.

The order of the day at the training homes varied according to the season and its effect on outdoor work. Commencing at 5 o'clock the day would generally be divided into four hours of manual work, two hours' study, where those unable to read and write would receive tuition, and three 'meetings'—sessions during which the Bible and doctrines and principles of The Salvation Army would be explained. Being new to Christianity the cadets had to learn a great deal before becoming officers and being sent out to take charge of a corps. But what the early officers may have lacked in education, they certainly made up in devotion, zeal and sacrifice. No less than 62 cadets were commissioned from the Bareilly Training Home in 1898.

In spite of the rate of literacy being so low two editions of *The War Cry,* one in Hindi and one in Urdu, were published monthly in the North India Territory, with a combined circulation of 1,150, each issue containing eight pages a little larger than foolscap size and sold for a pice, equivalent to the old farthing. All were sold!

*   *   *

As the work progressed it was thought necessary to divide the existing four territories into smaller units for easier oversight, having now throughout India and Ceylon no less than 1,484 officers, cadets and employees, 566 corps with 1,214 outposts, where meetings were held regularly, 361 schools and social institutions.

In May 1899, seven territories were established. Commissioner Higgins, father of General Edward J. Higgins, was at the time Resident Indian Secretary, a post he filled for seven years from 1898 till 1905, succeeded by Colonel Jang Singh (Hammond) who occupied the position till 1907.

Lieut.-Colonel Nurani (Clara Case) was appointed in charge of Central India Territory with headquarters at Ahmedabad.

Brigadier Yuddha Bai (Catherine Bannister), Punjab Territory with headquarters in Gurdaspur.

Major Yesu Das (Hipsey), North India Territory with headquarters in Lucknow.

Brigadier Yesu Ratnam (Stevens), South India Territory with headquarters in Nagercoil.

Major Sukh Singh (Blowers), Madras Territory with headquarters in Madras.

Major Bahadur (Hunter), Maharashstra Territory with headquarters in Poona.

Brigadier Jeya Kodi (Johnston), Ceylon Territory with headquarters in Colombo.

Ceylon had at this time 179 officers, 55 corps, 165 outposts, two social institutions, one industrial school and 39 day schools. Village schools were gaining in importance and many of the officers throughout India and Ceylon taught the village children besides running their corps. Two hundred and fifty-five qualified teachers were also employed with 21 inspectors who supervised the work. A total of 10,436 children were on the registers, and 650 boys and girls resided in the 12 industrial schools.

That India's poor are made poorer by the money-lenders' extortionate rates of interest is a known fact. Weddings are expensive. Money has to be found for the dowry and marriage feast. The only way for most poor people is to go to the money-lender and for the rest of their lives be in his clutches. The interest is so high that the original loan can never be repaid and a man's debts are often passed on to the eldest son. If the father dies before the daughters in the family are married, the responsibility for their weddings also falls on the son, and if he happens to have a few daughters himself, he is in real trouble. It is a vicious system which strangles a man's self-respect and stifles his zest for life.

To remedy this situation of constant debts, William Booth suggested putting up village banks as part of his scheme for helping the poor. In June 1899, the Indian *War Cry* reported that two village brotherhood banks had been successfully opened in the Telugu country and that three others were to be floated during the following month. Here the villagers could borrow at a low rate of interest and in this way be freed from the grip of the traditional money-lenders.

The idea was also to help villagers situated on poor unproductive land to purchase good land and establish new villages, by lending them capital which could be repaid at a low rate of interest payable within a certain number of years. The scheme quickly developed and village brotherhood banks were springing up in many parts of India.

A 1906 report:

'Already we have in operation 22 village banks. In one village the people were so grateful for what had been done for them in this way, that they have been collecting money amongst themselves and have purchased a piece of land, valued at about 100 rupees, which they presented to The Salvation Army.'

Seven years after these banks were established by The Salvation Army, the government passed the Co-operative Credit Societies Act, '. . . with the special view to helping agriculturists, artisans, weavers and others requiring assistance in their trades and occupation to obtain financial help at reasonable rates.'

The Salvation Army brought their branches under the new law and accounts were put under the supervision of the government registrar and annually audited by him. Establishment of central banks to provide capital for the village banks was advocated by the Army. One such was set up in Bombay at the territorial headquarters with Staff-Captain Ranjit Singh (Colledge) acting as secretary.

After some years the need for village brotherhood banks no longer existed, the government having got the better of the money-lenders and the Army closed its banks, having initiated the deal.

9

The healing ministry, (I) (1895-)

'IT was love for people,' these are the words with which Miriam Richards commences her fascinating book on The Salvation Army's medical mission, *It began with Andrews.* It was love for people which led Bramwell Booth, son of The Salvation Army's Founder, and its second General, to visit the workmen's cottages near Victoria Park, where he found a dying mother with a little baby boy. It was love for people which made Bramwell's sister, Emma, accept responsibility for the little orphan, and when the time came for her to marry and accompany her husband, Commissioner Booth-Tucker, to India, the 15-year-old boy, Harry Andrews, pleaded to go with them. Harry became an officer in Bombay at the age of 17 and was appointed to Nagercoil to assist Major William Stevens.

In a country as vast as India, besieged, as it was in the early part of the century, with outbreaks of cholera, smallpox and typhoid and with thousands dying of malaria, it stands to reason that existing medical aid could not cope with demands.

It was love for people and concern for their physical and spiritual welfare which led young Harry Andrews to use the 'healing virtues' which he possessed, to bring relief to the suffering around him. Realizing his aptitude, Mrs Major Stevens set aside a bathroom at the end of a veranda where Andrews put his simple remedies. Here people came to him, and he eased their pain and brought down fevers.

When Bramwell Booth heard about this he arranged for Harry to take a dresser's course at a London hospital. Returning to Nagercoil a year later he set up a dispensary on a site purchased with a donation of £50 given by a friend and called it The Catherine Booth Dispensary, in honour of the Army Mother.

The double door to the bathroom which housed the first dispensary is preserved to this day, and has a place of honour in what is now the workshop for artificial limbs in the rehabilitation department of the Catherine Booth Hospital. On it is written, 'These doors admitted the first patients for treatment by Harry Andrews in 1895.'

This was the beginning of The Salvation Army's medical work which today operates seven general hospitals, two leprosy hospitals and 12 clinics throughout India, and eight medical welfare centres in Pakistan.

Going back to the beginnings, January 1901, *India's Cry* (as *The War Cry* was called for some years) contained the announcement that the General, 'ever on the alert to meet the growing need of the Army in India', had appointed Ensign (Dr) Percy Turner to India. It was as a young medical student in 1887 that Percy Turner was first attracted to The Salvation Army. Listening to Mrs Bramwell Booth's holiness teaching in Exeter Hall made him decide to be 'a real follower of the Cross'. When Harry Andrews heard about the young doctor who was now a Salvation Army officer he contacted him while in England and impressed upon him the need for his medical skill in India.

After a period of further medical study Ensign Turner, taking the name of Dayanasen (Loving Kindness), arrived in Nagercoil to take charge of the hospital in embryo and was assisted by Staff-Captain Andrews (Sekunder—the Brave One). On 27 April 1901, the stone-laying ceremony of the Catherine Booth Hospital took place and the stone was laid by the Prime Minister of Travancore State, V. I. Kesava Pillai.

The General had in mind that Dr Turner should give simple courses of medical training to suitable officers, both Indian and non-Indian, which would prove useful in isolated villages. As it happened, a more ambitious scheme was launched. With financial aid from the Maharaja of Travancore a four-year medical course was started. Three Salvation Army officers were recognized as registered medical practitioners in Kerala State, Brigadier T. C. Chacko, Senior-Major S. Gnanaiah and Senior-Major J. Manuel, all giving valuable service over many years.

The role of pioneer was resumed by Major Harry Andrews in 1903 when he was transferred to Gujarat in a non-medical capacity.

However, famine had brought plague in its trail, and Andrews' compassion was again aroused by the need around him for a medical centre. *India's Cry* recorded: 'The purchase of land at Anand for a hospital has been completed and one ward will be ready in a month's time.' In March 1904 Commissioner Higgins (Senior) presided over the stone-laying, and before the year's ending the official opening of the hospital took place. The cost of the building was met by Canadian-born Miss Julia Emery in memory of her sister and the 50-bed hospital was named The Emery Hospital after her. As the work increased and responsibilities became heavier, Bramwell Booth decided that Harry Andrews should be given the opportunity of qualifying as a doctor and sent him to America to take a degree in medicine and surgery.

As a qualified doctor, Harry Andrews returned to India in 1912, again to pioneer the Army's medical work, establishing a hospital in Moradabad in the United Provinces. A further gift from Miss Emery, this time in memory of her father, provided for the major cost of the hospital building, and it came to be known as The Thomas Emery Hospital. It was officially opened on 7 March 1913 by Sir H. Weston (later Lord Weston), then Governor of the United Provinces. During two world wars the hospital was, with its doctors and staff, placed at the disposal of the military authorities, caring for wounded and sick soldiers returning from the battlefield.

At the end of the First World War trouble arose on the North-West Frontier of India and the military authorities requisitioned the help of Dr Andrews. The December 1919 edition of *The War Cry* reports: 'Lieut.-Colonel Sekunder (Dr Harry Andrews) killed in action.'

'When Bramwell Booth promised a dying mother in the East End of London that he would look after her child, no one could have remotely imagined that there would be a gathering at the Royal Army Medical College, Millbank, 29 March 1965 honouring that orphan boy,' wrote Colonel (Dr) Dan Andersen, The Salvation Army's medical advisor, and himself a long-time medical officer in India. The occasion was the unveiling of a painting of the scene where Captain Henry J. Andrews, IMS, won the Victoria Cross, to be kept as a permanent memorial in the VC's room. Brigadier Sir John Smyth, Bt, VC, MC, chairman of the Victoria Cross and George Cross Association, was officer commanding during the action in which Captain Andrews lost his life. Sir John gave a vivid picture of the dangerous situation in which a convoy was placed when a group of Waziris gained control of the heights above the narrow Tochi Valley along the convoy route. He witnessed personally Captain Andrews' complete disregard of his own safety in bringing in the wounded to a first-aid post and then placing them in an ambulance. When all the wounded were safely in the ambulance, Andrews was killed outright as he prepared to join them. In death, as in life, Harry Andrews lived up to his Indian name—Sekunder, the brave one—and to him The Salvation Army owes the foundation of its medical missionary work—because he cared for people.

In 1921, after 21 years of outstanding service Dr Turner and his wife left India. On the occasion of his farewell from Catherine Booth Hospital his successor, Dr William Noble, read an address containing a brief outline of the progress of the CBH from the day it was but a small dispensary to the present vast institution known for many miles around as a place of healing. Special days were highlighted—the doctor's wedding day, the Maharaja of Travancore's visit, the day the medical school was opened, the opening of branch hospitals.

During Dr Noble's time the capacity of the hospital rose to 500 beds; it expanded to a complex medical centre of 46 buildings (later added to by Dr Harry Williams), adequately equipped, with various departments of medical science. Five more branch hospitals were added to the existing four to reach the people in villages with no medical aid. Colonel Noble returned to India while officially designated 'retired' and served as Chief Medical Officer of the Emery Hospital, Anand, a continuation of the 44 years he had given to Salvation Army medical work in India. In recognition of this, the university at which he studied and gained his first medical degree, Emory, Atlanta, Georgia, USA, made him Honorary Doctor of Humanities. He was also awarded the Order of the Founder for having 'pioneered Salvation Army leprosy work in India'.

On the medical staff of Catherine Booth Hospital was an outstanding woman doctor who for more than 30 years served humanity—Dr Sara Daniel. Lieut.-Colonel Vera Williamson, who as Superintendent of Nurses worked closely with Dr Sara, writes this tribute to her:

Lieut.-Colonel (Dr) Sara did not choose medicine. She was a teacher. She gladly gave herself to God as a Salvation Army officer, following in the steps of her pioneer father. In those early days The Salvation Army picked her out and asked her to go to the Christian Medical College in Vellore, to qualify as a doctor under the great Doctor Ida Scudder. Doctor Scudder, since deceased, remembered her as 'quiet, but one of my good ones. She worked very hard, and was so sincere, I liked her.' The attraction was mutual. Lieut.-Colonel Sara remembers 'Doctor Ida' with the kind of remembering that brings a light to the eyes.

' "Doctoramma!" The women of India are rising nobly to the challenge of today, and serving their country well. When Lieut.-Colonel (Dr) Sara Daniel gave herself, as a girl, for the help of the people and the salvation of the world, such bold self-giving was rare and unpopular. Many will rise to greatness, but few will have lived so broadly, so richly, so deeply as our Doctor Sara.'

The Emery Hospital in Anand reached a peak under the energetic and capable administration of Dr A. Bramwell Cook. His skill as a surgeon became well known all over Gujarat and far beyond and patients flocked to the hospital. In *The Salvation Army Year Book 1940* Captain Cook writes:

Officially the hospital has 100 beds, that is, beds arranged around the walls would give that figure. On a recent Sunday a census of in-patients showed that we had 178 and four orphan babies. Overcrowding? Yes, but the need must be met. Fortunately, generous veranda space nearly doubles the capacity of the wards. Frequently both the out-patients offices are occupied at night by people who hope to secure accommodation in the morning.

Extensions made during the 21 years Dr Cook spent in Anand were a maternity wing in 1937, and a tuberculosis hospital in 1941. A training school for nurses was opened in 1943. Dr Bramwell Cook asserts:

I do not know of any profession more satisfying and rewarding than being a medical missionary. It is the grandest in the world, for it combines in one the two noblest—the ministry of the body and ministry of the soul. It makes the heart of a missionary rejoice to hear a patient say, 'I have never had love shown me in my life before. If the Christian God is a God of love, I want to be a Christian.'

Stanley Beer's first experience in tending the sick and the wounded was when posted to the Royal Army Medical Corps during the First World War. Military service took him to India where he became acutely aware of the need for 'physical healing and spiritual guidance'. Upon demobilization Stanley Beer entered

The Salvation Army's training garrison in Clapton, London expressing his willingness to serve in India. With five other officers he was sent to Livingstone College, Leyton, London, for a brief course in first aid and elementary medicine, before embarking upon his missionary career. He sailed for India on the SS *Calypso* in company with over 100 other missionaries, landing in Bombay, November 1921. His connection with the Emery Hospital in Anand was not in a medical capacity, he was appointed cashier. But while fulfilling these duties during the day he spent his evenings and many night hours reading medicine, literally burning the midnight oil in the days before Anand had electricity. Eventually acquiring a thorough knowledge of the X-ray apparatus he became the hospital X-ray technician. Later he closely watched Dr Bramwell Cook, who was appointed in 1931, at work in the operating theatre and in every way accumulated as much medical knowledge as possible. Army leaders became aware of his bent for medical work and decided to give him the opportunity of studying medicine in Bombay.

Prior to this it was necessary for him to take the matriculation examination, so Stanley Beer attended the local high school in Anand—in addition to his duties as manager of the hospital. He was then nearing the age of 40—a family man with four children.

After matriculating, Stanley Beer took up medical studies in Bombay, while Mrs Beer ran the Byculla English Corps. After three years Major S. Beer, LCPS(Bombay), returned with his wife to Anand hospital qualified to practise. Scarcely had he reached his goal when a calamity befell him; his already impaired eyesight began to deteriorate rapidly and he was faced with blindness. With indomitable courage Dr Beer faced a sightless future; he would never admit defeat. Once more he set himself to study, first to master Braille then to take a three-year course in physiotherapy at the Royal National Institute for the Blind, London. When qualified he and his wife returned for further service in India. That was September 1950. An influential Hindustani newpaper had a headline, 'Dr Beer Returns', but what was even more precious to the returned couple was a telegram from Anand saying, 'Welcome home!'

The new physiotherapy department with equipment donated by the Royal National Institute for the Blind, and further donations from the Wadia Charities, met a real need. Up to 50 patients were treated daily and Dr Beer's hands had now become his eyes.

In June 1955, while on annual leave in the Salvation Army home of rest, situated in the beautiful Nilgiri Hills, Stanley Beer was suddenly taken ill and died. Everyone who knew Stanley Beer drew strength from his courage and was cheered by his irrepressible good humour and unflagging optimism. He would never admit to having any particular virtues—not even patience, which he more than anyone was forced to practise—'I'm just plain stubborn,' he would say with a smile.

*   *   *

Many names could be mentioned of the Indian staff of the hospital in Anand who have given a lifetime of faithful service. Suffice it here to mention three, all belonging to the one family: Brigadier Punjalal Limba, the father, served on the hospital administration until retirement. The son, Brother Devdas Punjalal, was nursing tutor until he retired, but is still very active as a local officer of the Anand Central Corps. The daughter, Brigadier Grace Punjalal, retired in 1980 from the post of superintendent of nurses, which she had held for many years.

The present hospital administrator, Brigadier David Hiralal, started his service at the hospital as a nurse, but has for years held the responsible appointment of administrator. These and many others are the mainstay of our hospitals.

10

Booth-Tucker's second term (1903-)

FROM America came the tragic news in 1903 that Commissioner Booth-Tucker's wife, the Consul, had been killed in a train accident on 28 October. No one can estimate the sorrow this brought to the Commissioner and the six children left motherless. Muriel, who as an officer served in India, was the youngest of the family and only two years old at the time. The sympathy and prayers of many, including Salvationists in India, held the family up and God gave strength to face life with faith and courage.

When attending the international congress in 1904 Booth-Tucker expressed to William Booth his desire to return to India where he felt his most important work was to be done. The General at first rejected this request feeling that Booth-Tucker's particular gift of administration was necessary at International Headquarters. So for three years Booth-Tucker filled again the position of Foreign Secretary. During this time he married Lieut.-Colonel Minnie Reid, an outstanding officer who at the time of her marriage was in command of The Salvation Army's work in Ireland. They shared the same Indian background, Minnie Reid's father being at one time Acting Governor of Bombay and two of her brothers in the Indian Civil Service.

The wedding took place in South Tottenham Citadel, London, and was conducted by General Booth. Although the service was of a semi-private character, representatives of almost every department of Salvation Army work were present, together with a number of friends and relatives, including the bride's brother-in-law, Sir Frederick Cunningham. The General spoke in appreciative terms of the competent and self-effacing labour of both the bride and bridegroom—of the bride's devoted service not only in England, but also in Belgium, France, Switzerland and Italy. He also referred movingly to the bride's affection for his daughter, the Consul, and of her desire to care, as a mother, for the Consul's six children.

As Foreign Secretary Booth-Tucker brought his new bride to Ceylon and India for a visit of inspection and meetings in January 1907. The Indian *War Cry* relates an episode in Ceylon:

> Mrs Commissioner Booth-Tucker had her first bullock-bandy ride from Potuhera to Talampitiya, and first experience of crossing the paddy fields in bare feet, plunging through mud puddles, crossing bridges comprised of a branch of a tree, at other times jumping across running streams. All this, done by the uncertain flickering light of torches, giving a smattering of danger to the adventure, made the whole thing quite enjoyable.

> The visit to our Swamiwattee Estate followed the next morning. Rains of the previous day, and heavy dew during the night, left the path muddy and slippery. Bare feet being the quickest and easiest means of locomotion, the Commissioner led the way, and apart from two or three blood-sucking leeches fastening upon them, everything went off well. The meetings were full of interest and glorious spiritual results.

It would seem that Mrs Booth-Tucker was thrown in at the deep end by this experience, but she was a woman of high spirits, adventurous and with great personal resources, and would possibly have enjoyed it immensely. They also visited many towns and cities in India. In the interest of discussing the Army's social programme the Commissioner was granted interviews with the Viceroy, Lord Minto, the Governor of Bombay, Lord Lamington, and other provincial governors and also the Maharaja of Travancore, besides a number of other important officials who may be said to control the government of the country. They discussed with evident interest the various plans which The Salvation Army had introduced for the social welfare of India.

No doubt this visit stirred Fakir Singh's (Booth-Tucker) longing to be back among the Indian people, fighting their cause, being in the front line, leading them to a new life in Christ; for his first love was—and remained to the very last—India. Once again he raised the question with General Booth, this time putting his petition in black and white. The letter was printed in the August 1907 issue of the Indian *War Cry*:

My Dear General,

Your visit to the East, and the unparalleled reception which you have been accorded, have seemed to stir up my whole heart and soul afresh in regard to the vast needs and possibilities which lie before the Army amongst these oriental nations. My own recent trip to India has also

85

made me realize more than ever the wonderful opportunities which await us there.

While I deeply appreciate the responsible position at the Chief's side at International Headquarters, which you have called me to occupy, I nevertheless feel impelled to offer my services once again for India, where I feel that my knowledge of the country and its languages, gained after many years' experience, would be of special use to the Army.

You will remember, dear General, that the cause for my recall from India, in 1891, was the sudden and serious illness of the dear Consul, and her consequent inability to remain. Apart from this I never felt that my term of service was completed, and it would be both a satisfaction and a joy to me, if you would permit me to return, even if only for a few years.

You could reckon on both me and my dear wife doing our very utmost to push forward the interest of the War, and to carry out your wishes in regard to the same. We can, as you know, make suitable arrangements for the children, so that their health may be thoroughly safeguarded.

Ever devotedly,
Your Son and Soldier under the Flag,
(signed) F. Booth-Tucker.

The General, realizing at this stage that to keep Booth-Tucker from India would be folly, gave consent that he should resume leadership of the Army's work in India, relieving the then Resident India Secretary, Colonel Hammond, of his post, appointing him back to Britain. The special terms of Commissioner Booth-Tucker's appointment as the General's representative in India was: 'giving general oversight and taking control of all the work in India and Ceylon especially of contemplated developments and extensions. The appointment will not, however, in any way interfere with the responsibility of the existing territorial commanders.'

Commissioner Booth-Tucker accompanied by his wife and children arrived in Bombay 27 September 1907. Mrs Booth-Tucker came to be known as Dutini, meaning Light. They were warmly welcomed by a number of officers at Carnac Bunder. Immediately upon landing the Commissioner, ever in a hurry, hastened off to secure some property for a new factory for the rapidly increasing hand-loom business. This transaction settled, he sped on to headquarters at Bori Bunder where a breakfast was prepared, after which a private meeting was held.

Booth-Tucker found on his return to the land he loved no less than 1,700 officers, cadets and teachers had been raised within the country. His absence from India for 16 years, including eight spent in the United States, had modified his thinking somewhat, and the extreme tactics of youth had become more moderate. The begging bowls were no more, officers were paid a salary, though no more than to pay for the barest necessities. To clarify the current position Booth-Tucker sent out a manifesto naming it:

The Call of the Indian Battlefield

The officer who comes to India now is in a different position from those who came a few years ago. Other officers laboured, and he enters into their labour. Others planted, he reaps. He takes charge of troops who already exist. In former times those who preceded him came to create—a far more difficult work. He now comes to organize, train, improve and lead to victory some of the spiritually finest fighting material of the world. To whichever territory he or she may be appointed the officer will find a blessed and devoted band of Indian officers, intelligent, earnest, devoted, with local officers, soldiers, juniors, day schools, boarding schools, village halls, social institutions, the wonderful machinery which the Army succeeds, with God's blessing, in creating wherever it goes.

The possibilities and needs are overwhelming

What hinders us from advancing at a far faster speed than we are doing? Simply the lack of leaders. India could absorb 1,000 such tomorrow, and be ready to receive 1,000 more. She needs not merely spiritual leaders, apostles, prophets, but she needs also those who will consecrate themselves to her temporal needs, and help us to solve the problem of self-support by means of agriculture and industries. We want weavers, skilled mechanics, carpenters, engineers, farmers, dairymen, gardeners, doctors, nurses, teachers for our schools. In fact, there is a wonderful opening for the indirect preaching of the gospel by the average Salvationist of consecration and intelligence. Good musicians would also be of great help to us. The two or three boys' bands that have been organized have been a wonderful help to our work. Needless to say, we want also literary help, those who have the pen of the ready writer.

Count the cost

Of course, nobody should come who has not counted the cost. The Indian War involves much painful sacrifice and the facing of constant danger. Death and disease seem to have chosen India for their headquarters. Plague, cholera, smallpox, typhoid and malaria claim their constant victims.

To the family man, the suffering of his loved ones must necessarily be a constant source of sorrow. It is the keenest form of sacrifice, though the thoughtful care of the General and Chief of the Staff has now made it possible for non-Indian officers to send their children to the hills for their education. This, however, involves the trial of constant separation. (The children being away, often 1,000 miles from home, for 10 months in the year from the age of five.) To the non-Indian officer India means sacrifice, there is no blinking this fact. Although arrangements are now made for him to get his salary regularly it is not what other Europeans in India are accustomed to receive. But to place him on a level in this respect with other organizations would be to delay India's salvation by many years, and to take away what is one of the Army's chief glories and a special link of fellowship with our Indian comrades. If you want to be a successful soul-winner you must be prepared for sacrifice. You cannot abolish the Cross. Christ Himself could not. You cannot.

The speed with which Booth-Tucker put things into operation was astonishing. Within a month of his arrival in India he had transferred the headquarters for all India and Ceylon from Bombay to Simla, having secured an excellent location for the new headquarters and hall facing the Mall adjoining the Bara Bazaar (big market). The opening took place on 27 October, exactly one month after his arrival to the very day.

In 1906 it was decided by General William Booth that a central training home for India and Ceylon was to be opened in Madras. Here young men and women from any part of the sub-continent or Ceylon, with a knowledge of English and a desire to spend their lives for God and their fellow-men, would receive training through the English medium. The training home was also open for existing officers who desired further training. 'Officers of any rank, desirous of improving themselves and thus qualifying for staff positions will be eligible, and will be allowed to retain the use of their title, while being treated exactly as cadets.'

The training home was opened 28 December 1906 and came under the supervision of the territorial leader, Lieut.-Colonel Yesu Ratnam (Stevens), with Brigadier Gnana Prakasen and other capable officers as teachers. Captain Arivanandham (Howard), son of the Chief of the Staff, Commissioner Henry Howard, was one of them. A brilliant and gifted young man, he was devoted to the cause. He died of cholera within the year of his arrival. Captain Kira Bai (A. Hanna), grand-daughter of the Baptist pioneer missionary of Burma, Adoniram Judson, having joined The Salvation Army in America, was appointed to the central training home in Madras, taking the place vacated by Captain Howard.

88

The commissioning of the first cadets from this training home took place in the great Victoria Hall in Madras in January 1908 and was conducted by Commissioner Booth-Tucker.

The central training home was later transferred to Bombay with Major Jeya Prakash (Henry Gore) as training principal, succeeded by Major Dana Das (H. Pimm Smith).

One other central training centre was set up in 1956 in Trivandrum where Dana Das's son, Major Premanand (Don A. Smith) was principal. Cadets from that session serve today as divisional commanders, heads of institutions and as superintendent of nurses at the Catherine Booth Hospital at Nagercoil.

*   *   *

Part of India was again afflicted with famine in 1907-1908, and in several localities prices of grain had gone even beyond those of the last famine at the turn of the century. The government was doing all it could to help the situation, yet millions died of starvation.

Booth-Tucker's second term of service was characterized by a more practical programme. His evangelical zeal had in no way lessened, rather it had become all-embracing. Seeing again the extent of human suffering he realized more than ever before that 'salvation means bringing health—physical, mental and spiritual—to every man'.

To help ease the food shortage in the famine-stricken north, he sent large consignments of cassava flour (sun-dried tapioca) from south India and demonstrated its usage in public gatherings in Simla by special lantern lectures. In trying to combat the widespread scourge of malaria a quinine league was formed, which was duly recommended by the Deputy Commissioner of the Punjab, the league having no less than 45,000 members.

An 'Arbour Day' was inaugurated on Empire Day, 24 May, when in every suitable Army centre trees were planted for the purpose of shade, fuel, fruit, timber or silk growing. In malarial districts eucalyptus trees were chosen. This practice is still kept up, but the date is changed to 2 July, Founders' Day. In Kerala (land of the coconut), formerly known as Travancore, 5,000 coconut saplings were planted on Salvation Army properties on Founders' Day 1979.

Booth-Tucker, like William Booth, was never afraid of using unconventional methods if he thought it would serve a useful purpose, so he sent for a shipload of cats from England as a preventative measure against plague, reasoning that where there were cats there would be no rats—the main spreader of this dread disease. Lieutenant Makwit (Mohanand) of Russia, who had passed through the London training garrison, was sent in charge of the first consignment of cats for India. It seems to have caused certain comments, for Booth-Tucker, justifying his plan, wrote in the Indian *War Cry*:

> When the proposal was made in London to send a shipload of cats to India, to fight the plague (that is the rats) many wise people were amused at such a preposterous idea. Now that the Japanese Government has taken up the project and is importing cats in tens of thousands from Europe, to fight the vermin in Japan, these wiseacres will admit there was more in this novel plan than they had imagined.

From early times India's most important traditional industry has been the manufacture of cotton goods. In almost every village the click-clack of the hand loom could be heard from morning to night. When factory-made cloth from Britain and other countries started to flood the village markets, the ancient system of partial self-support by home-made and home-sold industries was upset and millions of village weavers were deprived of their living. To try and revive the village industries, and thereby help the people, The Salvation Army took steps to improve hand-loom weaving. Staff-Captain Prem Das (Maxwell), skilled in things mechanical, was appointed to live among the weavers of Gujarat, study their art, and improve their methods. Maxwell invented a new and fast loom which could produce four or five times the quantity of cloth woven on the old hand-loom. A vastly improved warping machine was also designed. The loom was simple to handle, which meant it could be operated easily by the women and elder children, thus bringing in more money to the family. Sales depots were set up and annual sales and exhibitions were arranged to help in selling the cloth. This helped to bring industries back to the homes in the villages.

A factory for producing these looms was set up in Byculla, Bombay. The Governor of Bombay, Sir George Clarke, paying a visit to the loom factory, discussed means of making the loom available to the poor in the villages. It was exhibited in many cities and won first prize in Ahmedabad, Calcutta and Madras. It soon

Left: Commissioner Frederick Booth-Tucker

Above: Captain Henry Bullard before sailing for India in 1882

Below: Tranvancore Salvationists welcome Booth-Tucker

Above: Opening ceremony of extensions at Catherine Booth Hospital, Nagercoil

Below: Sinhalese corps officers on campaign

found a market, orders came from the Maharaja of Kashmir, the Raja of Jahangirabad and many others. Government jails in many towns were sent supplies, as were missions even as distant as the Armenian Mission in Iran.

It became necessary to train weaving masters, and schools were set up. Sir Louis Dane, Lieutenant-Governor of the Punjab, who had seen the Maxwell hand-loom in operation and realized its usefulness to the villagers, placed a large fortress in Ludhiana at the Army's disposal. It was formally opened in December 1908, as the Sir Louis Dane Weaving School and became one of the most important institutions of its kind in north India. An account of the opening reads:

> When the morning sun was flinging its rays across the loopholed battlement of the fortress, Sir Louis and Lady Dane's state carriage and four drove through the grand old gateway of the castle followed by his retinue and staff. A *shamianah* (pavilion) had been erected for the occasion. Commissioner Fakir Singh (Booth-Tucker) read an address of welcome, expressing thanks for the personal interest manifested in the enterprise by His Excellency. The lieutenant-governor replied, expressing his surprise to see how well advanced all the arrangements were in such a short time and gave reason for confident hope in the future of the school.

The inventor, Ensign Maxwell, was married to Ensign Bussy (Jit Bai) shortly after this event. After a honeymoon of two days, one of them spent attending officers' councils, the bride returned alone to her new home at the loom factory in Bombay, while her husband went on a 'flying' visit back to the newly-opened weaving school in Ludhiana. The first officer-in-charge of 'the Fortress' was Brigadier Gnana Dasen (Alfred H. Barnett) who was later replaced by a Marathi officer, Major Yesu Chandra, who held many responsible posts throughout India.

It is interesting to contemplate that at the time when Gandhi made the *chakkar* (the spinning wheel) the symbol for his campaign to raise the status of the low castes, Maxwell's Salvation Army looms had already been in use for many years in Indian villages.

The fact that the Salvation Army hand-loom could work in silk and wool, as well as cotton, enabled the weavers to vary their output according to the conditions of the market. Booth-Tucker studied the current market and found that silk weaving was a more

91

remunerative occupation and a careful survey of the industry was made. It became obvious that greater skill was required for the production of silk. Visits to the various silk-producing countries, France, Italy, China, Japan and Kashmir, were made by Booth-Tucker and his wife, experts were consulted and books on the subject collected. It became evident that to make a success of this new venture it would be necessary to commence from the very first stage—growing the mulberry trees, rearing silkworms, reeling the silk—until finally the silk cloth could be woven.

It happened that a silk farm belonging to the great Parsee industrialist and philanthropist, Jamsetji N. Tata, had been set up in Bangalore. Some 50,000 rupees had been spent in starting the industry but it had not achieved the expected result. His sons, Sir Dorabji and Sir Ratan, approached Booth-Tucker after the death of their father and offered the whole property to The Salvation Army as a gift, believing that the Army, with its organization behind it would be able to make a success of the scheme.

The Tata Silk Farm, as it was known, was situated at Bangalore in the Mysore district famous for its silk-worms. Very soon a school for silk production was functioning with Ensigns Veera and Dev Kumari (Graham) in charge, later replaced by Staff-Captains Diriyam and Veera Sundram (Jackson). More than 100 pupils at a time studied the making of silk from the first to the final stage. It proved a great success and silk farms were established in other places.

In Ceylon the government handed over the Peradeniya silk school to The Salvation Army with Captain Bhagwandas (Jorgensen) as manager. A silver medal was won for their craftsmanship. Another sprang up in Moradabad, and in the forest of Changa Manga near Lahore, famous for its mulberry trees, a silkworm rearing centre was instituted. From Simla came the news, October 1915, 'We have been able to acquire a splendid property as silk farm and institute, 1,000 feet below the ridge, in a charming valley.'

The Bangalore Tata Silk Farm was ranked as the premier silk school in India and won many medals, among them a gold, for its excellent workmanship. Brigadier Jackson (as he became later) did much to bring the institution to this high standard during the seven years he and Mrs Jackson laboured here. They lost their first-born, a son, and thought it wisest to leave the younger children—four daughters—in the Children's Lodge in Clapton, London, a Salvation Army home where missionary officers' children were looked after while the parents were serving abroad. In those days there were no cheap air fares or students' concessions and the children did not see their parents for many years. Grace Jackson, one of the daughters, now retired as Lieut.-Colonel, looks back on her childhood. She was four-and-a-half when her parents left and 13 when they returned, the First World War preventing their coming to England. She, with her sisters, shared in their parents' sacrifice, but she says, 'While we lost something we also gained something, being in the centre of the Army in its development days. Granted, there was about the home a Victorian atmosphere, but we never blamed our parents for leaving us, we knew they were doing something great.'

Eventually silk weaving ceased to be a productive industry, as man-made fabrics started to flood the market, and one by one the places were closed down. The last report in the Indian *War Cry,* November 1928, indicates, however, that at that time the Bangalore silk farm was still operating, visited by the territorial commander, Colonel Muthiah, for inspection, and saw Ensign and Mrs Aanesen busily engaged at the farm.

Yet another 'away from the factory and back to the home' scheme, which has been successfully carried out for many years, was the needlework industry. In the villages around Nagercoil thousands of women have been taught lace-making and embroidery under the supervision of officers and teachers at the women's industrial home, and the articles produced in the homes marketed for them. Major Daphne Clair (from Australia) and Major S. Sarah, daughter of Tamil officers, spent many years in this work and were much loved and respected by the women and girls, Sarah, as Brigadier, taking full responsibility later.

Most, if not all, of the women's industrial homes as well as girls' boarding schools were supported by the handwork produced by the women and girls. In a country like India, where 80 per cent of the people live in villages, cottage industries were of the utmost importance in giving a necessary supplement to the meagre family income. It gave opportunity for all family members to earn their bit, at the same time allowing the mothers to stay at home, and so preserving the sanctity of home life.

'Religion is too often merely theoretical and unpractical,' said

Booth-Tucker, 'we must make ours apply to the everyday details of our people's life and work. Silk farms, weaveries, fruit farms, rescue homes, settlements, schools, hospitals, farm colonies, etc, all play their part in the great work of uplifting the poor and bringing them into the light and liberty of the gospel of Christ.'

One practical issue which could not be overlooked was that headquarters also needed money to keep the great machinery going. While the work in the main was subsidized by International Headquarters, to supplement it officers known as 'financial specials' were given the task of travelling around the country asking for subscriptions. These officers are worthy of praise. An early report from 1897 recounted by Adjutant Radha Bai (Marsh) reads:

> On a recent tour through the Punjab, Captain Roshni Bai and myself left the Northern Territorial Headquarters with a list of places to be visited, with no information regarding billets, etc, and 10 rupees (less than £1 sterling) for our travelling expenses.

Two other women, Captains Grose and Goddard, showed ingenuity by taking with them a magic lantern when they started off on a collecting tour in the hills of Ceylon in 1903.

> We set out full of faith for a successful time, taking with us the magic lantern by the aid of which we hoped to raise funds to replenish the 'War Chest'. The lantern proved a great help. There were a variety of slides, comprising part of the life of Christ, scenes from the Boer War, pictures relating to the late Queen Victoria and the coronation of King Edward VII. On Sundays, there being no Salvation Army centres, we arranged a small indoor meeting and then an open-air meeting. In some of the outlying stations visited, many remarked how seldom they had visits from anyone interested in their eternal welfare.

These officers were not only 'financial specials' but also travelling evangelists whose spiritual ministry brought blessings to many.

11

Far and near (1908-)

AT the beginning of the 20th century the Army in India acquired land and property in various places. In June 1908, 13 acres were purchased in Ahmednagar in the Maharashstra and planted out with various crops with a view to further development. Fariabagh, as the locality is called, became an important and thriving Army centre with a divisional headquarters, training college, schools and hostels.

Six hundred boys and girls are currently attending the William Booth Memorial School. To see these children at morning assembly is a sight that warms the heart—smartly uniformed, eager and alert, they take their places forming straight lines in the spacious compound. Assembly commences. A group of girls comes on to the platform to lead the singing. They sing one line and the rest of the children repeat it, the words are from the 13th chapter of 1 Corinthians—the 'love chapter'. Another girl reads from the Bible, a teacher prays, the Lord's Prayer is repeated by all. In closing, a declaration of allegiance to their country is recited. What better foundation could the young people have on which to build their lives!

Also in the year 1908 the Bombay headquarters was transferred from Bori Bunder, as the government requisitioned the premises for an extension of the railway adjacent to it. The Army acquired another property, known as Victoria House, just opposite Byculla Bridge. This was a large three-storey building, suitable also for accommodating the central training home, which was therefore transferred from Madras. Colonel and Mrs Blowers (Sukh Singh and Mithri) were appointed in charge, besides being territorial leaders.

All in all, in the year 1909, the Army had in Bombay, its birth-place: a territorial headquarters, a central training home, a civil,

95

naval and military home in Colaba Causeway, a rescue home for women at Mazagon and a loom factory and weaving school at Byculla. In Anand a site was acquired for a new training home for Gujarati cadets. Halls were being built throughout India and Ceylon, actually 254 within a period of five years. The number of village corps in India in 1910 totalled 777 with 433 primary schools attached. The General raised a fund of £5,000 for the purpose of providing halls at an average cost of £17 each, which would make it possible to put up about 300 halls. Those were the days when a little went a long way! Besides the promised help from the General's fund, soldiers were expected to contribute material and labour, or raise money by donating grain which was sold and turned into cash, so that up to 20 per cent of the actual cost would be raised locally. In 1910 an important development was the opening at Byculla, Bombay, of the King Edward Industrial Home for stranded Europeans and Anglo-Indians.

By now the Movement had acquired numerous properties, so in 1911 an association called The Salvation Army Property Company Limited was formed to administer these on a proper business footing.

To help Salvationists get their own land The Salvation Army bought 2,000 acres in the Punjab, some 180 miles south of Lahore, in what is now Pakistan. The cost of the land was 500,000 rupees (about £32,000). Plots were sold to colonists, payment being made in instalments over a period of 30 years, after which they became the owners. Staff-Captain Wafadar (Hackett) was appointed the first manager. When the colony, Shantinagar (Village of Peace), was officially opened by a flag-hoisting ceremony on 28 May 1916 an eye witness said, 'There was nothing to see but jungle.' One man came prepared to deposit 400 rupees for one square of land (25 acres), but when he saw the jungle he said, 'I shall only venture on half a square, if I lose that I shall still have 200 rupees.' He had his regrets for within four years the land was brought under cultivation and proved excellent for crops of various kinds.

The village was built up in the centre of the colony, 100 acres of land being reserved for that purpose. Each colonist has built his own house and enclosed his compound with a boundary wall. A meeting hall, manager's bungalow, officers' quarters and dispensary were also erected and in the middle of the village a deep well was sunk.

The village is a pattern for all the villages around for cleanliness and orderliness. All work is suspended on Sundays. The hall seats only 500 so men and women take turns, the men's meeting in the morning and meetings for the women in the afternoon, while the evening meeting, with a smaller congregation, is for both sexes. The collection plate is usually augmented with a basket in which rice, flour, cotton or eggs are placed. Sunday-school for the children is held in the large compound, each class seated in the shade of a tree. Even more important than the large gatherings on Sunday are the cottage meetings held in the homes of the colonists four evenings a week, where they gather in small groups for Bible study and prayer. A church bell, donated by the church at Jhang, calls the colonists for prayer at sunrise before they go to the fields for their daily labour. Ensign Dindar (William E. Carter, later Colonel and Territorial Commander for India East) succeeded Staff-Captain Hackett as manager of the colony and further developments were made, schools and a hostel for boys were built. A canal, constructed by the government, runs the length of the colony and assures a constant supply of water, which banishes any fear of failure of crops, different from so many places on the subcontinent which are dependent on the monsoon rains. The livelihood of over 4,000 people in Shantinagar is secure. They are now owners of their own land, while the Army continues to see to their spiritual and educational needs through the corps, the girls' high school, boys' boarding hostel (the boys' high school was nationalized some time ago) and the dispensary. Commissioner Arthur Holland, present Territorial Commander of Pakistan, writes: 'There is every prospect of Shantinagar remaining a live and vigorous expression of Salvation Army work.'

A mark of confidence was shown to the Army in 1924 when the judicial headmanship of a large portion of land in the Punjab of upwards of 25,000 acres was handed over for the purpose of establishing a colony similar to that of Shantinagar. The name of this colony is Amritnagar.

The pioneer spirit of the officers in the early part of the century brought them into ever new fields of opportunity. Two centres were opened in the Himalayan range in places with romantic sounding names such as Chini in Bashir State and Ani in the Kulu Valley. In 1911, Adjutant Jang Singh (E. Walker, later Lieut.-Colonel) was appointed to Chini Medical Institution on the borders of China and Tibet. The Adjutant had for some time been understudying Brigadier (Dr) Andrews. Newly married to a wife full of missionary zeal, they started off to their new appointment on a 12-day trek over the mountains. Muleteers had gone before with provisions, so they felt sure of a well-stocked food supply on arrival. The road was steep and as they reached a higher altitude the mountain path was covered in snow. The Adjutant was attacked by a malady common to those unused to travel in the mountains—and fainted. Mrs Walker resorted to prayer and her faith was rewarded. An old man came walking down the mountain path, seeing their dilemma he stopped and being familiar with the symptoms worked a quick cure. When, eventually, after the 144-mile-long walk they caught sight of the tiny village of Chini, their provisions having been used up, they looked forward to a substantial meal, being sure that the muleteers had arrived before them. To their dismay they discovered that neither provisions nor their luggage had arrived. No food was obtainable in Chini, for the natives had barely enough for their own needs and in any case would neither give nor sell to strangers.

The next four days the Walkers lived on water and three apples. At last someone was persuaded to give them some siftings from his flour and some home-made butter, and they made bread with this. Later they obtained a basket of potatoes and in this way they were able to hold out for 48 days when at last the muleteers arrived. Having been occupied with other business, which they had deemed more important, the muleteers had brought the Walkers' provisions when it suited them. The hill people soon learned to appreciate the strangers among them and the help given in times of sickness. The clinic's reputation spread and people started coming for treatment from remote places in Tibet.

Adjutant Yesu Prakash (Frank Mortimer, later Lieut.-Colonel) and his wife succeeded the Walkers. Mortimer was a gifted linguist and translated John's Gospel into the local language. By this means the word of God would reach remote mountain villages where the gospel had never been heard. Other officers worked for some years in this isolated post, including Adjutant and Mrs James Edwards and Adjutant and Mrs Dimberg, but financial consideration and lack of suitable officers made it impossible for the Army to keep the clinic going and it was eventually closed down.

In Ani in the Kulu Valley a mission station had been established by the Rev Marcus Carleton, a Presbyterian from America. Having obtained land from the government in this secluded valley, he brought in a number of boys from the Punjab, who had been orphaned during a famine, and set them to work on the land. Later, Christian girls, who were also orphaned, were also brought from the Punjab and eventually a Christian community was formed. Some years after the death of the Rev Carleton, his widow, who had carried on her husband's work, negotiated with Commissioner Booth-Tucker about taking over the work and The Salvation Army bought the property. Major Hannah Carr (Nirmala) and Staff-Captain Hansine Weie (Deva Priti) were appointed. Self-reliant and practical these officers possessed the special qualities such an appointment demanded. Hannah Carr had nursed the Army Mother during her last two years of illness and when Emma (the Consul) left for India, the Founder consented to her request to accompany his daughter. Hansine Weie hailed from Norway, was a good administrator and eventually became the Chief Secretary of the Women's Social Work in Britain with the rank of Colonel.

Another Norwegian, Mrs Commissioner Herbert Mitchell, living in retirement in London, has the unique experience of being able to look back on years spent in Ani in the enchanting Kulu Valley. She came out to India in 1921 with the Calypso party with 125 other missionary officers. When she arrived at Simla headquarters she was given her appointment to assist Adjutant Prema Bala (Mrs Costly) in Ani.

Ani lies 65 miles from Simla and the only way to get there in those days was by rickshaw or by foot. No rickshaw was available at the time, so Klara Muskaug, as was her name, set off on foot, accompanied by the wife of the manager of the Simla depot, Mrs Captain Jørgensen (a Danish officer). From Simla, which is 7,000 feet above sea-level, the road rose to 9,000 feet at Narkanda, then descended steeply to Luri which lies at 2,000 feet, up again 1,000 feet to Ani situated 3,000 feet above sea-level. Klara had not been told that mountaineering was part of missionary service and with her best Sunday shoes found the descent worse than the ascent. At night they stayed at Dak bungalows, rest houses originally put up for government officials. The journey took four days. During the three years Captain Klara Muskaug was stationed in Ani she did the journey on foot three times with only a coolie as company carrying her luggage. When passers-by on the road saw this young woman walking alone, they would invariably ask: 'Where is your husband?' and Klara, with a smile, would answer, 'He is waiting for me!'

Life was busy and satisfying at Ani and did not leave any time for brooding over loneliness or isolation. The corps, farm, day school, dispensary, and government post office took up all the hours of the day and some of the night as well. Two hours were spent daily in the school room and services were held three times a week in the little church. They grew grain and made bread with home-made yeast and made their own butter. Eggs and vegetables were sold to the local market. In the fruit season, preserves and jam were made from apples, pears, peaches and oranges. It was packed and despatched by coolies to Simla for sale at the Army depot.

Mrs Adjutant Costley, the officer-in-charge, was a capable, energetic woman. It was through the testimonies of two Indian officers visiting her homeland, Sweden, in the year 1887 that she heard the call to India. She left with the very first party of Swedish officers, nine in all, in 1888. In India she met and married a British officer, Captain Costley. Their life together was short, the Captain died before the birth of their first-born, a daughter. Mrs Costley carried on bravely in various appointments whilst bringing up Kathleen, who became an officer and married Captain Charles Green (later Colonel). Together they served in India for many years and Mrs Costley, Kathleen's mother, spent part of her retirement in their home, leaving India in 1938 after 50 years in the country.

The last officers to be appointed to Ani were Captain and Mrs Stanley Williams from Canada. The difficulty in finding officers suitable for this unusual type of work and the greater need for officers in expanding places led the Army to withdraw from Ani. Arrangements were made with the Church Missionary Society to give spiritual oversight to the Christian families, but the society did not wish to take over the activities of the mission, so the land and buildings were sold to the local *Rai* sahib (landowner) in 1932.

In a recent book entitled *Kulu,* written by Penelope Chetwode, daughter of a former commander-in-chief in India, and wife of Sir John Betjeman, is a description of a visit she made to Ani in 1964. She relates meeting with one of the local residents, a Christian, who told her that his father had worked as a catechist for the Rev Carleton; also that after The Salvation Army left, the Christians had built themselves a stone chapel. This information points to the permanence of the work done by former missionaries and Salvation Army officers.

In 1912 the Army in India celebrated its 30th anniversary by an exhibition and sale of work held in Bombay. Colonel and Mrs

Blowers (Sukh Singh and Mithri) had leadership of the territory. The town hall was engaged for the occasion and Sir Richard Lamb, ICS, opened the exhibition. Here was an optical demonstration of what, with God's help, The Salvation Army had been able to accomplish during the brief span of its Indian existence.

At this juncture it may be appropriate to give a detailed account of the work in India and Ceylon:

Indian and Ceylonese officers, cadets and employees	2,285
Missionary officers	207
Corps and outposts	2,763
Village day schools	450
Children on rolls	10,000
Industrial homes for children	18
Accommodation in industrial homes	800
Settlements for criminal tribes	11
Men, women and children in settlements	2,300
Farm colonies	5
Rescue homes for girls	4
Industrial home for stranded Europeans	1
Loom factory and weaving schools	19
Silk farms	5
Hospitals and dispensaries	8
Total social institutions	124
Persons cared for in institutions	4,520

Nineteen-twelve was also the year that General William Booth, the Founder of The Salvation Army, was promoted to Glory. Many joined in mourning the loss of a great man. His visits to India were vivid in many minds, his compassion for the poor and his plans for their betterment had awakened a new consciousness in the country.

His last message, when leaving Ceylon on his way to Australia in 1905, could apply to every part of the Indian sub-continent:

> In carving out and making your fortune, and increasing the prosperity of the country—which I have no doubt, and which repute says far and wide, you are doing—don't forget your souls—don't forget eternity —don't forget God!

In connection with William Booth's passing the Hindi *Punch* wrote:

> We record it with pride, that it was reserved for an Indian and a Parsee, follower of another faith, to be the first to suggest opening a

101

subscription list for a world memorial in which all countries benefited by the General's work, should be asked to participate. As a nucleus of the needed fund, the generous Parsee, troubled with no narrow religious prejudices, and realizing the magnitude of the departed crusader's noble work, offers 6,000 guineas as his personal contribution. We bow respectfully to Mr Rattan Tata for so faithfully and generously keeping up the ancient tradition of his father's honoured house.

Bramwell Booth, who for years had been his father's right-hand man as Chief of the Staff, became the General. In 1922 he visited all the main centres in India and Ceylon and met with people in all stations of life, the rich and the poor, and people of different religions. Great crowds gathered to hear him preach the gospel of Christ. At the end of his tour he affirmed, 'More and more I see that it is the Spirit of Jesus which is the real attraction.'

12

Restoring the 'lost sheep' (1908-)

A DAY in the early part of 1908 marked the conception of one of the greatest and most successful enterprises in the history of The Salvation Army in India—the transformation of criminal tribes to decent, law-abiding citizens. The criminal tribes of India represented a form of crime which is almost unknown in other countries, consisting of entire families devoted from the cradle to the grave to a life of crime. A child born to a family within these tribes automatically became a 'criminal', the caste system making it impossible to change caste. In the Punjab alone no less than 21,000 male adults were registered under the Criminal Tribes' Act. Crime maps kept by the government showed that the tribes' favourite habitat was the sub-Himalayan region of north India; Madras Presidency also having its quota, all in all numbering from one to three million people scattered throughout India.

To know their origin one must go back in history, some are said to be 'the direct descendants of the pre-Aryan aboriginal owners of the country, whilst others formed the bulk of the plundering armies which overran India previous to British rule'. Government had for many years been trying to control them but without success. They were a constant drain on government finances and a danger to the community. Their cunning was legendary, their exploits often cruel. They had nothing to lose.

It was while Booth-Tucker was conducting a congress campaign at Bareilly that he was approached by Mr Tweedy, Commissioner of Rohilkhand and member of the Government of the United Provinces, with the request that The Salvation Army would undertake reformatory work among the criminal tribes. Booth-Tucker agreed, and the matter was submitted to the Lieut.-Governor, Sir John Hewett, who suggested that one tribe should be entrusted to the Army, and if it proved successful other tribes would be committed later.

103

A start was made by opening a settlement for 300 Doms who were under the charge of the police at Gorakhpur. A set of buildings, which had been police lines, was placed at the Army's disposal and Brigadier and Mrs Hunter (Bahadur and Ratna Bai) were appointed to take charge of the settlement. The Doms were the most unpromising of human material, unruly, inveterate drunkards and gamblers. It was the practice when a Dom died to put a coin in the fist as a token that there would be something with which to start gambling on the other side of the dark river. Domestic affairs were confusing to say the least; when a husband went to jail, as often happened, the wife would take to herself another husband 'to protect her virtue', so she would say. When the first husband was released from jail he would claim his wife back, but if the second husband objected they would fight it out between them and the victor would win the wife. The children would seldom know who their real father was.

To find work for the settlers was of paramount importance. When first they were told to work they laughed scornfully. 'Work?' they said. 'We never work, we dance and sing.' It was indeed raw material the officers were dealing with. Brigadier and Mrs Hunter gave themselves to the task of reforming these men and women by showing them God's love in action. Gradually they took to weaving, using the Maxwell loom, and were paid for their work—even when they spoiled the material—and as they became more proficient their earnings rose, and with it their self-respect. Silk-weaving was allocated to the more expert among them. *Dhurri* (cotton carpet) making, which many of them had learnt in jail, was another line of work; sewing classes were started for the women. As other settlements were established, other kinds of work were introduced such as carpentry, dairy farming, irrigation projects, stone quarrying and agriculture.

In May 1914 when Brigadier and Mrs Hunter and their two children were returning, via London, from homeland furlough in Canada in company with a large party of Salvationists on its way to the international congress, the SS *Empress of Ireland* on which they were travelling met with disaster. The liner was rammed by a collier in the Gulf of St Lawrence and sank within minutes. One hundred and twenty-four of the Canadian delegation were drowned, including the entire Hunter family. The names of Brigadier and Mrs Hunter will live on in Army history as pioneers of a very specialized work.

Adjutant and Mrs Pimm Smith (Dana Das and Dana Bai) succeeded the Hunters at Gorakhpur Settlement. They had with them their two small children aged five and three. The Indian *War Cry,* June 1912, records: 'These two children accompany their father to the Gorakhpur jail the first Sunday in each month and there, in their childish way, sing Hindustani choruses to the Dom prisoners.' The missionary career of Commissioner Don Smith (R), being the younger of the two, started early!

The government, well satisfied with the behaviour of the Doms under Salvation Army care, wanted the work extended. Two other tribes, the Haburah and Bhantus, were settled on the outskirts of Moradabad, 100 miles north-east of Delhi. Rehabilitation work among the Haburah tribe proved successful. Under the management of Major Jivanandham, an Indian officer, the land was brought under cultivation by the sinking of wells. The industries were extended, and during the First World War the women were engaged in making uniforms for the military department.

One settlement after another was established and Booth-Tucker could report, 'We have already 29 settlements, the total population being 8,000 men, women and children. The buildings occupied by these tribes include three jails, two fortresses, one police line, four opium *godowns* (warehouses), an abandoned railway settlement and several villages and tracts of agricultural land.'

The wife of Brigadier Solomon Smith, recently promoted to Glory, has left an account of life in a criminal settlement and the inside information of an incident which stirred the imagination of people not only in India but in Britain—the capture of Sultana—the Robin Hood of the Terai Forest—which was televised in the film *The Long Duel* and written about in Jim Corbett's *My India.*

Brigadier and Mrs Solomon Smith were appointed to work among the Bhantu tribe in Najibabad Settlement in 1922. Mrs Smith takes up the story:

> Leaving Lahore at 5 pm we arrived at Najibabad station at 2 o'clock the following morning. We were met by an Indian clerk who directed us to a waiting bullock-cart where two armed policemen stood waiting for us. My heart sank as I climbed into the cart with my husband and two-and-a-half-year-old son. The four miles' journey took two hours as the

cart creaked along the rough road in the lonely jungle. By the light of the moon we could see in the distance the impressive outline of the old fort which would be our future home—an old Moghul fortress, its massive walls still bearing the shell marks from the Indian mutiny. We passed a police *chauki* (post); the big iron gates of the fort were opened and locked behind us. We realized that this was the toughest settlement of all the Army settlements. The Bhantu tribe, being known as the most notorious outlaws, often resorted to violence.

After breakfast, a roll call was taken and it was discovered that a considerable number had absconded. These men, about 40 of them, had been in the settlement only a few days. Sultana was their leader. He had gathered round him 100 kindred spirits all armed with guns. This gang lived in the forest, terrorizing the villagers in the district if they did not accede to their demands. Their fearlessness was legendary and won the admiration of some who looked upon Sultana as an eastern version of Robin Hood. There were rumours that the gang climbed the walls of the fort at night and brought their loot to the settlement, handing it over for their wives to hide.

One day a letter came from the police asking us not to allow anyone out that day as a search was to be made. Thirty policeman came into the settlement, dug up the floors and part of the mud walls of the houses where the criminals lived. They found thousands of rupees worth of jewels, gold, silver ornaments and 2,000 silver rupees besides currency notes. The money was left where it was found, as it could not be identified as stolen, the rest confiscated.

We were later informed by the government that a special dacoity force of picked men with Police Superintendent Freddy Young as the head had been authorized to catch Sultana and his men, and we were asked to give every possible assistance to the police. Freddy Young called on my husband and told him of his plans. Early attempts were unsuccessful. Despite swift raids and night-long ambushes Sultana and his men always managed to escape. Eventually, after many months the special police force surrounded the robbers' camp at dawn and Sultana, with most of his men, were taken prisoner.

Freddy Young sent a telegram to Solomon Smith asking him to meet a certain train. On this special train was Sultana, a very small man, and the rest of the gang in handcuffs and leg-irons, all chained together. Sultana said when he saw my husband, 'Smith Sahib, are you a padre or a policeman?' The reply was, 'A padre.' Sultana then said, 'You are a fool, Sahib. I could have shot you many times when you came to check at night with your torch. I aimed my rifle at you, then thought—no, I will not waste a bullet, for if I shoot him, who would take care of our wives and children?'

106

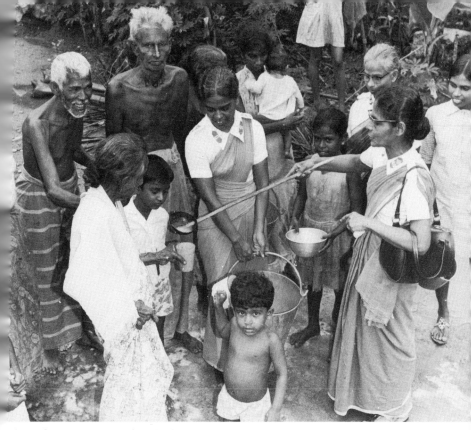

Above: Soup distribution near Colombo, Sri Lanka, 1974
Below: School children in South Eastern India, 1980

Left: Pakistani delegate to the 1978 International Congress

Above: The Maxwell loom

Below: Children of William Booth Memorial Schools, Ahmednag
1980

It was not Smith Sahib but Sultana who was a fool. Had he stayed inside the settlement, who knows, he may have mended his ways like so many of the others and would not have been hanged with eight of his men. The rest were deported for life to the Andaman Islands.

Two girls were born to the Smiths at the Najibabad Settlement, but in 1926 they contracted smallpox and died. Within the same week a boy was born. He, too, died of the same dreadful disease which had also affected Mrs Smith. Mercifully she recovered.

In January 1913 Staff-Captain Mackenzie (Anandham), later Commissioner and international secretary, received his appointment as superintendent to pioneer the work amongst the criminal tribes in the Madras Presidency. The first settlement to be opened by the Army was at Sitanagaram, an old railway colony near Bezwada. The second was Bethapudi, later named Stuartpuram after the Governor of Madras Presidency, Sir Harold Stuart. On the opening day when he stood before a group of wild, suspicious, resentful tribesmen, who had been brought in by the district police, he took them as representing the whole tribe numbering thousands in the Telugu District and, presenting them to Staff-Captain Mackenzie, he said: 'Take these, Salvation Army. I give you 20 years to do for them what has to be done.'

Stuartpuram became the largest of all settlements with some 3,000 settlers, situated on about 2,000 acres of land. The railway line passed through the colony with the station some four miles away from the settlement. In response to a plea of the settlement manager a station was built within the settlement and Stuartpuram station is today one of the regular stations on the line.

Schools for children were set up in all the settlements to train, teach and direct them into a new life, which gave the greatest hope for the future. The two schools at Stuartpuram Settlement became in course of time staffed with men and women teachers who had come up through the settlement schools, passed through their training and returned to teach the next generation. Yesu Ratnam, BA, whose name means Jewel of Christ, was brought up in the Stuartpuram Settlement. He received a grant from the government to enable him to continue his studies at Madras University. Giving his testimony at the settlement he said, 'You know who I am and what I was. I thank God that he helps me to live a pure life. All I am today I owe to Him.'

Many are the Salvation Army officers, national as well as missionary, too numerous to mention by name, who have had a vital part to play in the work of rehabilitating the outlaws of India. By their example of Christian love, lived out in daily contact with the settlers, a new dimension of living was shown them. They were told of a Saviour's love, a love which drew them away from their former wicked ways, a love which got behind their defences and lifted them up on a new level of life and gave them hope for the future.

Sir Harold Stuart had said, 'I give you 20 years.' In fact, it took a little longer, though not much. A generation later the same families still farmed the same land, producing better crops and better handicrafts than their parents, but the great difference was that they were criminals no longer. They were free citizens of a free India. The settlement is still there, but it is a criminal tribes settlement no longer. Instead, it is the Salvation Army land colony, Stuartpuram, with a Salvationist manager guiding the business affairs and looking after the spiritual welfare of several thousands of colonists, many of them Salvationists and a number of whom have become officers.

Colonel Edwin Sheard's name is well known among Salvationists through General Coutts' fascinating story, *He Had No Revolver.* In 1927, when an Adjutant, Sheard was appointed to take a party of Bhantus, who were being deported by the government, to the Andaman Islands. Among them were Sultana's men who were serving life sentences. Resettling them on this remote island with their families and The Salvation Army to look after them, it was felt there might be some hope of restoration. The group of islands is situated in the Bay of Bengal more than 600 miles from Calcutta. *'Kala pani,'* black water, the prisoners called it, referring to the intervening sea which would now sever them from the mainland.

Having already worked among the Bhantu tribe in the Moradabad Settlement, Sheard was well acquainted with their peculiarities. Fauj Singh was Edwin Sheard's Indian name, meaning 'Lion of the Army'. No doubt a lion-heart was required for such an assignment, but in other ways Sheard followed more the peaceful ways of the lamb.

When he and his wife arrived at Port Blair with 60 convicts in chains, their womenfolk and children, the police officer receiving them said to Fauj Singh after the chains of the prisoners had been removed, 'I would strongly advise you to sleep with a revolver under your pillow.' The police officer must have wondered at the reaction to his kind suggestion—not a word, just a smile—for the 'Lion of the Army' possessed no revolver, but a far more effectual weapon, which he used daily in all his contacts with the prisoners—the most powerful weapon in the world—the power of love. As manager, Sheard had to plan the settlement. A village set-up was drafted out and each hut detached with sufficient land for a vegetable and fruit garden. A completely new way of life was to be taught to the settlers. Services were held regularly on Sundays and during the week, attendance being entirely voluntary. Progress was slow because of their fear of each other, but gradually a change took place. Some made a new beginning as they committed their lives to Christ and received His forgiveness.

In the cottage meetings held on the verandas of their humble homes, in the dim light of a hurricane lamp hanging from the low roof, Fauj Singh would kneel on the mud floor beside the penitent, leading him into a new life in Christ Jesus. 'It was a great joy to watch the development of many fine qualities in the men,' writes Edwin Sheard in the little booklet *Sergeant-Major in the Andamans,* 'honesty in business, consideration for others, kindliness, and many other traits unknown to them in the old days. They had been described as "the worst criminals and the most uncivilized savages in north India": experience proved that, given sound opportunity for development, even the worst criminals are capable of the finer things of life.'

After five-and-a-half years in the Andamans the Sheards were transferred and Staff-Captain and Mrs Arthur Hughes appointed, later succeeded by Major and Mrs Francis (Santosh and Phul Bai). Few may have heard of William Francis and his wife; they deserve special mention for their heroism and Christian devotion. For nine years the Major lived in the Andamans. He and his wife were still serving in this isolated and lonely appointment with only the Bhantus for company and mail delivered only once a week, when the war came and the islands were occupied by the Japanese. Mrs Francis was evacuated to India, the Brigadier (which was now his rank) chose to stay with his people. It was not long, however, before he was deprived of his freedom and eventually sent as a war prisoner to occupied Burma. When the war ended he was a sick man. He was evacuated by boat to Calcutta where he hoped to be reunited with his wife. It was too late. Deprivation during the many years had taken its toll and he died just before the ship came in to

Calcutta harbour. He was buried in Calcutta with full Salvation Army honours. Brigadier William Francis had counted the Bhantu tribes people dearer than his own life.

Lieut.-Colonel W. Bramwell Baird, who has made a comprehensive study of The Salvation Army's work among criminals in India, has supplied the following information:

> From the opening of the first settlement at Gorakhpur in July 1908 until the close of the work after the Second World War was almost exactly 40 years. It took two generations. By the 1930s much of the work of reclamation had already been accomplished and the young people growing up under the Army's care were free from the taints of crime.
>
> During the war years the work in Moradabad and Bareilly was terminated and the premises adapted to other Salvation Army purposes. Both are still busy centres of Salvation Army activities and the new officer training college at Bareilly is a fitting memorial to great accomplishments of the past.
>
> By 1945 only a few settlements remained. In the north Kanth was closed in 1947, leaving the land to the people. Changa Manga and Kassowal had both been handed over earlier. In the south Sitanagram and others had been terminated some years before. Only Stuartpuram remained.
>
> By the end of 1948 all the tribesmen had been freed, the centres of activities were closed or used for other purposes and officers were transferred to other appointments. A whole community, the lost sheep of a by-gone civilization were brought back to the fold of good citizenship.

The Indian Government recognized the Army's services for the criminal tribes by awarding Kaisar-i-Hind medals to a number of officers. Among these were Colonel Edwin Sheard, Brigadier Solomon Smith, Brigadier William Francis and Major Leslie Gale (later Lieut.-Colonel).

Ensign Thomas Green (Prem Sagar), father of Colonel Charles Green whose last appointment on the sub-continent was as Territorial Commander of Pakistan, received the Order of the Founder in 1923 'for marked devotion in his work in an Indian criminal settlement—undergoing painful operation in giving portions of his skin in an attempt to save the life of a criminal tribesman's child'.

13

Farewell to India (1919-)

COMMISSIONER Booth-Tucker, who all his life had enjoyed robust health, fell prey to an illness in the early part of 1919 which made it necessary for him to return to England. He was now 66 years of age. He never went back to India again, but was given a less exacting position at International Headquarters from which he later entered retirement. He was promoted to Glory in 1929. There can be little doubt that Booth-Tucker was both the founder and the architect of The Salvation Army in India and Ceylon. For 20 years—first a period of eight and then 12—he had directed all operations. The man who in his young days in India had been imprisoned at the instance of his fellow countrymen was, in 1913, invested with the Kaisar-i-Hind gold medal by the viceroy at a reception in Simla. But of more consequence than any gold medal was the satisfaction of knowing that at the time of his leaving India there were 2,500 officers and teachers carrying on the work of proclaiming the message of God's love in nearly 3,000 centres. He also had the gratification of seeing the Army making its entrance into Burma during the latter part of his leadership. Commissioner and Mrs Booth-Tucker (Fakir Singh and Dutini) sailed from Bombay in May 1919.

In March of the following year the Simla headquarters was closed down and a rearrangement of territories and leaders took place. For many years Army work had been under the direction of eight territorial leaders, in part responsible to Commissioner Booth-Tucker as Special Commissioner for India, and in part to International Headquarters. The General now decided to appoint three Commissioners responsible directly to International Headquarters, in three territories. The administrative centres were:

Lahore (Northern Territory), Commissioner Jai Singh (Henry Bullard);
Bombay (Western Territory), Commissioner George Punter French;

Madras (Southern Territory including Travancore and Ceylon), Commissioner Sukh Singh (Arthur Blowers).

Commissioner George French was territorial commander for less than two years. When touring Gujarat he contracted smallpox. He fully realized that his last hour had come, and finished off his affairs with a precision and care which could have been possible only to one at peace with his Maker. From time to time he asked his comrades to sing for him and he repeated right through the beautiful 23rd Psalm, his voice ringing firm and true as he came to the lines, 'Yea, though I walk through the valley of the shadow of death, I will fear no evil: for thou art with me.'

After the Simla headquarters had closed down, the corps and depot continued for some years. Simla being a hill station and the seat of government during the summer months the population fluctuated with a great influx of people during the summer and very few residents in the winter. The Indian *War Cry* of July 1929 reports:

> The Territorial Commander, Lieut.-Commissioner Muthiah, conducted two meetings at Simla Corps, the evening one was announced to commence at 10 o'clock. The meeting closed at 1 am! The corps has an individuality of its own. No other corps is quite like it. Adjutants Karan Singh and Karini (Meredith), who are in Simla for the summer months, have thrown their hearts into the work as has their Indian assistant, Lieutenant Sena Putra.

An all-India audit office was set up in Poona in connection with the forming of the three territories and Lieut.-Colonel Charles Baugh (later Chief of the Staff) was appointed in charge. He would be directly responsible to International Headquarters by undertaking the audit of accounts of the newly-formed territorial headquarters, submitting his reports to the Chief of the Staff in London.

The Poona office also published the monthly English language Indian *War Cry*. Each territory sent in its material which was edited by the auditor or his assistant. Many outstanding officers have done service in this office. They were always welcome visitors as they travelled from territory to territory, not only as auditors but also for their personal influence.

In 1968 the *War Cry* office was transferred and literary and editorial offices set up in Madras with Lieut.-Colonel Jean Gould

112

as Literary Secretary and Brigadier S. A. Paul, Assistant Literary Secretary and Editor of *The War Cry*. In 1980 the South Asia Literary and Editorial offices moved to Bombay.

A writers' workshop, under the leadership of Jean Gould, took place at Nasik, March 1964, when Lieut.-Commissioner Gwendoline Taylor was the guest speaker. The setting up of this workshop came from the desire to bring something tangible out of the series of writers' study courses which had been conducted on a territorial basis for several years. The writing project for that first workshop was on the topic 'Christian Behaviour'. In addition to the main project, biographical sketches of Indian pioneer officers were also attempted, some of which have appeared in the London edition of *The Officer.*

The second writers' workshop was held in August 1967 at the Mar-Thoma Youth Centre, Adoor, in south India. The Bishop, Mar Theophilus, who lived in the same grounds, showed his interest by attending some of the evening programmes and by praying with the delegates on the morning of their departure. Brigadier (later Commissioner) Kathleen Kendrick, at the time secretary for missionary literature, was the guest speaker on this occasion and gave a series of lectures on 'Writing History'. Lieut.-Colonel K. Yesudasen gave nine lessons on 'The Epistle to the Hebrews.' An editors' conference followed this event, in which editors from each of the South Asian territories took part.

The Poona IHQ Audit Office was transferred to Delhi, the capital, in September 1977. The transfer was undertaken by Brigadier J. Milton-Rand just before his retirement. He was succeeded by Major Gordon Becker.

*   *   *

In 1921 a group of Indian girls took Europe by storm. It was only to be expected that people flocked to see and hear them—20 lovely youngsters with long, black, glossy hair and big, brown eyes. Wherever they went, whether in the British Isles or Scandinavia, they drew large crowds. They were girls from the Salvation Army boarding school in Satara, some 200 miles south of Bombay, children of Salvationist parents. Two Swedish officers were in charge of the party, Ensign Ellen Olsson (Khushi) and Ensign Emma Johansson (Kamala Bai), who were 'mother' and 'auntie' to the children. The singing of Indian *bhajans* to the accompaniment of tabla and sitar fascinated the listeners, but to hear the young girls speak so convincingly of what Jesus meant to them, their bright faces alight with an inner joy, brought a hush over the congregations. Sulochana was one of the party who said in one of the meetings:

> I would like to tell you again and again that I belong to a living God and I follow Him daily. I feel I cannot do enough for Him. In the Christian cemeteries in India are the graves of missionaries who have given their lives to carry the message of Jesus to my people. I want to thank you for what you have done for my country.

Sulochana wrote home to her parents that all the wonderful things she had seen and heard in England had deepened her longing and determination to return home and spend her life in telling the people of India about Jesus. Sulochana's parents, Major and Mrs Shirsath, became officers from Poona in 1897. They were newly married and the bride only 14 years of age. Mrs Shirsath, a lively 97, can look back on 83 years of officership and on having reared a family of 16 children.

Sulochana came back to England in 1923 as a cadet of the Conquerors Session. When she was 30 she took charge of Satara Division, the first Marathi woman officer to hold that position. Her cheerful spirit and charming manner endeared all to her. In a country where all women are expected to marry, Sulochana chose to remain single so as to give herself, wholeheartedly, to the work. As superintendent of the women's industrial home in Bombay her service to the women and girls was an expression of her love for God. Lieut.-Colonel Sulochana Shirsath gave 43 years' service as an officer in the Western Territory. Of the 20 girls from Satara School who went to England, 18 became officers. Others, besides Sulochana, have given a life-time of faithful service to God and the Army. The influence of Khushi and Kamala Bai, who trained the children in the boarding school, and later the cadets in the training garrison and the officers in their divisions, will live on for ever in the Maharashstra. These two Swedish officers came to India together with 52 other officers who were sent out in 1914 in what was called 'The Scandinavian Party'. Brigadier Ellen Olsson (Khushi) served 33 years in India and Lieut.-Colonel Emma Johansson (Kamala Bai) 38 years.

With the many newly-opened criminal tribes settlements and other institutions and expansion of evangelistic work there was a constant demand for more officers. India's need was paramount among Salvationists in many western countries. General Bramwell Booth mustered 128 officers from various territories and chartered a small, but comfortable vessel, the SS *Calypso* to transport the party to India. Officers from the Continent and Scandinavia had come to London some months earlier and were accommodated at the staff college, in North London, where they were given a course of lectures and language study.

A month prior to sailing, two great farewell meetings were held in London, one at the Metropolitan Tabernacle, the other at Clapton Congress Hall. Both gatherings were led by the General which added significance to the occasion. Other farewell meetings followed in various towns in the Midlands. Everywhere these gatherings were preceded by mammoth marches with bands and banners, the farewelling Salvationists being the centre of attraction in their colourful Indian uniforms.

The ship left from Hull on 17 October 1921. Life on board the *Calypso* was, as for the other big parties that had been sent out, similar to a busy training school. Immediately after breakfast each day the missionaries hurried off to prayers, and from prayers to a lecture on such topics as 'Early Days of The Salvation Army in India', and 'Preservation of Health in India'. Doubtless by now knowledge on that subject had increased since the days of the early pioneers of whom too large a proportion died. After lectures came the all-important language classes. English was taught to those who came from non-English speaking countries. Time was scheduled for private study, singing and music classes—in short, plenty to guard against anyone being homesick.

Flying the Army tricolour flag at the masthead, the *Calypso* docked at Bombay on 11 November 1921. That evening at their welcome feast they were introduced to the custom of eating curry and rice without the use of spoon or fork, sitting on the floor. Within days this memorable party had broken up to find their way to appointments in various parts of the great sub-continent, Ceylon and Burma.

Officers sent to the Madras Province received a most cordial welcome from the Governor of Madras. Lord Willingdon wrote:

> Most gladly I write you this note to give a warm welcome as Governor of the Presidency, to Commissioner Blowers and his 30 officers who are

coming to assist in furthering the wonderful work which The Salvation Army is already doing in our province.

I have seen so much of the activities of The Salvation Army during the years of my life in India. I have expressed myself so often in terms of appreciation of those activities, that I think it is hardly necessary for me to say to Commissioner Blowers and his party that, in the future as in the past, the great work which The Salvation Army is doing in this country shall receive all sympathy and encouragement from

Yours sincerely
Willingdon

Commissioner and Mrs Arthur Blowers (Sukh Singh and Mithri), having done more than 70 years' combined service in India, left the country in November 1924 after a sincere and fond farewell. They called him 'a pioneer of pioneers' and his wife certainly shared that title. The Commissioner continued to work for India and the neighbouring countries as the international secretary, a position he held for many years. In 1937 he was admitted to the Order of the Founder for distinguished service.

In January 1922 an Eastern Territory was created, which included Burma, with Colonel Hira Singh (Edgar Hoe) as Territorial Commander and Lieut.-Colonel Jivanantham as Chief Secretary. Headquarters was set up in Calcutta. For further effective oversight, the Ceylon Command, which had formed a part of the Southern Territory, became a separate territory with Colonel Harry Millner as Territorial Commander and Major L. G. Krasse as Chief Secretary. Ceylon had at the time 46 corps, 85 societies/outposts, 153 officers and cadets, 56 employees and teachers, 16 schools and five institutions. A special feature in Ceylon (Sri Lanka) is the large proportion of women officers, partly accounted for by the fact that, unlike India, no pressure is put upon the daughters in a family to marry if they wish to remain single. A greater reason by far would be the women's and girls' institutions on the island which have produced many fine officers. Of the officers-in-charge who have trained the girls two deserve special mention, Brigadier Laura Gale and Brigadier D'Silva. Brigadier Gale received the Order of the Founder in 1976 for: 'Having for 40 years cared for the social, moral and spiritual needs for women and girls at The Haven, Colombo.'

In April 1924 the Southern Territory was divided into two territories, the Madras and Telugu Territory with headquarters in Madras and Colonel N. Muthiah as Territorial Commander, while

116

headquarters for the Southern Territory was set up in Trivandrum with Commissioner Blowers as Territorial Commander until September when he and Mrs Blowers left India and Lieut.-Commissioner Mrs Annie Trounce took over the leadership. Mrs Annie Trounce was early widowed and left to bring up her two daughters. The elder, Muriel, with her husband Colonel Victor Thompson served many years in India. For 12 years Lieut.-Commissioner Mrs Annie Trounce was Territorial Commander for the Southern Territory, following in the footsteps of another woman warrior, Colonel Clara Case, who had been the Territorial Commander from 1905 until 1917.

In Calcutta, on one of the city's busiest thoroughfares, a new territorial headquarters and central hall was opened on 4 July 1928 by Sir Stanley Jackson, the Governor of Bengal. The property, 37 Dharamtala Street (now called Lenin Saranee), was acquired at the cost of five lakhs of rupees (£37,313). The governor was presented by the builder with a gold key, the handle of which was wrought in the design of the Salvation Army crest. A large number of distinguished citizens was present. The building was one of General Bramwell Booth's 70th birthday memorial schemes. Replying to the territorial commander's, Lieut.-Commissioner Ewens', address of welcome, Sir Stanley Jackson said:

> I am very pleased to have this opportunity of taking part in the opening of this fine building today—you are rightly proud of the progress your Movement has made during the 60-odd years of its existence. I have always been greatly impressed with the businesslike way in which The Salvation Army manages its affairs and as an organization, there is nothing of the same character which can claim to be superior. One of the greatest claims for appreciation of your work is that you get down to a class of people which few others touch.

This occasion would have delighted Commissioner Bullard, looking back, as he could, to the very first efforts of establishing Army work in Calcutta. And the two young women pioneer officers who in desperation sent out a plea for help through the Indian *War Cry* in 1883:

> No besieged, starving garrison looked and waited so earnestly and expectantly for help to drive the enemy from the gate, as your forlorn comrades at Calcutta. The enemy says we may as well give in at once, that no help will come. They see our strength is nearly gone, but praise God, we work, listen and are still believing.

So God honours those who wait on Him and trust His promises.

14

Beautiful Burma

BURMA—a land of sunshine, luxuriant foliage and flowers, soft warm winds, gaily plumaged birds and daintily dressed men and women. The women in pure-white lawn jackets (*aingyi*) with pretty buttons, over a sarong (*loongyi*) of soft material in pastel shades, silk scarf to match and velvet sandals. The men also in *aingyi* and *loongyi* but of slightly thicker material, on their heads brightly coloured silk-scarves knotted over the ear in a jaunty fashion.

The religion of Burma is Buddhism. The countryside is studded with pagodas and *kyaungs* (monasteries), a common sight is to see monks (*hpyngyi*) with shaven heads and loose-flowing yellow robes, carrying orange-coloured umbrellas and begging bowls, starting out in the morning to collect their daily food offerings (*sun*).

Felix Carey, son of William Carey, 'The father of modern missions', was the first Protestant missionary to land on Burma's shores. But of him it was said, by his disappointed father, 'Felix has shrunk from being a missionary into an ambassador,' as he left his mission and joined King Thebaw's staff. Adoniram Judson followed soon after in 1813 and rightly bears the name 'The Apostle of Burma'. He laboured for six years before he won his first convert and after 10 years could count only 10. For 20 years he worked diligently to accomplish the task of translating the whole of the Bible into the Burmese language.

The Karens, one of the many races that inhabit Burma, originally from the northern mountainous district, had a tradition that a man with a book in his hand should come from the west, who would bring peace and prosperity to their people. They saw in Judson and his Burmese Bible the fulfilment of this prediction, and when Judson left Burma after a ministry of 37 years thousands of Karens had accepted the gospel of Christ. But while the Karens 'received the word gladly' the Burmans of the plains remained aloof and indifferent.

It had long been a cherished hope of Salvation Army leaders to commence work in Burma. Adjutant Taran Das (Ruben Moss) was in January 1915 sent to survey the land, while at the same time collecting funds for the Army's work in India. He conducted meetings where opportunities were given and in one place was asked to address the Young Men's Buddhist Association. After hearing accounts of the Army's success in the reclamation of criminals the Buddhists guaranteed financial aid if such work could be done in their country. The prospect seemed reasonably bright. Moss reported to Commissioner Booth-Tucker who, always expecting quick results, sent back a telegram:

YOU ARE APPOINTED TO OPEN OUR WORK IN BURMA STOP PROCEED ON THESE LINES STOP (1) OPEN WOMEN'S RESCUE HOME (2) JUVENILE PRISONERS' HOME (3) A CENTRAL CORPS (SD) BOOTH-TUCKER COMMISSIONER

In the meanwhile Mrs Blowers (Mithri), whose husband at the time was Chief Secretary for India and Ceylon under Commissioner Booth-Tucker, set out from Simla with a small party of women officers. When this party of brave women arrived in Rangoon, April 1915, they soon got down to business. Meetings were held in the YMCA hall and the English Baptist church which were kindly placed at the Army's disposal. Mrs Blowers preached and also explained the reason for the Army's arrival. Very soon a suitable house was secured for a women's social institution.

A few months later Major and Mrs Leib (Uttam Das and Uttam Dasi) were appointed to take charge of Rangoon Division to further develop and organize the work which had already been started. The Leibs and their daughter Lily arrived in Rangoon on 9 October 1915. When Major Leib approached the Burmese Government presenting the Army's plans to commence social and evangelical work in Rangoon he was received very cordially by the Lieut.-Governor, Sir Harcourt Butler, KCSI. Suggestions for the reforming of criminals were laid before the governor and it was decided to give them a trial. The government was to release to the Army adolescents nearing the completion of their prison sentence in the hope that under the Army's care they would be influenced for good.

The first reform home was officially opened on 13 March 1917, by Sir Harcourt Butler, who showed a personal interest in the venture and donated 1,000 rupees as a grant towards the Army's work. Two years later the institution was visited by the Inspector General of Prisons for Burma, Lieut.-Colonel Knapp, IMS, and being favourably impressed with the work done he suggested that extensions should be made and greater facilities provided. A new and larger building was acquired, standing on three acres of land, two of which were put under cultivation by the inmates. In the workshop, cane-work and carpentry were taught, which found a ready sale in clubs and homes all over Burma.

Since the Army seemed to be able to handle the young delinquents Mr Morgan Webb, Secretary to the Government of Burma, conferred with the officers regarding the extension of the scheme, and later nine murderers, with other long-sentence men, were handed over to the care of The Salvation Army.

Mrs Adjutant Foster (Gulam Bai), who with her husband worked among these young men, gives a glimpse of daily life in the home:

A message comes from Insein Jail notifying us that a dispatch of three prisoners, under armed escort, is timed to arrive at the institution between 11.30 and noon. My husband is away in Rangoon on business, my two little ones are asleep in their cots, the drowsy quiet of midday heat predominates. It is 12 o'clock, through the stillness comes the clank, clank of chains. Three prisoners are passing under the arched gateway with their armed escort. The prisoners, with shaven heads, are dressed in the coarse clothing of the jail, handcuffed, and with heavy leg-irons clanging at every step they take. They are chained to each other at the waist and linked on to the police, one on either side of the three prisoners with loaded rifles, a third with fixed bayonet brings up the rear. The little party clatters over the stone entrance along the veranda, here they line up in front of me, the police ground their rifles and come smartly to the salute. I am handed a long official document which I sign and return. They salute and depart, leaving the prisoners in my care.

My husband arrives back and the prisoners are set free from their chains. It is briefly explained to them why The Salvation Army has received them. They are exhorted to be good boys, obey the rules of the home and to stand up and act like men. Each one is then given an *aingyi* and *loongyi* and a silk headscarf, which makes them feel respectable, for however down-and-out a Burman is he must have a silk scarf for his head, or he is not a Burman. The rapid change that takes place in the appearance and lives of these men is amazing to see.

120

'When the time came for the young men to leave the home, they were given a set of tools and a Bible. Many of them asked for a song book, too, and we did occasionally get news of boys who, having returned to their village, gathered their friends around and read the Bible and taught them the songs they had learned in the home,' says Brigadier Mrs McQuilkin who, with her husband, was also stationed there.

In January 1921 a new central hall and divisional headquarters was acquired in Lewis Street. The Chief Judge of Burma, Mr Justice Robinson, supported by Commissioner and Mrs Bullard, was at the opening. Meetings were held on the Sunday in both the central hall and at the YMCA. 'Two souls were converted during the month and one soldier enrolled,' reads the report. Burma was always a hard field. The Christian teaching of self-denial and the discipline of Salvation Army soldiership does not have a general appeal to the easy-going, pleasure-loving Burman. So much more worthy of respect are the few who in isolation have taken up their cross to follow Jesus.

The first Burmese candidates who offered for officership in The Salvation Army were Ba Maung and his wife in 1928, 12 years after the Army commenced work in Burma. Both came from strict Buddhist homes.

By 1921 there were three corps in Rangoon District: Central Corps in Lewis Street—English speaking; Dunidaw Corps—Telugu speaking; Kalabasti Corps—Tamil speaking. Officers from the Madras Territory came over to minister to their own people in the two last mentioned corps. Later a purely Burmese-speaking corps was opened at Kya Kwe Thet.

For administration purposes Salvation Army operations in Burma came under the Eastern India Territory and were directed from the Calcutta headquarters until 1928. In May of that year the General decided to make Burma a separate command. Lieut.-Colonel Jeya Das (Hancock), who had done 28 years' service in India, was installed as officer commanding. Two years later, when he retired, it was announced that the Burma Command would for the present be regarded as an independent division, directly responsible to International Headquarters and Major Gayuna (Wilby) to be divisional commander.

In August 1922 the Army took over a soldiers' home from the YMCA in Maymyo in Upper Burma. Here in beautiful

121

surroundings and bracing air, servicemen could relax and find a retreat from the rigours of military life. Sunday services were held, which to many brought memories of home. The officer and his wife saw not only to the temporal needs of the soldiers, but through their ministry many left renewed in spirit as well as body.

The same year a corps was opened in Mandalay 600 miles north of Rangoon. King Thebaw had his palace here until 1885, when he was exiled to India, where he died. On one occasion, during his exile he sent £5 as a donation to The Salvation Army with an expression of his good wishes. Mandalay is the religious centre of Burma. Daily, 11,000 *hpungyies* arrayed in their saffron-coloured robes would sally forth in the early morning carrying their begging bowls. The appearance of The Salvation Army Indian uniform of red jacket and khavi *dhoti* or sari roused great curiosity. Some said they were the seventh religion and the last and would cause fire to come down to earth. Others wondered whether they were a travelling circus, and one person, believing this, asked to be allowed to come into the hall for two annas! It was not until 1922 that the uniform was changed to Burmese dress of white *aingyi* and navy blue *loongyi* which was more in keeping with Burmese taste.

In connection with General Bramwell Booth's 70th birthday celebrations a new women's industrial home was built in 1927. In those days Rangoon was called one of the most cosmopolitan cities in the world and young girls and women of all nationalities found temporary shelter in the home—American, British, Japanese, Chinese, Indian, Anglo-Indian and Burmese. A report states: 'Several have done well, while some have married!' For over a quarter of a century Brigadier Catherine Sørensen and Major Louisa Reading (Danish and English respectively) served at the women's home. Assisting them for many years was a gifted Chinese girl, Eva Kimlin, who became an officer.

Major Thomas Hood, whose first wife died in Mandalay, was sent to pioneer the work in Pyu. He wrote:

> My wife and I went to Pyu quite alone, without even a translator. The district lies in Lower Burma, in the wet zone where the monsoon rains last six months. When travelling at such times one has to take off one's shoes and socks, tuck up one's clothes above the knees and trudge mile upon mile through slush and mud of the paddy fields—no proper roads—the rain pelting down. Most of the village houses are built on stilts, usually of bamboo.

Two young women officers followed the Hoods, Captain Rose Flood from Australia and Captain Freda Saltmarsh from England. Their quarters was a rambling wooden building on stilts, the jungle fast encroaching underneath where snakes and giant lizards made their home—sometimes making their way 'upstairs'. At night the oil lamp was encircled by flying-ants and other insects humming in harmony with the zooming of mosquitos which were legion. But Rose and Freda disregarded these minor inconveniences, they enjoyed their work and were happy when visiting their Burmese and Karen officers stationed in various villages. In their company they walked from village to village, crossing rivers by the help of bamboo poles, selling Gospels, preaching the good news.

Land was bought at Pyu for a new divisional headquarters and a training college at Toungoo when Brigadier (later Lieut.-Commissioner) Arthur Hughes was the officer commanding from 1933 to 1939.

When Burma became involved in the Second World War the Burmese Government ordered all foreign women and children to be evacuated. Major Reading of the women's industrial home relates her experiences:

> I had to think and plan for the girls under my care in those terrible days before Burma fell. Rangoon was being evacuated. I got as many girls as possible fixed up with friends and relations and those, for whom I couldn't find suitable places, I took with me to Kalaw in the Shan States, where we have a home of rest for officers. Here in the grounds the government had built a large bamboo hut for evacuees. March 1942, the Japanese armies were getting nearer, other plans had to be made. The Chinese and Indian girls I had with me I dare not leave behind, it was too late to trek to India over the mountains and I could help no one by staying. I approached the evacuation committee and arrangement was made for seven of my girls, my Chinese Captain and myself to go by air to Calcutta. After a terrifying day and night on the train we arrived at the airfield. We left Burma on the night of 31 March arriving Calcutta in the early hours of 1 April 1942.

Among the women officers evacuated was Brigadier Mary How, who had become well known in the ruby mines and business houses of Burma, as the Army's energetic and cheerful collector. Mary How took up an appointment at a boys' home at Bongaon on the borders of what is now Bangladesh, from where she was very shortly promoted to Glory, having been an officer for 40 years, 22 of them spent in Burma and India.

The men officers stayed on in Burma till they were forced to leave and had to make their escape through the mountains of north Burma, through occupied territory, along steep and dangerous paths over to India. The wives, who had been evacuated earlier, spent many anxious months with no news of their husbands until they arrived in Calcutta.

At the time when war interrupted the work of The Salvation Army there were in Burma, under the command of Brigadier Lownes, 27 officers and cadets, 127 soldiers, seven corps, and three social institutions. The small force was again put under the direction of Calcutta in the hope that the Eastern Territory might by some means be able to contact and guide the Salvationists there.

The first contact with Burmese Salvationists after the war was made by officers on red shield work who entered Rangoon hard on the heels of the re-occupation forces. Meeting up with the few faithful Salvationists while conditions were still disturbed and unsettled, these officers brought with them a new hope for the future and gave witness to a universal brotherhood in Christ.

Towards the close of 1946 Albert Orsborn, then General of The Salvation Army, appointed a Commission of Goodwill and Enquiry to visit India, Burma and Ceylon. Arriving in Rangoon December 1946, Commissioner Gore (International Secretary), Major Stanley Hannam (Under Secretary) and Brigadier Victor Thompson (Chief Secretary in charge of East India Territory) called on government officials and Church leaders. In an interview, the Governor of Burma, Sir Hubert Rance, expressed the opinion that the re-establishing of the work of The Salvation Army depended on the turn political events would take. There was no doubt that the country needed such social activities as the Army had to offer, but the future was uncertain.

However, the members of the goodwill commission were optimistic for the future, even though this field had never been one of the most productive, our witness among the people was valued. The loyal Salvationists who had remained faithful during war years could not be left shepherdless.

A survey revealed that headquarters in Lewis Street had been bombed and was lying in ruins. Within the shell of blasted walls a Chinese man had built a bamboo room. The Telugu corps was still in operation, the comrades holding on faithfully until an officer could be sent them from the Telugu country. The boys' home (former Juvenile/Adult Remand Home at Tamwe) was in good condition and used as a day school. The delinquents had been released at the start of the war. The women's industrial home had for a time, during the Japanese occupation, been used as a hospital. It was returned to The Salvation Army and the small depleted force of Salvation Army personnel used it as their headquarters. Meetings were held though attendances were few. Brother Judson, a naturalized Burman of Indian parentage, was of invaluable help to the handful of officers, being fluent in English, Burmese and Karen. A faithful Salvationist for many years he now holds a commission as Envoy.

Of the drama of the intervening war-time years there is little on record. We know that Adjutant Saw Kedoe, deprived of his uniform during war years and without a shirt to put on, had the Army crest tattooed on one shoulder and the Army flag on the other. A permanent witness to whom he belonged! Lieutenant Ma Lay May was widowed during the war, her husband died while trying to locate Salvationists round the country. Ma Lay May was advised to return to her village, instead she walked many long miles to get to the women's industrial home in Rangoon, because she felt that God wanted her to continue to work for Him in The Salvation Army.

In April 1947 Brigadier L. Clayson Thomas, familiar with Burmese conditions after his many years in the country, was appointed to re-establish the work. His observations at the time are interesting:

> Our arrival was not entirely welcomeless, as two national officers of our small pre-evacuation forces were in occupation of our former women's industrial home. Regular meetings are now being conducted from four centres, whilst modest beginnings have been made with both a children's educational centre and a women's industrial centre. But these are not the days of spectacular advances for The Salvation Army in Burma, for our rehabilitation programme coincides with Burma's new independence. National aspiration surges strong within Burma's indigenous peoples, and only time will prove to them that Christianity is not synonymous with imperialism. Patience and wisdom are called for concerning the eventual shape of the Army's 'things to come' in Burma. The Burmese are coming into their own and claiming their rights to solve their own problems and manage their own affairs. However, wise observers of the trend of events in Burma feel that eventually there will be a warm and reciprocal attitude toward those of us who are ready and

willing to co-operate with the Burmese in solving their many and varied problems.

The Fourth of January 1948 was a momentous day for Burma—a day of a great gesture and of a great experiment, when a sovereign power bequeathed independence to a group of people who had decided on self-determination. We who love and work for Burma wish her and her people well, and we of The Salvation Army pray that we may have a part in establishing this beautiful land in righteousness, peace and prosperity.

The first requirement was a new headquarters and central hall and premises were obtained in Bigandet Street. Seven Burmese officers rallied round the officer commanding and his wife. It was not easy going. Burma, in common with other newly-independent countries suffered the usual birth-pangs. But in spite of such conditions the Army, by divine aid, was able to maintain and in some instances develop the activities which had been re-established during the previous two years. An information and advice bureau was opened, accommodation was provided for refugee families as a result of the insurrection in the country. The Salvation Army headquarters became a distribution centre for relief sponsored by the Rangoon Charitable Society.

Other officers commanding followed Brigadier Clayson Thomas: Brigadiers Lawrence Fletcher, W. Wycliffe Sharp and Edwin Robertson. In 1965 many changes were taking place in the country, re-entry permits for people from abroad were no longer issued, so when Brigadier and Mrs Robertson's permits expired in the summer of 1965 they knew there would be no returning and the reins of Salvation Army leadership were handed over to Major Violet Godward. When in turn she was requested by the Burmese Government to leave the country in 1966 she handed over to Major Ba Sein, a Burmese officer of many years' experience.

Brigadier Cecil Dark who, with his wife, was among the early missionaries in Burma, wrote a tribute to Major Ba Sein after his promotion to Glory in 1971. The Brigadier, who was able to contact the Major during a three-day tourist visa visit when travelling in Asia in 1970, wrote of Ba Sein:

> For about four-and-a-half years Major Ba Sein faithfully supervised the work in Burma without contact with officers from other lands, with the exception of two or three visits of a few hours. It was my privilege to spend three days in Rangoon, much of the time with Ba Sein visiting the centres of Army work, attending a large gathering of Christians of all

denominations in what was previously known as the Scots Kirk. These were experiences I shall never forget.

Major Ba Sein was called to his Heavenly home a few months after this and Major Saratha Perieswami, a woman who is a teacher by profession, was given the responsibility of the Army's work in Burma as its liaison officer, a duty she has carried on faithfully right up to the present time besides supervising the girls' home in Tamwe. Few have been the contacts with the outside world.

In 1972 restrictions were eased slightly allowing visitors a seven-day visa and the International Secretary, Commissioner Arthur Hook, accompanied by the Under Secretary, Lieut.-Colonel Leslie Pull, paid a visit. As they touched down at Rangoon Airport a customs official said: 'Oh, The Salvation Army has come back—we are so pleased to see you; we still have your headquarters here.' Wondering just how many Salvationists had remained faithful they made their way to Tamwe. As they approached the hall the joyful sounds of a fanfare filled the air and the band of the boys' home greeted the visitors with a *Triumph Series* march as they entered the crowded hall. A tribute to Major Clifford Bowes, brother of the present bandmaster of the International Staff Band, who, when serving in Burma many years ago, trained the first boys to play an instrument.

The crowning day for the valiant soldiers of The Salvation Army in Burma was in January 1980 when for the first time in its history they received a visit from their international leader. As General Arnold Brown and his party drove up the flag-bedecked driveway of the boys' home, the strains from the boys' band rang out in no uncertain tones, 'Onward, Christian soldiers'—an apt expression of their determination and spirit of loyalty. Owing to restrictions the General was prevented from preaching in a public meeting, but a 'Family' gathering was arranged by Major Saratha and her workers, where the General reminded them of God's faithfulness.

The women of the home league expressed their welcome in song and the newest home league member, an 89-year-old, garlanded the General indicating Burmese Salvationists' affection. The highlight of this gathering was the commissioning of a Burmese couple, Brother and Sister Wallace, as officers of The Salvation Army. At the conclusion, after singing the Founder's song, the General prayed for God's protection and blessing upon this small and special battalion of His Army.

127

When the President of the Burma Council of Churches asked the General, 'Do you think that Salvationists around the world sometimes forget the little Army here in Burma?' the General was able to assure him that there are many who remember our valiant soldiers daily. As the General took leave of the little force at the airport he confirmed the promise: 'I won't forget you, nor will your comrade Salvationists around the world.'

When the International Secretary for South Asia, Commissioner Edwin Marion, visited Burma in September 1980 he commissioned two more officers, husband and wife, who are now caring for the young people in the children's home in Pyu.

15

'The strength of the hills is His also'

THE Lushai Hills, or Mizoram as the district has been called since 1954, lies tucked in between Bangladesh to the west and Burma to the east and is part of India. Ram means country and Mizo is the name covering all the different clans of which Lushai is just one. A day-long journey on a single track, narrow mountain road leads to the main town, Aizawl; gates regulate the up and down-going traffic. The villages scattered throughout the mountains can be reached only by foot.

In this remote area is a flourishing expression of The Salvation Army with an officer strength of over 100, and thousands of Salvationists. It was not through the efforts of missionaries from abroad that the Army took root in Mizoram, but by the initiative of one of its own sons—Kawl Khuma. His name means 'Overcomer of the Universe' and Kawl Khuma prevailed where lesser men would have given in. Rosalie M. Wheaton tells the full story of his life in *Kawl Khuma*.

The Mizo people having lived in isolation for centuries developed their own culture. Kawl Khuma, born in 1890, was brought up with the simple animistic beliefs of primitive man, in spirits dwelling in the jungle which surrounded his village, spirits to be appeased by offerings of cocks, pigs and other animals. It was not until he attended school in Aizawl that he heard the Christian gospel. The words of the Lushai pastor spoke directly to the 14-year-old boy and he decided there and then to become a Christian.

After passing the middle school examination in English he was accepted for training as a compounder by the local civil hospital. In his spare time he would go from village to village, together with a Christian friend, preaching the gospel of Christ, winning many converts. One day, sitting among a group of Christian friends, Kawl Khuma suddenly exclaimed, 'Let us form ourselves into an association of Christians and draw up a special set of rules by which to guide our lives. We could all live together in a separate community, and to give a better witness I think we should wear uniform.' After discussing the possibility of such a venture, they decided their uniform should consist of a khaki coat with a piece of red cloth sewn on the upper edge of the breast pocket.

Some time later, having donned the suggested uniform, the friends were sitting talking in the market square when two men came walking up to them. One of them, a shopkeeper and the first Lushai to have passed the matriculation examination, said to Kawl Khuma:

'You and your followers look just like the people of *Chhandamna Sipai* (The Salvation Army).'
'Who and what is the *Chhandamna Sipai?*' asked Kawl Khuma.
'They wear uniform and have a set of rules which discourages smoking and drinking and wearing jewellery and chewing betelnut. They have military ranks and there are many thousands of soldiers in countries all round the world. If you want to know more about it I'll lend you some books which I picked up when I was in Calcutta, they'll tell you all about it.'

Kawl Khuma was not slow in getting hold of the books, which happened to be *The Doctrines of The Salvation Army* and *Orders and Regulations for Soldiers.* Having studied English he had no difficulty in explaining what he read to his friends, who were amazed how close to their own idea of Christian living were the principles outlined in these books, and their first reaction was—how can we get in contact with The Salvation Army? Someone told them of Booth-Tucker being the leader and that his headquarters was in Simla in north India. Kawl Khuma wrote to him at once. When the reply came with an invitation to come to Simla, Kawl Khuma and his friend Pu Chalchhuna, with whom he had formed the little group of uniformed Christians, decided to make the journey together.

With only the clothes they wore and a jacket for additional warmth, the two of them set out on the journey of some 1,250 miles from Aizawl in the Lushai Hills to Simla in the Himalayas. The first part of the journey was in a small country boat, down the foaming rapids of the river, down through the jungle to the heat of the plains. After many days' travelling and not a few adventures, they at last reached Simla. They made their way straight to the Salvation

Army headquarters where they were received kindly. It was arranged for them to stay in the home of Salvationists until Commissioner Booth-Tucker, who was away at the time, could meet them. They used the waiting time well—attended meetings, took part in open-air meetings, and were greatly affected by the joyful expression of Christian faith.

Chalchhuna's health, unfortunately, was giving cause for anxiety, he had developed a cough followed by high fever. When admitted to the hospital the doctor diagnosed 'double pneumonia'. Kawl Khuma stayed by his friend's side on a mat on the floor. On the seventh day Chalchhuna passed away. He was given an Army funeral and Salvationists stood by Kawl Khuma in the loss of his dearest friend.

A few days later Kawl Khuma was called to Commissioner Booth-Tucker's office. 'Are you willing to travel to Bombay and undergo training in the Salvation Army training home, and then give your life in service for God in the Army?' asked the Commissioner. This was, of course, Kawl Khuma's greatest desire, the very reason why he had ventured out on his long journey, and seeing the Army at close quarters had strengthened his determination to become a Salvation Army officer.

Once again he set out, this time alone, on the journey to Bombay lasting two days and nights. Major Henry Gore, the training principal, bade him welcome to the central training home where 22 English-speaking cadets from different parts of India were preparing themselves for full-time service in the Army.

Kawl Khuma had only one idea in mind, and that was to go back to his beloved hills and open up the work of The Salvation Army among his own people when training days were over. Army leaders were not sure that the time was ripe for this. Two missions were already operating in the area and The Salvation Army did not want to cause any dissension. On the day of commissioning when the cadets, true to Army traditions, accepted the appointment given wherever it may be, Kawl Khuma was appointed to the criminal tribes settlement in Gorakhpur. He went with a heavy heart. Convinced that God wanted him to preach to his own people, he wrote after a short time and explained this to Commissioner Booth-Tucker, who released him from his appointment and allowed him to return to his home.

Arriving in Aizawl he was greeted with affection by family and friends, all eager to hear of his adventures in the great world beyond the hills, about which they knew so little, and especially about the international *Chhandamna Sipai.* Kawl Khuma hadn't been home long before he received a letter from Colonel Sukh Singh (Blowers), Chief Secretary for India and Ceylon, which stated:

> As we are unable at present to commence Salvation Army work officially in your district, we advise you to return to your former occupation. You will still retain your rank of Lieutenant, but we will be unable to pay you any remuneration. However, we shall constantly pray for you that the Lord may use you mightily in His service.

The reason for this letter was a refusal from the government to permit more than the two existing missions to operate in Mizoram. Kawl Khuma felt differently about it. He firmly believed that God had directed him to The Salvation Army and it was within this framework that he wanted to work. Many of his friends encouraged him. Together they constructed two large communal houses of bamboo and grass in Sawleng village. In order to support themselves they bought a couple of pack animals and set up a transport business carrying rice and other products for sale to Aizawl. Kawl Khuma was made responsible for the business.

Travelling at the creeping pace of pack animals over mountain tracks did not really suit Kawl Khuma's vigorous, daring spirit. He was happiest when, with a Salvation Army flag held high on a bamboo pole, he marched from village to village conducting meetings in Salvation Army fashion. He even got hold of a drum which delighted the gay, music-loving Lushai people. Marching to its beat behind the flag they visited Aizawl. A revival spread throughout the hills and thousands of animists turned in faith to Christ.

Kawl Khuma realized that instruction in the new faith was essential to make strong Christians. He wanted to put into the hand of every convert a copy of the *Handbook of Doctrine* and *Orders and Regulations for Soldiers* in their own language. But under present circumstances, living in a communal house and plying his trade, it was impossible. The Salvationists gathered in conference. It was decided that another should take over the transport business and leave Kawl Khuma free to translate the books. A friend let him use his cookhouse as a study (a shed separate from the main

132

house). There Kawl Khuma settled down to the difficult task of translating parts of the books which were applicable to his people, adding explanations where necessary. He also translated Salvation Army songs into the Lushai language.

When in April 1921 Lushai Salvationists heard that a training home was established in Calcutta, they applied for some of their young men to be admitted. Six candidates, under Kawl Khuma's leadership, left their mountain home for the great city, where they spent 10 months in training for officership. On their return to the Lushai Hills they established six corps from which quickly sprang 31 outposts in neighbouring villages. Many were converted and the work of The Salvation Army expanded.

A year later Kawl Khuma was called down to Calcutta. Complaints had been sent in to the government that Lushai Salvationists were causing disturbance among the people by interfering with the already established churches and headquarters was advised to withdraw its forces. On hearing this Kawl Khuma was grief-stricken. 'Many of our people were never Christians at all until we preached in their villages,' he protested. 'It is true that our earliest Salvationists, like myself, belonged to the mission, but when we gathered a few workers our aim was to preach to the unconverted, like William Booth did in London.' Upon his return home Kawl Khuma felt defeated when he had to pass on instructions: 'No uniform may be worn, the Salvationists are to be persuaded to amalgamate with the missions.' Kawl Khuma himself was given a new appointment as compounder in the Army's Bongaon dispensary in Bengal.

But the Lushai people, like their mountains, are rugged and firm. Their sense of loyalty is strong and constant. When the Salvationists were gathered together and the position explained to them, Lieutenant Lalkaithanga, who had been Kawl Khuma's right-hand man, exclaimed, 'I can never change my allegiance!' Many others declared the same and the group decided to continue to work for God as their conscience bade them, Lalkaithanga being elected their new leader. Six months went by, the faithful group preaching and teaching in the villages. Money had been collected toward the annual Self-Denial Appeal and sent to headquarters in Calcutta despite their unrecognized status. For the sum of 100 rupees (£7) a piece of land was bought in Aizawl and the stony, hilly ground levelled in readiness for a hall to be built.

Some months later, in the latter part of 1924, the Territorial

Commander of the Eastern India Territory, Colonel Stanley Ewens, accompanied by Kawl Khuma and two missionary officers, made the week-long journey from Calcutta to Aizawl to inquire into the allegations. Arriving at the outskirts of the town a large assembly of Salvationists met the Colonel and his party with cornets blaring, drums beating and the Army banner at the head of the procession, shouting 'Hallelujahs!' in holy joy.

Interviews were arranged with leaders from the Welsh Presbyterian Church who proved to be most friendly, and the superintendent of the hills, a government official, entertained the visitors. The complaints were evidently unfounded and after a while the authorities lifted some of the restrictions and officers were permitted to resume their ranks and uniform wearing. Headquarters advised the officers to take responsibility for the work in their home villages. A salt-selling business was organized by Salvationists to support the work.

April 1925 Kawl Khuma was released from his appointment in Bengal to return to the Lushai Hills 'to strengthen and encourage the faithful Salvationists'. It was not until the early part of 1928, however, that government permitted The Salvation Army to operate officially in the Lushai Hills, a change of attitude that had come about through Commissioner Blowers' representations to the Viceroy. There was great rejoicing among the Lushai Salvationists. No time was to be lost, eight candidates were immediately sent to Calcutta to be trained as officers. When they returned and joined the ranks of the formerly trained officers, several thriving outposts were upgraded into corps. Work among young people was organized. In 1929 the first 10 corps cadets commenced writing the set Bible courses. The red epaulet, which was the distinctive Lushai mark of uniform became more and more in evidence in workshops, schools and market places. Even babies brought forward for dedication in meetings had tiny red epaulets. In Aizawl a 'Temple of Salvation' was erected. Lushai Salvationists revelled in their new freedom and the work flourished. In February 1931 they could report of a 'fighting force' of over 1,000 strong, 10 corps, 22 outposts. Adjutant Kawl Khuma was the district officer and revered by all.

In 1941 the first session of cadets was trained in Aizawl. Major Jewkes from Calcutta gave oversight, Major Kawl Khuma was the resident teacher. That same year the home league for women was commenced. This became immensely popular among the industrious Lushai women. The Aizawl branch raised money to support motherless babies by gathering firewood and selling it in the bazaar. Annual home league rallies brought women from the scattered villages to Aizawl. Carrying babies on their backs they would walk for days—up hill and down dale—stopping overnight in the homes of friendly villagers.

In 1945 the Lushai District with 30 corps was raised to the status of a division and Brigadier Kawl Khuma designated the divisional commander. That year 2,572 rupees was collected for the Self-Denial fund.

In 1947 Lieut.-Colonel R. L. Rust (Vetha Dasen), an Australian, was appointed Territorial Commander for Eastern India Territory. A month after his arrival in Calcutta he planned to visit the Lushai Hills for a three-week campaign of meetings. With Adjutant Khara, a Lushai officer, they made the arduous journey up to Aizawl—first by train, then river steamer across the Ganges, then another train journey till they reached Silchar on the border of the Lushai Hills. The next 93 miles were done by jeep up the narrow mountain road. Earlier travellers had had to do this part of the journey on foot or horseback, so they counted themselves privileged.

Three memorable weeks were spent preaching the gospel in the scattered villages, witnessing many conversions, rejoicing in the sight of uniformed Salvationists testifying to Christ's power in their lives. By his wise teaching and whole-hearted salvationism Colonel Rust won many friends among the Lushai people.

The time for leaving had come and the Colonel and his helpers started on their homeward journey. They had not travelled very far down the narrow mountain road when suddenly, round a hairpin bend, the trailer swung over the edge of a precipice, pulling the heavier vehicle after it. They were hurled down the seemingly bottomless depth until a tree stayed them.

Brigadier Kawl Khuma's son, Lalruata, who was with them, managed to scramble from the jeep and despite injuries crawl up the steep cliff to the road. Adjutant Khara had an injured thigh, Colonel Rust was the most seriously hurt. He could neither move nor speak for the intense pain in his chest. With the help of other passengers Colonel Rust and Adjutant Khara were hoisted up to the road and driven to the mission hospital in Aizawl. A few hours later, as Brigadier Kawl Khuma and a mission sister sat beside him, Lieut.-Colonel Rust passed from this life. At the funeral the whole population of Aizawl and people from neighbouring villages came to pay homage to the Christian gentleman who, they felt, had given his life for them. Later a Rust Memorial Hall was built in Aizawl to honour his life and service.

Only four Salvation Army missionary couples have at different times been appointed to the Lushai Hills, thus sampling life with no electricity and only a very limited supply of water, using rain water for daily use stored in tanks during the monsoon, and keeping to a ration of one bucket a day in the six months off-rainy season. But inconveniences, lack of commodities and isolation were forgotten in the joy of sharing with these robust Lushai Salvationists the early spirit of the Army. The chosen four couples were: Adjutant and Mrs Dennis Parker, Senior-Major and Mrs Fred Coxhead, Brigadier and Mrs Walter Merry, Major and Mrs James Kennedy (now retired Colonels). The latter gave nearly nine years' service in the Lushai Hills. Major Kennedy's training in dentistry and Mrs Kennedy's qualifications as a nurse gave a plus to their spiritual ministry.

In 1950, leaving Senior-Major Coxhead to take charge of the 39 corps which had so far been established, Brigadier Kawl Khuma set out to pioneer the work among the people in Cachar in the south. The district was in a state of political upheaval following the partitioning of nearby East Pakistan from India. Thousands of Hindu refugees had flooded the town of Silchar, the capital. Communal strife between Hindus and Moslems expressed itself in arson. It was not an easy task for the 60-year-old officer and his wife to face this challenge, neither did a foreign language make it any easier. Kawl Khuma, however, was undaunted. When conditions became somewhat settled he set out to contact Lushai people who had moved to the district. He also commenced work in Manipur State. When in January 1956 Kawl Khuma returned to Aizawl to enter retirement he left this new opening with a soldiers' roll of 400 names.

General Frederick Coutts admitted Lieut.-Colonel Kawl Khuma (R) to the Order of the Founder in 1966.

> . . . because he with vision and tenacity pioneered and established Salvation Army work in the Mizo (Lushai) Hills and later in the Cachar District and Manipur State, and has rendered service which would have commended itself to William Booth.

In 1960 a 10-day seminar for officers was held in Aizawl under the leadership of Brigadier Don Smith, General Secretary, North-Eastern India Territory. The uniqueness of this occasion was that the first complete edition of the Bible in the Lushai language had just been published and copies had been brought up from Calcutta. Up to this time only the New Testament, the Pentateuch and the Psalms had been translated into the vernacular.

In 1962 Mizoram, which is now the Lushai Hills' official name, opened its own training college in Aizawl. The inaugural function was attended by Pu V. L. Tluanga, Chairman of the Mizo District Council; Pu Paul Zakhuma, Assistant Deputy Commissioner; Mr Roberts, principal of the Aizawl College; representative leaders from the Baptist, Presbyterian and Seventh Day Adventist Churches and many other well-wishers. The cost of the training college building was donated by the USA Central Territory. The first session of cadets comprised four married couples and four unmarried men.

In 1972 the government asked The Salvation Army to manage a school for the blind at Kolasib.

On 1 April 1978 it was a proud day for Mizo Salvationists, for then this province, which up to now had been part of the North-Eastern Territory, became a separate entity and named the Eastern India Command, under the leadership of Officer Commanding, Lieut.-Colonel Kapliana, and General Secretary, Major Chianghnuna, with command headquarters in Silchar.

'God is at work in the command,' reports Barbara Chianghnuna, English-born wife of the general secretary. She adds:

At a five-day campaign of meetings no less than 7,000 people attended and over 300 men and women sought God's forgiveness. In Aizawl Salvationists decided that something needed to be done about the notorious 'red light' area, near the Aizawl Bazaar Corps. The leader of the enterprise, Brother Hmingthanga, is himself a converted drunkard. The young women were first contacted on a 'one to one' basis and invited to the meetings. Brother Hmingthanga and his wife have opened their home for those in need of shelter and calls it The Goodwill Centre, other Salvationists assisting them and helping the new converts to find suitable employment.

This kind of practical caring is in the tradition of the early Salvationists in Britain.

The little group of stalwart Mizos who, in 1916, decided to form themselves into a fighting force for Christ, has now expanded into an army with seven divisions/districts, a training college for officers, where currently 33 cadets are doing a two-year training course, 8,943 soldiers, 107 active and 22 retired officers. In operation are 79 corps, 139 outposts and societies, a school for the blind, several day schools, two high schools with approximately 700 students in each, and four homes for destitute children, one of which is entirely supported by Aizawl Central Corps.

Communal riots in Silchar in 1979, during which the headquarters building was damaged, made it necessary for the administration to be transferred to Aizawl. In 1980, upon the transfer of the North-Eastern Territorial Headquarters to New Delhi (now called the Northern Territory), the Mizo staff of the Eastern India Command occupied the Calcutta headquarters from where at present the Mizo work is administrated.

Had Kawl Khuma not been true to his 'Heavenly vision' would the Army be found in Mizoram today? An interesting thought!

16

The healing ministry, (II) (1926-)

SIGNIFICANT advances were made in the medical field during the next decade. In Dhariwal, a small town in northern India, the management of the New Egerton woollen mills appealed to The Salvation Army to open a hospital to ensure medical aid for its staff and employees, promising six acres of land on a nominal rental of one rupee (less than 10 pence) per year. Ensign (Dr) Samuel Burfoot (Kalyan Singh), son of the pioneer officer Lieut.-Colonel Burfoot (Dayasagar), was appointed to establish the hospital. For three years he laboured in a room near the railway station until the completion of what is now the MacRobert Hospital, named after the founder of the British India Corporation, the then owner of the mill, Sir Alexander MacRobert, Bt, KBE.

The hospital was officially opened in January 1926 by Sir Malcolm Halley, then Governor of the Punjab. Dr Burfoot remained as chief medical officer until 1944 and was succeeded by a number of other dedicated Salvation Army doctors. The mill management has regularly sent a bill for one rupee for the rent of the land over the years, and the hospital pays up without a murmur.

During the time Dr William McAllister (now Colonel retired) was the chief medical officer emphasis was placed upon preventive medicine and this was continued by succeeding doctors. In 1972 a community health service was established by Captain (Dr) Walter Lucas with a team of five nurses, a doctor, a clerk and a driver. Its aim was total health care in the nearby villages, lowering of birth rate, infant mortality rate and malnutrition among children. Homes are visited by the nurses giving advice on health and family planning, treating minor ailments, vaccinating against various diseases.

Throughout India and Pakistan there are many thousands of poor people suffering from eye diseases and blindness which can be cured with proper medical treatment. In the Punjab the prevalence of blindness is very high due to the severe, dry heat in the summer with seasonal dust storms, infection carried by flies, dietary deficiency and the custom of rubbing soot round the babies' eyes to 'beautify' them. The poor have neither the knowledge nor the means to visit ophthalmic hospitals in large towns or cities, so eye camps are set up in the villages.

The mobile eye services of MacRobert Hospital, with a full team of 16 members with equipment and vehicles financed by Christoffel Blinden Mission, West Germany, commenced a regular service in 1973. The team works continually for nine months, visiting remote mountain areas such as Jammu, Kashmir and Himachal Pradesh during summer months, concentrating on the villages in the plains during the winter.

Eye camps, or field hospitals, are set up wherever accommodation is available—in Sikh *gurdwarah* or Hindu temple, in schools (while the children have their classes in the open), or an owner of a big house will vacate one or two rooms to be used as an operating theatre, even former raja's palaces have been allotted for the purpose. Camps are usually of 10 days' duration. Three days for clinic and selecting patients, one for operating, during which time up to 100 operations may be done. The team then moves on leaving one doctor and nurse to continue treatment, dressing and general care. This over, they catch up with the rest of the team which has started another camp elsewhere. Team members return to the area for follow-up care later.

The spiritual impact of this labour of mercy is not to be underestimated, for the work is done by divine compulsion following the example of Christ who healed the sick and gave sight to the blind. A Sikh gentleman, who had put part of his house at the disposal of one eye camp, brought out his copy of the Bible, saying to the visiting officer, 'I have read it right through, it is my most treasured possession'.

'There is no greater thrill than to see a blind man given sight,' declared Captain (Dr) Walter Lucas, who had come to the hospital in 1970, and who did so much to increase its services during the short time he was there. 'Early in his life Walter Lucas, born in 1939 in Australia, became known as a man with a tremendous capacity for action,' writes Leslie Rusher, 'an irresistible impulse to work swiftly and efficiently.'

In August 1973, a brief 34 years later, crowds of Indian villagers packed into the compound at the Salvation Army hospital at Dhariwal, to look upon the simple wooden casket covered with a white cloth which contained the body of the young doctor, and to pay their respects to one whom they revered for the selfless service he had given to their people. Walter Lucas had been suddenly taken ill and a few days after an operation his life on earth had ended. Olive, his wife, gathered their three children around her and told them that Daddy had gone to Heaven. She then opened the Bible and through her tears began to read, 'Let not your heart be troubled,' the children weeping with their mother while listening to the words of hope and assurance. They were still weeping, when Helen, eight years old, and the eldest, said, 'Mummy, what about where God said He will wipe away all tears?' That truth, coming with such simplicity from the lips of a child, eased their heartaches and helped to change the night of sorrow into a morning of hope.

In January 1975 Olive, with her children, returned to the mission field and served for some years as a teacher at the Salvation Army Howard Institute in Rhodesia (now Zimbabwe). During October 1976 she paid a visit to the MacRobert Hospital in Dhariwal to take part in a ceremony conducted by the Territorial Commander, Colonel Jaikumar Makanji, marking the opening of a new theatre complex in memory of Walter Lucas.

*   *   *

Of all the suffering that besets humanity the plight of the leper is surely the worst. Shunned by his fellowmen and his family, he is regarded as unclean. The disease which eats into the very bone and flesh mars and disfigures the unfortunate victim, making him a grotesque sight from which others turn away with aversion.

But Jesus, who came to redeem the world, also reached down to the leper and touched and cleansed him. Sending out his Twelve apostles He commanded them: 'As ye go, preach, saying, the kingdom of heaven is at hand. Heal the sick, cleanse the lepers.' At the three leprosy hospitals operating in India, the Army endeavours to carry out that injunction.

A leprosy hospital had been in existence at Bapatla in Andhra,

141

north of Madras, for a number of years, maintained by a mission board in America. Because of lack of personnel The Salvation Army was asked to take it over. The transaction took place in October 1928 when it was officially handed over to Colonel N. Muthiah, Territorial Commander of the Madras and Telugu Territory at the time, and Captain C. N. Sena Putra was appointed the first superintendent.

On the island of Venduatthy, off the coast of Ernakulum in the Cochin State, 200 lepers were housed. They had very little medical care and scant supervision. The government woke up to the fact that more ought to be done for them and buildings were erected to accommodate 300 lepers on a piece of jungle land of about 160 acres at a place called Adoor—now Koratty. The Salvation Army was asked to take charge. Dr Margaret Round from England, who served for many years at various Army hospitals in India, was appointed medical officer there for the first six months, until an Indian doctor obtained special training for the work. This hospital was managed by The Salvation Army until 1955 when it was handed back to the government.

Leprosy is endemic in the southern part of India, it affects both rich and poor, young and old. As general hospitals would not admit persons suffering from leprosy there were hundreds of sufferers who were not treated for the disease. Turned out of their homes they had no other choice but to live on the streets begging their food. In 1936 The Salvation Army opened a hospital for lepers at Puthencruz. It was the fulfilment of a long-cherished dream of Lieut.-Colonel (Dr) Noble, Chief Medical Officer of the Catherine Booth Hospital at Nagercoil. For years he had prayed and worked for it, knowing the great need for such a hospital in north Travancore.

Brigadier Mable Poole was the matron for many years and will be remembered for her compassionate care for the lepers. Lieut.-Colonel (Dr) K. C. Joseph, who was promoted to Glory in 1980, was medical superintendent of the hospital for 28 years and his name will ever be connected with the Evangeline Booth Leprosy Hospital, Puthencruz. Son of Salvation Army officers and a fourth-generation Christian, he obtained his medical degree at Miraj after which he served at various branch hospitals of the Army before being appointed to Puthencruz. Both he and his wife were greatly loved by the leprosy patients whom they served selflessly for so many years. Their four children were born in the leprosy colony. At his own request Lieut.-Colonel Joseph was buried in the leprosy cemetery.

In Salvation Army hospitals patients are not only given medical treatment, but the staff endeavours to show them the love of God in action, for it is His love which compels them to serve. Abdul, a young Muslim boy, accepted Christ as his Saviour because he had seen Christ in the life of the Indian nurse, Adjutant Moses, who tenderly cared for him during the many years he was bedridden. Petros, a one-time Hindu, full of leprosy, blind and often in pain, had a ready smile. In spite of his afflictions he said that God's grace was helping him daily.

When patients have been bacteria negative for a period of 12 months the doctor gives them a certificate which states that they have been treated for leprosy, but are now symptom-free of the disease and no longer infectious and can leave the hospital. With their scant belongings tied in a cloth or put in a box, a few rupees and their precious certificate, they set off for home. Their hopes are high for they believe there will be loved ones waiting for them now they are cured, and life will have a new start. Alas, for many of them this is not so; their hopes are dashed to the ground, for no one, not even their family, will receive them and all that is left for them is to join the great mass of beggars infesting the highways.

Palami was a young Hindu in his early 20s, shy, refined and lovable. With others he left the hospital with his certificate, said goodbye to his mother who was also a patient, and made his way back to relatives and friends in his native village. But he was not welcome, to them he was a 'leper' and unclean, cursed by the gods. He could not find work for no one wanted a leper, he could not beg for he was too shy, he could only starve. After a time he crawled—actually crawled—back to the hospital, where the superintendent found him lying near the gate. He was given food, they tried to revive him but he did not want to live. He was frightened of life and the stigma of leprosy, and the following day he died. His broken-hearted mother did not weep, but with a bewildered look sat holding the hand of her only child, repeating, 'Why?—Why?' 'The lepers need not only mercy but justice,' said Brigadier Hilda Plummer who related this tragic incident.

As a young officer Hilda Plummer (Jivi Ratnam) volunteered for leprosy work and the outcome of that dedication was a lifetime of caring for lepers. She served at different times at all three leprosy hospitals, being appointed superintendent of the Evangeline Booth Hospital at Bapatla in 1950. Retiring in 1960 she chose to remain in India. 'If I had 50 years to spend in India I would do just the same for the leprosy patients and would have them all happily looked after,' were her words on the occasion of her being awarded the Order of the British Empire.

Close to the village where she spent her retirement lies Bethany Colony, a village of some 400 inhabitants. All, except the children, are former leprosy patients now living a normal family life. Each family has built a small hut for itself. Here Brigadier Hilda Plummer (R) helped with childbirths and continued to care for those to whom she had devoted her life. She was promoted to Glory on 17 April 1980 and in compliance with her wish, her body was taken to the leprosy hospital. From there leprosy patients respectfully carried the coffin to its resting place in the leprosy hospital burial ground, to a place Hilda Plummer had previously chosen. Compelled by love she gave her all without reservation.

*   *   *

When in the 1930s Colonel H. B. Colledge, Territorial Commander, Madras and Telugu Territory, was considering extending the medical work in the territory, Mr P. V. Krishnaiah Chowdhury, local member of the legislative council, persuaded a local farmer, Pamulapatti Paranthamiah, to give a five-acre site from his banana field for the purpose. The site was at Nidubrolu, 15 miles from the Army's leprosy hospital at Bapatla. The name of the hospital was to be The Jubilee Hospital for Women and Children to celebrate the first 50 years of Salvation Army service in India. Lieutenant and Mrs Albert Sena Putra were appointed to an empty shell of a hospital, the Lieutenant as business manager and Mrs Sena Putra, RN, as nursing sister. (Later Sena Putra became Chief Secretary, Western India, with rank of Lieut.-Colonel.)

With the arrival of Captain and Mrs Clesson Richardson from America, both qualified surgeons, the hospital was declared open on 29 November 1935 by Lord Erskine, Governor of Madras. When General Evangeline Booth visited the institution a year later the name was changed to The Evangeline Booth Hospital.

Extensions, both in land and buildings, brought the 30-bed hospital up to a 92-bed general hospital with facilities for surgery,

144

general medicine, obstetrics and paediatrics and a rapidly developing public health outreach programme. Whereas before one or two doctors covered every aspect of the work, there are now specialist doctors for each department. The two-year course, leading to the qualification of auxiliary nurse/midwife, has been upgraded to a RN/RM four-year course.

The hospital report for 1975 quotes Pope Paul VI in his encyclical on development: 'Development is for the whole man, it is not only concerned with man's economic status, but with the social, cultural, moral and spiritual being as well. . . .' The latest change at Nidubrolu Evangeline Booth Hospital is the transfer of the place of worship to the centre of the hospital quadrangle as a constant reminder that the most important aspect of development is the spiritual dimension.

When a cyclone struck the south-east coast of India in November 1977 both Nidubrolu and Bapatla hospitals were affected. The tornado swept over the land uprooting trees, destroying buildings, levelling everything to the ground. A tidal wave 18 feet high crossed the coast to the north of the Nidubrolu hospital exposing the town to the fury of winds estimated at between 100 and 125 miles per hour. Many of the hospital buildings were damaged, including the generator room which had its roof blown off. The immediate priority was for electricity and dry wards to accommodate the injured, some of whom had come from Komali where the church building had collapsed, killing over 80 people and injuring many more of those who had taken shelter there. A feeding programme at five centres was organized by Captain George Scott, the hospital administrator, where 8,000 people were supplied with one meal a day for two weeks, the local Rotary and Leo Clubs providing the money. Thousands of people were inoculated against cholera and typhoid. Later a large-scale programme of re-housing the homeless was undertaken.

At Bapatla leprosy hospital the boundary wall was completely demolished. Former leprosy patients living in the nearby Bethany village crowded into the hospital for safety, as the cyclone totally destroyed their village of bamboo huts. Brigadier Hilda Plummer, who lived in the neighbourhood, sheltered well over 100 in her little house. The total number of dead is unknown but the estimate given is 80,000. Whole villages were laid waste, a grinding stone or a torn piece of clothing in the thorn bushes were in some places the only indication that this had been the site of a busy village. The staff at

Bapatla worked with the government in organizing mass vaccination, chlorination of wells and disposal of carcasses and, in co-operation with World Vision and other agencies, in the distribution of clothing, food, cooking utensils and money. Kerala and Sri Lanka were also affected by cyclones and help given to the sufferers.

A young English Salvationist, Graham Griffiths, son of Colonel Maurice C. Griffiths, the then Territorial Commander for Western India, came to give help on a more permanent basis, helping the farmers in the rehabilitation of the land. Graham lived in Dindi village for three years in a one-room house of timber and thatch, without amenities of any kind—a present-day pioneer. The 2,000 acres of land round the village had been spoiled by sea water, drainage ditches had to be dug and the fields leached with fresh water and chemicals until the land would again be arable. Oxfam provided money for the scheme, on which up to 200 people per day were employed.

When Commissioner Edwin C. Marion, International Secretary for South Asia, visited Dindi in 1980, a meeting hall, which had just been completed, was dedicated for public worship.

'In our age', said Dag Hammarskjöld former Secretary-General of United Nations, 'the road to holiness necessarily passes through the world of action.'

* * *

Captain Ludvig Andersen (Daya Ratna) had the distinction of being the very first Salvation Army missionary sent out from his native land, Norway. He arrived in Ceylon (Sri Lanka) in 1893 where he helped to pioneer the work, later being transferred to the Maharashstra in western India. Preaching and teaching, he walked from village to village, clad in Indian garb and carrying his violin with which he accompanied the singing of Marathi *bhajans.*

'Major Ludvig Andersen and his wife laid the spiritual foundation of the Salvation Army work in the Maharashstra,' said a senior American missionary in Ahmednagar. Their three children inherited the same love for India and, becoming officers, gave many years' service in the country.

The son, Daniel, qualified as a doctor, and with his doctor-wife,

146

Sølvi, also from Norway, returned to the scene of his childhood—Ahmednagar. The hospital they were appointed to in April 1939 was well known to Dr Andersen. As a boy he had often heard it referred to as the *Dagadai Davkhana*—the stone hospital—because of its solid stone structure. Formerly belonging to the American Marathi Mission, lack of funds and personnel had forced its closure. During General Evangeline Booth's visit to India in 1936 arrangements were made for The Salvation Army to take it over, in faith that doctors would be found. That mission hospitals were still needed was established by a survey carried out at the time which indicated that India's total medical services, including government, private and mission hospitals, reached only about 30 per cent of the people.

A skilled surgeon, Dr Dan Andersen provided facilities for major surgery which, up to that time, had been practically unavailable for the population of over one million, except for those who could afford to travel to hospitals 75 or more miles away. Women patients were only too glad to have a woman doctor to go to, and Dr Mrs Andersen worked tirelessly for their welfare.

A nurses' training school was built in 1944, the government meeting 50 per cent of the total cost. The Lady Colville Nurses' Home, named after the wife of the Governor of Bombay, was said to be, at that time, the best building in Ahmednagar. English is the medium of instruction and the training given is recognized in Great Britain. Nurses from all parts of India have been trained at the Ahmednagar hospital. 'The first few weeks can be frustrating, even hilarious, until the students understand the English mode of speaking,' says Major Ruth Goodridge, present nursing superintendent. Not only must the student-nurses do their studies in English, but those who come from other language areas also have to learn to speak Marathi, as only very few of the patients understand English. Training is not free as it is in some countries. Students have to pay for books and tuition and during the first year pay towards their board. This is the recognized procedure in hospitals in India, but as many of the students come from poor homes, it is often a financial struggle for the family.

Although tuberculosis affected at least one per cent of the people of the district, which meant at a rough estimate at least 10,000 patients with active infective lung disease, there were no wards set apart for specialized treatment. After the Second World War money was raised and tuberculosis wards with 60 beds were built and opened by Rajkumari Amrit Kaur, then Minister of Health for India. Preventive measures were also taken by getting the co-operation of the school authorities in Ahmednagar city and tuberculin-testing all school children, vaccinating those susceptible.

Dr and Mrs Andersen served the hospital for 21 years after which Colonel Andersen took up the appointment as the first Missionary Medical Secretary at International Headquarters.

Other doctors came to serve at the Evangeline Booth Hospital in Ahmednagar, among them a young man, Dr Murray Stanton, with his wife, from New Zealand. While doing his internship at the Catherine Booth Hospital in Nagercoil, Murray was moved by the need of the people around him and decided to return as a missionary officer using his medical skill for the people of India. His wife, Janee, shared his convictions. After being commissioned as Salvation Army officers in London they were appointed to the Ahmednagar hospital. 'Murray Stanton not only showed himself to be a man of great depth and capacity,' writes John C. Waite in *They Ran to Him,* the story of Dr Stanton's short but radiant life, 'he demonstrated also that he was a man of tender sympathies and understanding, with a sense of humour that drew smiles from staff, patients and others. He obviously enjoyed life. His cheerfulness and confidence encouraged all he met.'

Did Murray Stanton have any premonition that his life was to be cut short? Visiting the cemetery one day, where Peter, the young son of Dr Bramwell Southwell, a former chief medical officer, lies buried, Murray Stanton pointed to a large tree with spreading branches near the grave. Half jokingly, half in earnest, he said to Raju, the driver who had brought them there, 'If I should die in Ahmednagar, see that I am buried under that tree, that lovely, living tree; no concrete.'

A few months later Murray's body was laid to rest under that tree with its spreading branches. Taken ill at the end of April his funeral took place 13 May 1972, the day that he died. Captain Murray Stanton died of a liver disease at the age of 32. The hospital staff was to suffer another loss in Shirley Millar (wife of the Hospital Secretary, Captain Millar) who died of cancer six months later. These events were a severe test of faith for many who questioned why young people who had so much to give in God's service were taken. Murray Stanton had had an answer in words he said some years previously:

Suffering and death are no argument against the love of God. I agree with the old-time Salvation Army belief that all men are subject to suffering and death. Of the two, death is of the least concern to the Christian. It is the doorway by which one passes into the fullest communion with God.

*   *   *

Walk down any big city in South Asia and you will soon become acquainted with one of the acute social problems in this part of the world—the beggar problem. A little girl, barely more than four years old, is seen flitting from person to person on a Calcutta street, her thin arm outstretched, her big brown eyes in her pinched face pleading. *'Baksheesh! baksheesh!'* she cries, copying the lament of all beggars. Then patting her little bare, brown tummy above her tattered skirt, *'bhukhi hun!'* (I'm hungry). A passer-by tosses a coin towards her, she grabs it and scoots off in the direction of a porch. Here sheltered from the mercilessly hot sun, lies an old man, not more than skin and bone. He is obviously near death's door. It is the child's grandfather, her only relative. The money the child earns through begging goes towards food to try to keep them both alive. The pavement is their home.

This is but one case out of many thousands in countries where social security is unknown. In the above instance the little girl was received into the Salvation Army home for girls at Behala, a suburb of Calcutta, while the old man was granted his request—a railway ticket to return to his village to die, knowing that his granddaughter was cared for.

Colombo in Ceylon (now Sri Lanka) is said to be the first eastern city which has attempted to grapple seriously with the beggar problem. In 1907 begging on the streets was made an offence by law, empowering the police to clear the streets of the beggar population. A house of detention was set up with two branches. One entirely under police control for receiving, sorting and classifying the vagrants. The other, for the care of the sick, the physically handicapped and helpless vagrants, under Salvation Army management. Here the blind, the deaf and dumb, the crippled and mentally deficient were taken care of.

In Bombay the deputy commissioner of police, having learned that a large number of beggars were dying of starvation on the streets, convened a meeting of the citizens of Bombay with the

149

object of forming an organization to help such people. A committee was formed, and in 1920 a temporary shelter was set up in a former military camp, housing 130 handicapped beggars. The Salvation Army was asked to manage this establishment. Many of the beggars were sent to the camp by the police, but the majority were initially collected from the streets by members of the committee accompanied by an Army officer, the municipal health department giving the loan of horse and motor ambulances for conveying the beggars from street to camp. Whole families came with five or six children, in some cases the parents both blind. Major Anand Rao, a devoted Marathi officer, and his wife attended to all the daily needs of the inmates. This was the beginning of the work among beggars in Bombay—among 'the least, the lowest and the lost'.

In 1938, the Governor of Bombay, Sir Roger Lumley, with Lady Lumley, opened Bombay's memorial to King George V, an infirmary for destitute incurables, under the management of The Salvation Army. The beggars' camp, which for some years had been situated at Rowli Hill subsequent to the temporary set-up at the military camp, was now transferred to a location adjoining the infirmary. The new home for the destitute is named after Lady Dhanbai Jehangir, Sir Cowasji Jehangir having donated two lakhs of rupees (£15,380) towards the scheme.

Brigadier Hilma Mantyla (Astha Bai), a Finnish officer, was put in charge of these twin institutions, ably assisted by Major Eva Andersen (Supriti) and a capable Indian staff. Having completed the mammoth task of organizing and getting the place into running order, Astha Bai gave 14 years' devoted service to supervising the admission and rehabilitation of hundreds of beggars and of tending the incurables in the infirmary. With it all she found time to transform the barren compound into a beautiful garden. Other officers have through the years given their service and their love to these unfortunates whose lives were nothing but misery, who have never had anyone who cared for them. To be told that God's love reaches down to the very lowest was almost beyond their understanding.

Bhagrita was one of the patients in the infirmary. For six years she had been lying on her back with a damaged spine. She learnt to read during this time and was given a New Testament. When the officer who was teaching her came to her bed one day, Bhagrita excitedly said, 'I have found such a beautiful prayer, it begins like this: "Our Father, who art in heaven." ' She had at last found a Father who loved her.

Appointed by The Salvation Army, Alex and Mary Queen, a devoted Christian couple, had the management of the institution for a number of years. Alex Queen was a natural mechanic while his wife was a capable nurse. During their term of service new ventures were experimented with to employ even the severely handicapped. One such was a special gadget for bunching safety-pins. This has been proved most successful and is occupying the inmates even to this day, enabling them to earn a little money.

Rabindranath Tagore wrote in Gitanjali:

> My heart can never find its way to where thou keepest company with the companionless among the poorest, the lowliest, and the lost.

The present superintendent, Major Jean Brown, a Canadian officer and qualified nurse, has found the way for she says, 'I do enjoy this work so much, and it is good to be here.' One of her competent helpers is Mr Ashirvad Christian, a Salvationist, who has given outstanding service for 33 years at King George V Memorial Infirmary, thus providing the only continuous link for the Army. He is highly respected by all, including the government authorities. A Marathi officer, Brigadier S. Torne, now retired, has also given devoted service for many years as camp manager.

In 1980 the number of destitutute people in the institution was 180, who had been sent by the police for periods of two to five years. Twenty-eight chose to stay on after their period of detention and worked in the vocational training centre. One man with only hooks for hands bunched safety-pins, another with only a left arm sewed button holes by help of his mouth, a third operated a sewing machine with only a stump of an arm.

When asked if any manage to make a living outside the institution Major Brown told of a young boy with no legs who, during his stay in the home, had managed to save a little of the money earned. With it he has 'set up shop' outside one of the government hospitals and from his small stall on the pavement he sells biscuits and potato-chips to people visiting the hospital.

Mother Teresa, who has devoted her whole life to the poor, states:

> All the desolation of the poor people, not only their material poverty, but their spiritual destitution, must be redeemed, and we must share it, for only by being one with them can we redeem them, that is, by bringing God into their lives and bringing them to God.

17

War and peace

HAPPILY, India never became a battlefield during the Second World War but within its borders troops were trained, waiting to go into battle further east and military camps were dotted all over the country. In such places The Salvation Army operated its red shield centres for the benefit of members of the forces. Salvation Army officers within the country were at first assigned to these posts, later being reinforced by a party of officers from Britain under the leadership of Lieut.-Colonel Thomas Ward, and from Canada Major John Nelson (later Colonel) with others.

The red shield centre nearest to the fighting line was at Ramkophalong close to the Burma border. Here, among war-weary men, where fighting was at its toughest, Major and Mrs Fred Jewkes and Major Nellie Horning set up a little oasis in the wilderness of war. Bamboo *bashas* were erected for quarters, canteen and recreation room. General Sir Philip Christensen honoured the opening with his presence.

'No one will be able to estimate fully the value of these officers in the area,' said one of the servicemen, 'there can hardly be a man of the 14th Army who passed that way and has not reason to give thanks for the work of these comrades.'

When Burma was retaken these three officers, together with an Indian Salvationist, Ganga Prasad (now treasurer at Calcutta Central Corps) went with a military convoy into Rangoon to set up canteens. It was while they were there that Brigadier William Francis of the Andaman Islands (having been interned in Burma) was brought from the death railway, sick in mind and body. As mentioned previously he was evacuated to Calcutta, but died before the ship reached port.

In Calcutta, Major Leslie J. Russell (now a retired Colonel), son of early pioneer officers, formed a brass band of the many Salvationist servicemen stationed in and near the city, Adjutant Arthur Hook (later International Secretary for South Asia) succeeding him as bandmaster. On the last day of 1944, 40 men gathered at the social service centre, Lower Circular Road, in readiness for a six-week tour of the Arakan front. 'It was commenced with a grand watchnight service,' writes Harry Pepper in his articles in *The Musician*. Throughout the first week rehearsals were held every day, led by the bandmaster, Adjutant Dennis Parker (Leslie Russell and Arthur Hook having been transferred from Calcutta). The band travelled by train, by lorry and by river steamer down the River Ganges, through fertile plains, through 'tiger country' and barren mountains to places such as Silchar in Assam, Chittagong and Cox's Bazaar, in what is now Bangladesh, and to Ramkaphalong where the Jewkes and Nellie Horning operated the red shield centre. Here the bandsmen spent an evening at a lonely RAF site, the most forward Fighter Command station at the time. They played at hospitals, where wounded soldiers had just been flown in from the fighting around Mandalay. A musical programme was given in a natural amphitheatre, cut out of a hillside, where about 1,500 men listened with keen attention. Here and there they met up with Salvationist bandsmen stationed in isolated camps who were delighted to join the band and share the fellowship.

At the end of his article Harry Pepper writes:

> The band has travelled 3,000 miles and played to about 10,000 servicemen. We went on a mission and we believe the mission was fulfilled.

Red shield hostels in Bombay and Ahmednagar were taxed to capacity, over 40,000 meals a month were provided. But the mission of the red shield services was not only to provide servicemen with canteen and recreational facilities, it was to remind them that in a war-torn world of hatred there still existed goodness and love, pointing them to the One who holds history in His hand. It is impossible to estimate how many were helped spiritually through the red shield services, but we know of at least four who are now serving as officers in the ranks of The Salvation Army. Audrey Prior, now Mrs Major James Northey, wife of the Assistant Literary Secretary, IHQ, came to India with the WAAF, and as a result of her contacts at the New Delhi Red Shield Club she decided to become a Salvationist and was sworn-in by Major Joseph Ashley, the officer in charge of the club. It was to an Indian congregation in New Delhi that James Northey, serving in the RAF, preached his first sermon.

Two New Zealanders joined The Salvation Army in Calcutta, Lawrence Weggery and David Jackson. Both were fighter pilots with the Royal Air Force serving on the Burma front. Warrant Officer David Jackson, who had first met The Salvation Army in Canada and England, cemented his link with the Army in Calcutta because of the spiritual fellowship they offered. After returning to his native New Zealand he decided to become a Salvation Army officer and entered the International Training College, London.

Flight Lieutenant Lawrence Weggery was sworn-in as a Salvation Army soldier in Calcutta Central Corps. He married Enid Arnland, daughter of Danish missionary officers, and took her to New Zealand where they became officers. Enid's mother, Mrs Brigadier Jenny Arnland, 'who was involved in red shield work at Sudder Street, was a great influence in both David's and my own life, probably personifying the warmth of salvationism which attracted us both to the Movement', says Lieut.-Colonel Lawrence Weggery, now a divisional commander at Wellington, New Zealand.

Brigadier and Mrs Arnland were travelling home to Calcutta by train from their annual furlough in Naini Tal in 1951, when the Brigadier, who had been unwell for some time, was suddenly promoted to Glory. In God's providential care, two strangers offered Mrs Arnland their help. She was glad that one of them was from the Arnland's home country, Denmark. Mrs Arnland continued her service in India until retirement, having then completed 35 years in the country.

Frank Ockleston had never had close contact with The Salvation Army before going to India with the RAMC. In Poona Brigadier Emma Johansson and Major Cath Jarvis (now a retired Lieut.-Commissioner) made 3 Napier Road into a home for 'the boys' and Frank was invited with others of his unit. The result was that Frank became a Salvation Army soldier. 'Commissioner Herbert Mitchell (International Auditor in Poona at the time) became my spiritual counsellor, then and subsequently,' are Frank's own words. As an officer Ockleston returned to India together with his wife and for 10 years used his skill as a radiographer at the Catherine Booth Hospital in Nagercoil. Major and Mrs Frank Ockleston have since served as corps officers in the British Territory.

While Indian troops fought valiantly on the side of the British in both world wars, at the same time Indian nationalism was growing within the country. Mohandas Gandhi, of whom it was said 'he made humility and truth more powerful than empires' had started his freedom movement in 1919, hoping to gain independence for India through *Satyagraha*—Truth Force. But while Ghandi exhorted his followers to practise non-violence, his movement became increasingly marred by incidents of bloodshed and force. His own death occurred at the hand of an assassin in 1948.

In 1938 Mohammed Ali Jinnah, head of the Muslim League, began to agitate for a separate Muslim state, fearing that under a predominantly Hindu rule the Muslims would become second-class citizens. This brought about violent outbreaks between Muslim and Hindu communities and delayed for some years the already promised independence.

In 1947 the Viceroy, Earl Mountbatten, invited the Territorial Commander Northern India, Lieut.-Commissioner Herbert S. Hodgson and his wife to the viceregal lodge at New Delhi. They were entertained to luncheon, after which the viceroy led Commissioner Hodgson to his office where he told him that India would be given independence and divided into the two dominions of India and Pakistan. He pointed out that changes in Salvation Army administration would be necessary as it would not be possible in future to control affairs in India from Pakistan. (Up to that time, for administration purposes the whole of Punjab, the United Provinces and Delhi had come under the Lahore head-quarters.) The viceroy recommended the establishment of a new headquarters in New Delhi, retaining the present headquarters in Lahore for Pakistan. These suggestions were dispatched by cablegram to General Albert Orsborn, and the following territorial changes took place: Colonel Ivar Palmer was appointed to command the new Northern India Territory with headquarters in New Delhi. Colonel Arthur Hughes became Territorial Commander, Pakistan, with headquarters in Lahore, whilst Lieut.-Commissioner H. S. Hodgson was transferred to command the Western India Territory with headquarters in Bombay.

Independence became a reality at midnight 14 August 1947 amidst great rejoicing. But the demarcation of the frontiers of the two distinct nations turned jubilation into turmoil and bloodshed as Hindus fled the new Pakistan and Indian Muslims sought refuge in their new homeland. 'People were uprooted and driven like millions of dry leaves by a turbulent gust of fanaticism and blind passion,' said Mohammed Ayub Khan, one-time President of Pakistan, 'hundreds of thousands of men, women and children were butchered and the sub-continent was engulfed in a bloody civil war.'

The Salvation Army was operating on the Wagah border near Lahore giving help to refugees, the 'red coat' worn by the national Salvationists making them neutral in the conflict between Hindu and Muslim and their service was accepted and appreciated by the authorities. Many of the wounded and dying were brought to the Salvation Army hospital in Dhariwal near to the border on the Indian side.

In a refugee camp at Kalyan, south of Bombay, a Salvation Army goodwill centre was set up on the barren hills where Hindus, who had fled from Pakistan, were trying to make a new start in life, having lost all they possessed and seen many of their family members killed. Captain Margaret Barker and her Indian assistant, Lieutenant Esther Bai, lived among the refugees and ministered to their needs.

The tragic beginnings were eventually overcome, but left unavoidable scars on either side of the border, dividing families who for years were not able to see each other.

With independence it was natural that changes took place. Would there still be a place for The Salvation Army in India and Pakistan? General Albert Orsborn asked India's new Prime Minister, Pandit Jawaharlal Nehru, this question in an interview during his visit to India. The prime minister answered:

> Anyone who has the welfare of the Indian people at heart will be welcome amongst us, and The Salvation Army has certainly proved itself in this connection.

The Constitution of India gives full right to 'profess, practise and propagate the Christian faith', while proselytism is frowned upon. Jesus himself condemned it in the words to the Pharisees, 'Ye compass sea and land to make one proselyte' (Matthew 23:15). 'Proselytism is the getting of a man to change from one religion to another without any necessary change in character and life—it is a change of label, but not of life,' wrote the eminent India missionary Dr E. Stanley Jones. Conversion is different, it is a change of character, obeying the teachings of Christ, of love to God and love to man. No Indian convert should be any less Indian—but a better Indian.

The Salvation Army was not a foreign body but an integral part of Indian life. A quarter of a million Salvationists, led by some 3,200 officers in full-time service in over 5,000 centres, were professing their allegiance to Jesus Christ in the countries of India, Pakistan, Sri Lanka and Burma.

Evangelistic and educational work in the villages is now carried out almost entirely by national doctors. Indian Salvationists have qualified as teachers, doctors, nurses, dispensers and laboratory technicians and are giving efficient service in the Army's schools, hospitals and dispensaries. Indian officers made a great contribution to the reclamation of the criminal tribes. National officers serve as editors of *The War Cry* and other publications printed in 11 languages to meet the need of the sub-continent. At the territorial headquarters national officers serve in all departments, quite a number filling the posts of territorial commander and chief secretary. As far back as 1950 Lieut.-Commissioner S. Manuel, who hailed from Madras, was appointed Territorial Commander of the Southern Territory, the largest in the South Asian group with 1,200 officers.

Other changes took place after the war. In Pakistan Indian dress and names were not acceptable, so those with Indian names had to change them. Throughout the South Asian territories missionaries discontinued using Indian names. The *dhoti* was discarded in favour of trousers both in Pakistan and India. In the cities western dress was becoming the accepted thing for men so there was something ludicrous in seeing missionary officers walking around in *dhoties* while Indian bandsmen were dressed in trousers. The Indian uniform of khavi and red had served its purpose during pioneer days, but to continue wearing it would be a hindrance rather than a help, so the white uniform, worn by Salvationists in so many countries the world over, took its place, while in Pakistan grey is preferred. As for the sari, the most becoming and graceful of garments, that remains uniform for Indian and Singhalese women-officers, while Pakistani women prefer the more practical *salwar* and *kamiz*.

In Calcutta the women's and children's home at Behala was reopened by Mrs R. G. Casey, wife of the Governor of Bengal.

During the war it had been requisitioned by the government for an air-raid emergency hospital and later used for famine victims during the Bengal famine. The Matron, Major Eva Crann, was awarded the Kaisar-i-Hind medal in recognition of her selfless service.

18

Pakistan and Bangladesh

THE Islamic Republic of Pakistan, which came into being in 1947, was divided into two sections in accordance with the distribution of the Muslim population, West Pakistan and East Pakistan with 1,000 miles of Indian territory in between. East Pakistan became a separate independent state in 1972 taking the name of Bangladesh. Pakistan means 'the holy or pure land' in Urdu, the main language of West Pakistan, *pak*—holy or pure, *stan*—place or land.

In this predominantly Muslim state what did the future hold for Salvationists and other Christians? Reading the new Constitution the Prime Minister, Liaquat Ali Khan said:

> Adequate provision shall be made for minorities freely to profess and practise their religion and develop their culture, and to safeguard the legitimate interests of the minorities, and the backward and depressed classes. The minorities would in no way be hindered from professing their religion. They may look forward not only to a period of fullest freedom, but also to an understanding and appreciation on the part of the majority which has always been the characteristic of Muslims throughout history.

The Salvation Army's new territory of Pakistan consisted of 236 corps and 701 societies and outposts with 162 officers on active service, Shantinagar and Amritnagar land colonies and a girls' boarding school. All work was concentrated in the Punjab with Lahore as the centre.

Karachi became the new capital of West Pakistan and remained so until 1960 when it was transferred to Rawalpindi and later to the newly-built capital of Islamabad. Brigadier and Mrs David Walker were appointed to Karachi to open up work. Supporting new openings seemed impossible at the time, financial stringency jeopardized any advancement. The Walkers were up against it. Colonel Hughes, the territorial commander, wrote to the Brigadier:

I cannot tell you how it would grieve me to have to come away from such a tremendous opportunity as Karachi presents, but since the expenses are on our territorial funds and we are deeply in need, we just cannot afford to open new work without International Headquarters' assistance.

Brigadier and Mrs Walker held on tenaciously to Karachi, devoting their time to building up a corps programme and ministering to the many Punjabi Christians who had come to the capital to work but who had no pastor to shepherd them. In reply to the Colonel's letter the Brigadier said:

We have every intention of making this work self-supporting, but we have to build up gradually and teach our people to give. We assure you, with the blessing of God our position here will be fairly strong before we have completed our first 12 months. To retreat is most inadvisable as it will have repercussions on all our work in this country.

The General Secretary, Brigadier Wycliffe Sharp, and his wife came down from Lahore to help raise funds and eventually a divisional headquarters was established.

From being a relatively small coastal town with a population (1941 census) of 250,000 Karachi now has about 7 million and is known to be the fastest growing city in the world. Land is being reclaimed both from the sea and the surrounding desert. At the time of partition many migrants from India swelled the population and as industries developed people flocked in from the villages. As can be expected, such a city has the contrasts of the rich and the poor. *Busties* (slum quarters) line the railway tracks or cling to the edge of the barren desert where hundreds of thousands of people live in sub-standard and appalling conditions. Most water has to be carried from public taps or brought to them in tankers, few have electricity and sewage is non-existent. For anyone with a social conscience there is no limit to the work that needs to be done in the field of medical care, education and so on. To this end a dispensary was built in 1968. This has developed into a well-organized programme with specialized clinics for 'under fives', undernourished babies, family planning, ante-natal as well as gynaecology and general clinics. A medical mobile unit visits surrounding areas regularly. Other clinics were opened subsequently in Lyallpur (now Faisalabad), Hyderabad Sind, and Jhang, totalling seven with the already existing ones in Lahore and Shantinagar and with a rural clinic in the desert area of Thal. These clinics meet a great need, especially for Pakistani women who are

161

still reluctant to be treated by a male doctor. Nurses are desperately needed to augment, and in some cases replace, the present devoted band of nurses who serve with skill and compassion. When the clinic was opened in Faisalabad, the muezzin calling the faithful to prayer from the minaret of the mosque deemed the occasion important enough to make public announcement of the opening of the new Salvation Army dispensary.

In one of the slum quarters of Karachi, known as Mahmoodabad, a small school of 30-35 children was commenced in the corps compound by Envoy Matthew. The Envoy's original name was Syed Mazhar Hussain and Matthew the name he chose after his conversion. Herein lies a remarkable story. Syed was born in the East Punjab into a strict Muslim family, the youngest of seven brothers. As a young boy he showed great promise in his studies and was sent to a mission school, but he took strong objection to the Christian teaching. Proud to be a follower of the prophet, Syed was a true believer in the One God, and he resisted in every possible way any Christian influence, even actively opposing Christian activities. Much to his displeasure and chagrin his closest friend in school did, however, accept Christ, taking the name of Andrew as a sign of his new birth. Andrew's conversion became the first pointer in Syed's long search for truth.

In 1921 Syed left for England where he studied for a science degree at Birmingham University. While he was there he became obsessed with the idea of becoming a Muslim missionary and began studying comparative religion. He travelled in Europe preaching Islam. Later his journey took him to Mecca, the birthplace of the prophet and the site of the holy Kaaba, the centre of worship for all devout Muslims. But instead of this being the culmination of his heart's yearning, the zenith of all his expectations, he turned away dispirited and downcast.

In his distress he wrote to his old friend Andrew, telling him of his perplexity of spirit. Andrew wrote back advising him to study the Bible. 'It is written in the Koran,' he wrote, 'if a Muslim does not honour the *Zabur* (the Psalms), the *Tauret* (the Law) and the *Injil* (the Gospels) he is not a true Muslim.' And he added, 'Through reading these you will come to know the truth.'

Syed set his mind on studying the Bible from cover to cover, but he found no peace. His proud Muslim heritage would not permit him to accept Christ as the Son of God, the Saviour of the world.

He set out for the Middle East once again, hoping that there in the cradle of so many religions he might find the truth. Like Artaban, one of Van Dyke's fictitious Magi, Syed moved among the throngs of men in populous Egypt, looking up into the great countenance of the crouching sphinx vainly seeking for an answer to his search for truth.

Years went by and Syed was no longer a young man. He felt his search had been in vain. There was nothing left for him but to finish this meaningless life. In March, 1965, he stood by the sea wall of Manori, ready for the waters of the Arabian Sea to receive his weary body, when suddenly, as he was going to throw himself out, he felt two strong hands holding him back, making him stand on the shore away from the sea. 'And', says Matthew, as he calls himself now after his conversion, 'when I opened my eyes I knew it was the Lord whom I had been seeking, standing before me in white clothing.'

Matthew came to The Salvation Army where, as he says, 'Captain Maqsood loved me as a father and the behaviour of the Salvationists made me want to become one of them.' Matthew started gathering the children of the poor who had no schooling and taught them in the Army compound. 'You see, I have never married, but God has given me many children. It is important that they should know the Lord Jesus.'

At the time of starting the primary school no hall was available, but with the support of Christian Children's Fund of America a child sponsorship programme was developed and, as more children were added to the roll, classrooms in the form of nearby hutments, were purchased and more teachers employed. Today a primary school and a vocational training/education centre caters for 550 students from kindergarten up to grade 10 with a competent staff of 17 teachers. Carpentry, sewing and embroidery are some of the things being taught.

Matthew was given the rank of Envoy and is now in charge of a corps in the Karachi Division, probably the oldest active corps leader in the world. Looking like a patriarch of old with long, flowing white hair and beard, his face lit up with an inner radiance, his sparse body energetic for his great age, he never tires of telling of the One who is the Way, the Truth, and the Life.

The onslaught of a cyclone means death for many and

homelessness for even more. When one such devastating wind struck East Pakistan in November 1970 (now Bangladesh), a relief team of six officers, including two nurses, headed by the General Secretary, Brigadier Ernest Yendell, flew the 1,000 miles which divided East Pakistan from West Pakistan to Dacca the capital. The most seriously affected area, an island called Sashibhusen in the Bay of Bengal, was reached by boat. Here crops had been destroyed, frail houses demolished claiming many lives, corpses still unburied and carcasses of animals lying around. A young college student, who volunteered to guide and translate for the team, had lost five members of his family. Many similar cases could be told.

By use of helicopters and other means of transport food was getting through from government sources. Another most urgent need was clothing and this task was undertaken by the Army's team in addition to medical aid given by the two nursing sisters, Captains Vera Walker and Alina Vanninen. An elderly man, having heard that medical help was available, had come a distance of seven miles with a gaping wound in his leg caused at the time of the cyclone. Many practical problems had to be resolved in trying to rehabilitate the people of this stricken area. The Salvation Army moved in again later, but that belongs to the Bangladesh narrative.

The Army in Pakistan has seen many advances during the last decade. The old headquarters building, a club before the Army bought it many years ago, crumbling and unsafe, gave place to a fine modern building in 1969. It contains flats for officers and transit flats where travellers can enjoy clean and comfortable accommodation.

The Sunrise Institute for the Blind, Lahore, came under Salvation Army administration for some years at the request of its founder, Miss Marjorie Fyson, MBE, until government policies decreed that education was to be undertaken by the State. Subsequently Salvation Army schools were taken over with the exception of certain girls' schools, the Army still caring for the children in the hostels.

Besides the many newly-established medical centres, concern for underprivileged children resulted in homes being built in different parts of the country. In Lahore, a home for orphans and deprived children lives up to its name, Joyland, for here the children breathe the happy atmosphere of home. A similar home for boys operates in Karachi and attached to it is a community centre. A boarding hostel for girls at Jhang caters for 30 girls for whom adequate schooling might not be possible in the isolation of their native villages. A similar boarding hostel for boys is functioning at Sheikhupura. Many corps halls have been built. An annual feature in Pakistan is a 'cycle campaign' when a group of corps officers takes the gospel message to many villages and the spiritual life of the people is enriched.

A Salvationist from Shantinagar colony, whose work brought him to Rawalpindi, adjacent to Islamabad the new capital, commenced meetings in his home inviting friends and neighbours. As a result Colonel Gulzar Masih was able to enrol 40 people as soldiers of The Salvation Army. A new corps has been opened in the north where nearly a century ago the early pioneers had unsuccessfully tried to establish work.

Shantinagar and Amritnagar colonies have already been mentioned earlier. At the former a new hostel for boys has been built along with staff bungalows and new and improved accommodation for the dispensary. Almost all the land in the colony now belongs to the colonists. Thus those who were without land have become prosperous farmers. But man has to be constantly reminded that a full barn cannot save his soul, so the Army's religious and educational programme continues. 'It is our intention to develop and improve the work extensively,' says the present Territorial Commander, Pakistan, Commissioner Arthur Holland. 'There is every prospect of Shantinagar remaining a live and vigorous expression of Salvation Army work.'

A new medical welfare centre was opened in 1980 in Khanewal financed by Finland and the USA Western Territories. Major Alina Vanninen, who is Finnish and has already 13 years' service at the Shantinagar dispensary to her credit, is in charge. This provides a base for a mobile clinical service to surrounding areas.

It was with a sense of regret that the old training garrison, which had housed cadets for 51 years, had to be demolished. Alternative premises have been acquired on the outskirts of Lahore where cadets now receive tuition.

The home league and its noble efforts to combat illiteracy among women is mentioned in conjunction with the work of this branch in another chapter.

Let us take a last look at Lahore. Good Friday 1980. A large cross is seen on the roof of a house belonging to a Salvationist family. The husband is the son of venerated Pakistani officers, the wife is the grand-daughter of a converted Sikh. At night the cross lights up the darkness surrounding it, a witness to their Muslim neighbours of the Saviour of the world.

Easter Sunday morning sees the central corps hall, with sacred memories for Pakistanis and missionaries alike, packed to the last seat, children filling the space between the front seats and the platform. Dressed in festive garb of bright colours and with faces aglow, the atmosphere is one of jubilation as the large congregation lifts up the words in song, *'Phir ji utha hai Masih, Halliluyah!'* ('Christ the Lord is risen, Hallelujah!')

*   *   *

Bangladesh is one of the world's disaster areas. The flat, fertile delta which makes up the greater part of the country is intersected by three mighty rivers: the Ganges, the Brahmaputra and Meghna. During the monsoon, which brings an annual average rainfall of 100 inches, sending the rivers in spate, thousands of square miles lie flooded and the only way of getting about is by boat. Bangladesh teems with people. The population density is rated among the world's highest. Since partition with India the population has swollen and the 1980 figure was assessed at 82,710,000. For every 1,000 people there are 850 Muslims, 130 Hindus, 17 Buddhists, and three Christians (two Roman Catholics and one Protestant), according to the 1980 United Bible Societies Bulletin.

The 1,000 miles that separated East and West Pakistan were symbolic of many other things that divided the people: their language, mode of living, diet and dress. The people of the eastern wing are smaller of stature, a gentler race, given to the arts, as against the tall soldier-like people of the western region. A war for independence from West Pakistan was fought in 1971 and East Pakistan became Bangladesh—the Bengal nation. To control the monsoon floods is beyond the country's power, so the Bangladeshis must content themselves with being probably the world's most practised river boatmen. However, when the water subsides it leaves a rich, fertile soil where rice and jute are cultivated. But when devastating cyclones add to the deluge, as so often happens, thousands are rendered homeless and may even lose their lives.

166

This scant outline of the unique circumstances under which the people of this country live may help to give a better understanding of the service needed and given by The Salvation Army in co-operation with other organizations, and to form some idea by which constructive and permanent aid can be programmed.

Although The Salvation Army has only recently been operating here, the first relief team coming in 1970, Army history goes right back to the beginning of the century when India was undivided. The criminal tribes settlement at Saidpur and a boarding school for children of the settlement at Nilphamari operated right up to partition in 1947, when some of the people opted for India and the rest were cut off from headquarters in Calcutta.

Ravaged by war and another cyclone the country needed urgent help. A relief team, headed by Major Chianghnuna (present General Secretary, Eastern India Command) was sent from Calcutta early in 1972, following government acceptance of the Army's services. A mobile dispensary gave emergency medical aid, and reconstruction of houses was undertaken. To provide the homeless with immediate shelter *katcha* houses were built, made of bamboo and thatched roofs. For more permanent dwellings, *pakka* houses were erected with wooden frames and galvanized iron roofs. In this way no less than 17,000 people were given again a roof over their heads. A Dutch team, led by Major Eva den Hartog, concentrated during 1972-73 on the Faridpur area. The Major wrote in a letter a few days after arrival, 'Seldom have so many suffered so much as the people of Bangladesh. Many of the recognized disaster zones are populated only because people cannot find anywhere else to live.'

The USA sent Major and Mrs George R. Collins to administer the Army's relief and rehabilitation services in Bangladesh, with an office in Dacca, the capital. The Major could report that more than 1,250,000 people had been given food, clothing, housing, medical care and other aid during the first two years of operation. Major den Hartog took oversight of the work after Major Collins. A large-scale supply of relief goods from Holland was brought in by chartered aircraft organized through The Salvation Army and distributed to the needy with the co-operation of other relief organizations.

Flooding of the Comilla area in 1974 caused starvation and suffering and many were reduced to eating the leaves of banana and jute plants. Four feeding centres were set up and baby-food and milk distributed. Brigadier and Mrs Victor Pedersen from Australia took charge of the work in 1976. Tornadoes struck again in 1977 and floods brought further havoc. This was virtually unnoticed by the world press, but caused large-scale loss of crops and severe food shortage in many parts of the country. A home for physically-handicapped children was opened in Dacca. Canada sent Major and Mrs Ray Homewood on a short-term basis to give a helping hand. An emergency hospital in one of the most needy refugee camps in Dacca brought relief to thousands suffering from all manner of diseases.

Figures of relief work may mean little when one sits well fed in a comfortable home and it is difficult to enter into the sufferings of the poor and the homeless. Yet, the needs of Bangladesh had a world-wide appeal and many gave liberally. For those, it may be of interest to know what was accomplished through their giving:

Main features of Salvation Army service in Bangladesh since 1976

Houses built	—2,350 bamboo frame, thatched roof houses.
,, ,,	— 822 timber frame, GI sheet roof houses.
Schools built	— 21
Clinics built	— 5
Medical treatment	—More than 100,000 persons have been treated annually by the combined effort of Dacca and Jessore SA clinics.
Food distribution	—Large quantities of food have been imported, this has included 1,300 tons of high protein biscuits, milk powder, meal, etc.
Women's training and adult education	—This, combined with instruction in family planning, is given in Jessore and Mirpur.
Girls' home	—A home for 21 orphaned or deprived girls in Dacca.

Envoy and Mrs R. K. Biswas, Salvationists of four years' standing, have developed the corps work in Jessore and initially helped with relief work.

Early in 1977 an application was made to the government for registration under the Companies Act with a view to carrying out a full-scale Salvation Army programme. In April 1980 the Bangladesh Government granted the Army full registration—both as a relief agency and as a Christian organization, whose aim is 'the spreading of the Christian gospel'. This has given a new impetus to the work, for becoming a Christian does not mean accepting a foreign culture, but accepting Christ who was born in the East and who belongs to the whole world, through whom all men can obtain salvation, and enjoy a new, more satisfying life.

19

'In word and deed'

'INDIA has tried to fly with one wing, and she has gone round in circles,' said Gandhi many years ago, pointing to the fact that women had not been given opportunities to develop their potentialities, and as a result the country had not made the progress it ought.

'Whether among the higher or lower castes, you will never do very much for India', said Booth-Tucker, 'until you help the woman, for handicapped though she may be by customs and traditions, she is nevertheless the key to the situation.'

When Mrs Bramwell Booth, wife of the Army's second General, inaugurated the home league for women with its fourfold aim of fellowship, education, service, and worship, she was indeed divinely inspired. The influence which the home league has had on women in the south Asian countries is beyond estimation. The decision to include all women in the fellowship has done much to encourage women of other faiths to participate. In the home league there are no barriers: Hindus, Muslims, Buddhists, Sikhs, Parsees, Christians, rich and poor, young and old, all are welcome. The result is that countless women have found joy in fellowship, wider horizons through learning, satisfaction in service and a deeper meaning of true worship.

The annual home league rally is for many women the gala day of the year. From remote villages hundreds of women travel by horse carts, *tongas,* tractors and trains, or walk long distances to be present at their respective divisional centres. Embroidery and other handicrafts are prepared with skilful care and the set Bible portion memorized, all eager for their particular home league to win the efficiency banner. Bible stories are enacted with imagination and ingenuity. The meal between sessions is like a banquet, even though it may be served on banana leaves, and the fellowship is as warm as the curry!

The home league has also been the medium through which many women have learnt to read and write. An adult literacy programme has consistently been carried out in Pakistan for many years and hundreds of village women can now read Bibles given them at the completion of the course. Rally time is examination time. There is no age limit for the students, and it is heart-warming to see with what determination some elderly women struggle to learn the intricate, artistic Urdu script. 'Before, I was illiterate, now I can read!' exclaimed a grandmother, her wrinkled, careworn face transformed with joy. To her the Bible had become a living book.

The blessings which the home leaguers receive are shared with others and many are giving to the helping-hand scheme. In the South-Eastern India Territory Rs4,719 were raised in 1979 toward a motherless babies' home. Home league local officers in the Tenali Division, Madras and Andhra Territory, are helping to make their corps self-supporting. The Rs6,380 raised for the helping-hand scheme in this territory was used to purchase furnishings for the medical relief and rehabilitation centre at Dindi in the Divi Taluk, the Army's new opening in the area that was struck by the tidal wave and cyclone in 1977. Almost 5,000 women attended the series of home league rallies held during 1980, 76 women were enrolled as Salvation Army soldiers and 544 women decided to follow Christ.

With characteristic enterprise, home league women in Mizoram decided to be 'missionary minded' and help their sisters in another country. They produced the splendid sum of Rs6,000 to be sent to Indonesia, a commendable effort in an area where the majority have to depend for a living upon cultivation of their small, terraced rice fields.

In Rangoon, home league members have loyally upheld the aims of the league against adverse circumstances. Through the testimony of one of the members, the husband, attending an Army meeting for the first time, came forward and knelt at the Penitent-form seeking the same joy and peace which his wife experienced. During the war they both served with the Salvation Army red shield services in Upper Burma. When they heard that the meeting hall in Rangoon had been destroyed in a bombing raid, the husband gave money for a new Penitent-form to be erected when another hall was acquired. For to him this was the place where he had sought and found the Lord Jesus Christ.

In a vigorous message urging the women of India to grasp their opportunities, Mrs Commissioner T. H. Holbrook, as Territorial Home League President, Western India, wrote in *The War Cry*:

> Gone are the days when only men and boys learned new skills; we believe there is always a better way of doing things and our home league programme can be a definite help if we are willing to pass on to others what we have learned, practising all the time new methods ourselves.

New methods were introduced and old and proven ways revised when Mrs Commissioner Arthur Hook, wife of the then international secretary, held home league seminars throughout the various territories during 1978.

The fourfold aim of the home league is to work for better homes, for only through God-centred homes, where His love is expressed in daily living, can we hope for a better world.

* * *

Bordering on Tibet and Sikkim, in the far corner of the state of Bengal on an elevation of 4,000 feet in the Himalaya mountains, lies Kalimpong. The foothills abound with rich vegetation, brilliantly-coloured flowers and birds of many hues, and towering high above it all is the snow-capped peak of Kangchenjunga. But the 80 boys and girls of the Salvation Army Mary Scott School and Home are not able to enjoy this splendid scenery, for their eyesight is impaired. It is in fact a school for the blind, which was handed over to The Salvation Army in 1952 when Major Hazel Koerner took charge. The children are mostly from backward areas in Nepal, Sikkim and Bhutan, with Bhuddist and Hindu backgrounds, learning in this place to care for themselves and, in spite of their handicap, how to live as equal members of the community.

The school curriculum takes the children through to the government school final examination, successful students can study further at any of the training centres for the blind which are found in India. Many of the young men have taken the three-year course in physiotherapy in Bombay to which they have travelled alone, facing the three-days-and-nights journey with self-reliance, and are now serving in government hospitals.

Others have been trained in the teaching profession and have taken posts in Salvation Army and other schools for the blind. The headmaster and another senior teacher at the Mary Scott School are both former pupils. John Dick Khawas, the headmaster, holds the degrees of BA, BEd; Rongong has also obtained his MA in English

172

in addition to his already obtained BA, BEd degrees. Three other teachers, basic trained for the blind, are also former students. Ten teachers make up the staff and all are Christians.

The school can be proud of its academic achievements. Intiaz Ahmed gained his Bachelor of Law degree at the University of Bombay, where he was awarded a gold medal on two consecutive years, one for the highest marks obtained in the papers of Legal Theory and Property Law. He is now at London University in England reading for his Master of Law degree.

For the less scholarly, various handicrafts are taught at the school and many are able to earn a living in the workshop. Some of the residents are happy to stay on after school age, for this is their home.

Courage and determination are the characteristics of these young people, a standard set by Brigadier Dorothy Page, a Canadian officer, who during her 20 years at the school did so much to improve and develop it. Following the Brigadier's retirement in 1977, Captain Elsie Hansford from England is keeping up the same traditions. Sponsorships are given by various agencies among them The Royal Commonwealth Society for the Blind.

Music plays an important part in the daily life at the school, says Elsie Hansford. All the children love to sing and one can truly say 'the hills are alive with the sound of music'. Many different instruments are taught by the capable music master, who is one of the 'old boys' who came back after doing special training in music in Calcutta. A group of young Christians, led by one of the high school teachers, recorded a programme of music and presented the gospel message on the Nepali station of All India Radio. The school orchestra is popular at many local functions. Games are part of the daily curriculum and seeing the children chasing a ball one would have to look twice before realizing that they are blind.

In 1972 the school admitted 20 deaf and dumb boys because of the dire need of these unfortunates, 10 of them became boarders and training is given in tailoring, bookbinding and general handicrafts. In 1980 this department was transferred to Darjeeling where Elsie Hansford installed the children in Erin House, the former home of rest for officers.

As Kalimpong lies in a sensitive border area certain restrictions are imposed on the institution. No child is allowed to change his or her religion until the age of 18 years when, if so desired, he or she can be registered as Christian. But no restriction is put on day-to-day activities so that morning and evening prayers are held regularly. Children from the locality swell the numbers at Sunday-school to over 100. Sunday afternoon and evening meetings are held to which visitors are also welcome. Open-air meetings are held in the town and nearby villages and often a group of older boys goes out to conduct meetings at other schools.

Sunday closes with an informal hour of singing and fellowship. Grouped on the lawn under the stars, when the weather is mild, they sit and sing and play their songs. They may not see the great mountains sketched in the moonlight but their inner eyes see the glory of a celestial city as they sing one of their favourite songs, written by Albert Orsborn:

> Let nothing draw me back
> Or turn my heart from Thee,
> But by the Calvary track
> Bring me at last **to see**
> The courts of God, that city fair,
> And find my name is written there.

In Bombay a hostel for blind working men was opened by General Arnold Brown, when as Chief of the Staff he visited India in 1973. The hostel has accommodation for 70 men. A similar institution was opened in Ahmedabad in 1978, and the same year a school for the blind was opened at Kolasib in Mizoram. Financial assistance from Christoffel Blinden Mission has made this service possible.

* * *

In a country with a population of over 625,000,000, increasing yearly by around 12.5 million, it may not be surprising to find a high rate of unemployment resulting in homelessness and misery. People by the thousands flock to the cities in the hope of finding work. Most of them are disappointed but linger on with a hopeful spirit, meanwhile setting up for themselves hutments on the city pavements, some remaining there even after a job is found. Occasionally they are cleared off the streets, but the squatters always return, they have nowhere else to go.

Salma was one of the many hutment dwellers in Bombay. Her home was a structure of pieces of tin, sacking and cardboard precariously put together, six by seven feet square. A social worker made enquiries into the conditions of some of the hutment dwellers and recorded the following:

> Salma was married when very young and has had eight children and thinks she is 30 years old. Her husband left her during the last pregnancy, as he could not feed the ever increasing family. Three of the children have died. The family now exists on the 25 rupees (£1.40) earned weekly by the eldest son, a youth of 15. 'In the hut there are no sanitary facilities', says Salma, 'so I must take my bath in the open, by the street pump, which means I must bathe with my clothes on and let them dry on me, and I'm always catching colds. We just couldn't survive without the free meal from The Salvation Army,' she adds.

With the support of Oxfam and World Church Services, The Salvation Army operates a free meal service in the city. The food is cooked at a social institution, the King Edward Home, from where over.1,000 meals are distributed daily in three different centres.

In Calcutta conditions are similar, with its vast population and no social security, people by the thousands are left starving. Here, until he died in 1981, Dudley Gardiner operated The Salvation Army's feeding programme through which thousands of free meals are given out daily. Known as 'the angel with the bushy beard' Dudley spent his days among the 'forsaken ones', and the children loved him.

When Dudley Gardiner, as a military major serving with British forces in Burma, was taken prisoner in the Second World War he was filled with a loathing of war and its destructiveness. He resolved that when his term of service was completed his life would take a different direction and become creative instead of destructive. In his search for a place where he could serve humanity he came to Calcutta in 1957. Here he found his destiny among the poorest of the poor. Working long hours he gave his service free, having discovered that in giving you gain. The former military officer was engaged in another kind of battle than the ones he previously fought. As Michael Quoist describes it, 'The battle for a better world is a battle of love, in the service of love.' Dudley Gardiner received the MBE in 1974 as a recognition of this work.

*   *   *

'Happiness is seen to lie, not in possessions, but in creative achievement,' wrote Commissioner (Dr) Harry Williams on the occasion of the 10th anniversary of the vocational training centre for the physically handicapped at Aramboli in 1978. That creative achievement is not only the way to happiness but also the secret of success is evident in this thriving institution.

It came into being through a series of deciding factors, clearly indicating God's guiding hand in the affairs of men. Harry Williams, Chief Medical Officer at the Catherine Booth Hospital at the time, was engaged in a programme of reconstructive surgery for lepers and physically handicapped persons. He realized that medical rehabilitation was not enough. When surgery and physiotherapy had done their best, there still remained the age-old problem of earning a living. The idea of a vocational training centre, where persons severely handicapped by leprosy and other diseases could be trained to become economically independent, was born within him. A donation of Rs40,000 for rehabilitation work, given through a chance meeting on board a ship bound for Liverpool, contributed to the initial expenses. The appointment to India of Lieutenant George Scott, an engineer-educationist, provided the technical skill. Mr Sundar Egbert, himself handicapped, became the sustaining drive in the venture. Sankara, an ex-leprosy patient and a blacksmith, supplied the initial workforce. A former branch hospital, 10 miles from Nagercoil, now redundant with the establishment of a state health centre, afforded suitable accommodation. A new workshed was put up, a few tools and machines obtained, and the experiment was on.

The work was built up slowly, at times agonizingly. Most of the trainees had through their incapacity lost confidence in themselves. To instil in them the motivation to become independent was of paramount importance, but not easy. Gradually a definite change of attitude became apparent, they progressed to a disciplined work-force capable of doing a day's work.

Training in the workshop was complemented by evening classes. Instruction was given in the basic 3Rs to the illiterates, English and arithmetic to the already literate, technical mathematics and engineering drawing to the more advanced.

A thriving concern was built up. From making the first wheelchair the volume of work increased to include hospital furniture manufacture on a large scale, with other jobs like poultry rearing and repairs of agricultural tools on the side. The instalment of heavy machinery made more advanced jobs possible, and making spare parts for textile machinery created a profitable business. Parts for loudspeakers and ticket-printing machines for a Kerala government department were also manufactured.

When lack of rain in the catchment area affected the generating of electric power and many industries closed down, this centre recorded an increase in turnover above the previous year by starting taking in more jobs involving hand work. Instructors and trainees, all either ex-leprosy or physically-handicapped people, showed their flair for innovation by doing many things without power and worked at odd hours when power was available. In 1975 a 25 kVA power generator was installed.

In 1974, Captain George Scott was transferred and Mr Sundar Egbert appointed in charge of the centre. As a child, Sundar became badly crippled by polio. After his father's early death Sundar was admitted to the Dohnavur Fellowship where he was taught watchmaking. The friends at Dohnavur arranged for him to be admitted to the Catherine Booth Hospital in 1962 and he received treatment under Dr Harry Williams, but remained dependent on his wheelchair. His firm belief in God made him sure that his life had a purpose, and a desire was awakened within him to work for other handicapped people.

When the idea of the vocational training centre took shape, it was to Sundar, who was then engaged in the Swedish Red Cross Rehabilitation Centre at Vellore, that Dr Harry Williams turned, persuading the director to relinquish Sundar for the new project. Sundar Egbert's drive and skill, linked to his indomitable spirit, have contributed much to the success of the centre. That he himself is handicapped has proved an advantage rather than a drawback. When disabled trainees lose courage they see in their mentor, who carries the same burden, the power to overcome.

The vocational training centre has received various State awards for being the best centre for the rehabilitation of the handicapped, and a cash prize was given for the best worker in the cured leprosy section. Sundar Egbert was also honoured in 1979 by receiving the Army's Certificate in Recognition of Exceptional Service.

By his side is his gracious wife, Sugantham, former secretary of the vocational training centre for physically-handicapped women at Nagercoil, herself also physically handicapped. They were married in the Catherine Booth Hospital chapel, the ceremony conducted by Captain (Dr) Herbert C. Rader. It was a joyous occasion where two people, in spite of disabilities, showed enough faith and courage to face life together trusting in divine power to help them build a home for each other. Their example has been an encouragement to others in like circumstances, for many of the lads who were trained in the centre have developed enough self-confidence to set up their own homes and support their families.

Two sister institutions to Aramboli were opened in 1971, one in Trivandrum for physically-handicapped girls. A princess of the Travancore royal family was present at the opening ceremony. Major Margaret Spooner, third-generation missionary officer, was the first superintendent and supervised the many skills being taught—bookbinding, weaving, embroidery, plastic work and tailoring. Added to this in 1979 was a printing press which is now undertaking to print all Salvation Army books and periodicals published in the South-Western Territory.

Another centre was opened in Nagercoil the same year where the existing women's industrial home was changed to a vocational training centre for physically-handicapped women. Brigadier Sarah, who for many years had been stationed at the industrial home and was looking forward to her already overdue retirement, was asked to pilot the scheme and it is to her credit that the transition was made so effectively. Brigadier Vera Williamson, who later took over the reins, after 25 years' nursing at the Catherine Booth Hospital, and subsequently became the chief secretary of the territory holding the rank of Lieut.-Colonel, says of her appointment at the vocational centre, 'It was to me the crowning joy of my career'.

The centre has 50 boarders; they include the blind, the deaf, former leprosy patients, the orthopaedically handicapped and spastics. The present superintendent is Major Edith Drøsdahl, a Norwegian officer-nurse. The healing process in the trainees, from an attitude of despondency and hopelessness to a buoyant spirit of confidence with which to face life anew, is a modern miracle. The aim is to return as many as possible to their own villages where they will build up their own trade taught in the centre. Sewing machines are supplied free in some cases, the more capable paying back the cost in easy instalments according to their earnings. Contacts are kept up after the women leave the centre. Quite a number are now self-employed, others have obtained work and a smaller number have married. One young girl, accepting the Christian faith, married a man cured of leprosy, also a Christian; they now have their own family.

The sheltered workshop is a place where the severely disabled with no home to go to, can be occupied and earn enough for their food plus a little pocket-money. All trainees, who can possibly hold a hoe, do two hours of gardening under the guidance of the farm manager. Cocoa trees have been experimented with and are now producing pods full of cocoa beans. A cow known as Shanti, a goat and her kid named Sally and Ann, after the donor's daughter Sallyann Hood, a medical officer at the Catherine Booth Hospital, give opportunity for teaching dairying skills.

A secretarial training school has gained government recognition, which means that candidates can enter for government examinations. In 1978 out of eight VTC examinees seven passed. Shorthand classes are given to those proficient in English; book-keeping is another subject taught. Men students have joined in these classes, two of whom are former leprosy patients, now qualifying as stenographers and secretaries. A far cry from the young Hindu lad, Palami, who though cured of leprosy could find no work and frightened of life and the stigma of leprosy died an untimely death.

The vocational training centres for the handicapped are activity-oriented, to help those who thought themselves useless to become creative, and through creativity find happiness and self-esteem. 'Physical handicap is not unmitigated evil,' says Dr Harry Williams, who was the initiator of these centres. 'I have seen the development of character which has been the direct result of such crippling.' To use obstacles as stepping stones is a hard lesson to learn and praiseworthy are those who achieve it.

20

Love must serve

AFTER William Booth's second visit to India in 1895 he sent out a memorandum in which he expressed his hopes for the future of the Army in India. Have his hopes been fulfilled? A short survey of so large an area, including Sri Lanka, Pakistan, Burma and Bangladesh, can give only an incomplete picture of what has been accomplished. However, a review of his six points might be helpful to see more clearly the progress made since Frederick de Lautour Tucker and his three companions landed at Apollo Bunder, Bombay, 100 years ago.

To secure and train converts was William Booth's first concern. Any organization attaining its centenary faces the tendency to live on memories—to glory in past victories. The desperate battles fought by the pioneers, nationals as well as non-nationals, were won through selfless devotion and sacrifice. Present-day Salvationists, numbering 200,220 in the area with which we are concerned, are reaping the harvest of their labours. But the Army cannot rest on past achievements, the battle against evil and ignorance, poverty and privation has to be fought constantly. Salvation Army soldiers cannot afford to be apathetic, they must be constantly on the alert, always ready to witness to their faith, always willing to offer their services, their love and concern for those in need.

When Dr Stanley Jones once asked Gandhi what he would suggest to make Christianity part of the national life of India Gandhi replied: 'That all Christians live more like Jesus Christ, that you practise your religion without adulterating or toning it down, that you put your emphasis upon love, for love is the centre and soul of Christianity.' Herein lies the message for today's Salvationist.

Within the last decade there have been many encouraging reports of evangelical outreach. In Mizoram, when Lieut.-Colonel Kapliana inaugurated the new district headquarters at Darlawn, a march of witness preceded the meeting in which 2,300 people shared in worship and at the closing moment of the meeting many knelt at the Mercy Seat seeking God's blessing.

In Sri Lanka (where the Army will be celebrating its centenary in January 1983) General Arnold Brown said during his visit in the early part of 1979, 'We must reach out or die out,' observing that at nearly 100 years of age The Salvation Army in Sri Lanka is not feeble but vigorous—100 years young in God.

'Cycle campaigns', in which a number of officers travel from village to village proclaiming the gospel, are annual events in the Punjab of both India and Pakistan. In south India a great cycle rally with more than 1,000 Salvationist cyclists, with flags and placards, travelled along the 200-mile highway from Kanyakumari in the southern Cape Division to Trichur in the northern Alwaye Division—a live demonstration of Richard Nuttall's 'Travel along in the sunshine on the King's highway'. Brigadier Nuttall, known in Army circles for his music, gave his life for India.

In the Madras and Andhra Territory a number of societies have sprung up, often due to the faithful witness of a lone Salvationist. Hyderabad is a new field of labour since 1962, and now has five corps. In Bombay a Christmas programme for all communities was organized by the Christian Council of Bombay on Chowpatty beach. With Byculla Central Corps Band supplying the music, carols were sung in Marathi, Hindi, Gujarati, Malayalam, Konkani and English. The Christmas story was presented in Hindi in song and Indian dance. Distribution of Bibles and Gospel portions plays an important part in the evangelistic programme. Special emphasis has been placed on the task of training new converts through literature and seminars.

The second point in William Booth's memorandum was improving the training of officers. The acceptance and training of candidates for officership has seen a radical change since the first days of the Army in India when a convert was given officer rank by the word of a leader. Gradually the minimum educational standard has been raised and most territories will now only accept candidates of matriculation standard. One territory requires two-year post matriculation. There are nine training colleges in the South Asia territories with 218 cadets. A two-year course of study in college, interspersed with corps work (pastoral work) is followed by advanced training through correspondence. Refresher courses for officers have also featured in the programme for many years.

Following the pattern of the International College for Officers in London, England, a South Asia College for Officers (SACO) was set up in Colombo on 30 January 1980. Twenty-three officer-delegates from the various territories benefited from a two months' course of study. The college faculty comprised Lieut.-Colonel Jillapegu Israel, BA, BEd, as principal, Brigadier Alice Stiles, MA, BEd, vice-principal, and Captain Margaret Burt, BRE(Canada), education officer. It is intended to make this a regular feature by which each year a number of officer-students can benefit.

The college programme aims to 'help officers look objectively at the world, the Church, the Army and themselves; to renew their vision of the purpose of our Movement and of their service for God within it, and to foster international understanding and fellowship'.

The most noteworthy outcome of the pioneers' work, commenced a century ago, is the great army of 3,313 officers and employees numbering 1,919 who are serving today. The national officers of India, Pakistan, Sri Lanka, Burma and Bangladesh will be carrying on the work of the Army, leading their own people strengthened by the international bond of The Salvation Army. Today the officers from abroad number only 74, plus six employees engaged mostly in administrative, medical and educational work, thus maintaining the spirit of internationalism, for the Army believes in a world-wide brotherhood of nations.

From the time of Colonel Weerasooriya and Commissioner Muthiah, India has produced its own leaders. Commissioner Joseph Dahya, son of an early-day convert in Gujarat, gave capable leadership in three different territories. As the Salvation Army representative he attended the Assembly of the World Council of Churches held at Evanston, Illinois, USA, in 1954, and the third Assembly at New Delhi in 1962, which was also attended by Colonel D. A. Sanjivi and Colonel (later Lieut.-Commissioner) B. L. Benjamin of Pakistan.

Other national leaders, to mention only a few, have been: Commissioner Samuel Gnanaseelan, ably supported by his wife, Nurani, daughter of Colonel Yesudasen, the Brahmin convert who brought the Army to central Travancore; Commissioner Pavureth E. George, the first Malayalee officer to become the Territorial Commander, South-Western Territory with that rank; and Lieut.-Commissioner Fazal Masih of the North-Eastern Territory.

At the international conference of leaders in Toronto, October 1979, Colonel Mannam Samuel, Territorial Commander, Madras and Andhra Territory (now commanding South-Western India Territory) expressed deep gratitude on behalf of his people for the ministry of former missionaries, and added in conclusion, 'We are determined to be faithful custodians of the salvation message they imparted to us.'

The cost of maintaining the work is of necessity heavy. Maintenance of present operations and their extension still calls for considerable financial support, and thanks are due to all who so generously have supplied funds over the years. It is, however, gratifying that more and more is being done by way of self-support and at present two-thirds of the financial cost of the work is raised in the countries concerned. The annual Self-Denial Appeal has over the last few years shown a remarkable increase, and self-support through stewardship has become the basis of financing local corps.

'Pay 1,000, nay 10,000, times more attention to the children,' was William Booth's third injunction. From the earliest days of the Army in India care of the children has been of primary importance. From as early as 1892 The Haven in Madras has taken in children in need of a home and today it is fulfilling the same purpose for which it was established. The need is still the same, and well-established homes such as the Calcutta Behala Home, Sion in Bombay, The Haven in Colombo, the Tamwe homes for boys and girls in Burma, Joyland and the Azam Town boys' home in Pakistan still meet a great need. Sponsoring agencies throughout the world meet part of the maintenance of the children.

The primary schools in the villages, instituted in the early days to give children of lower castes the opportunity of learning, have in most places been replaced by state schools. In Pakistan boarding schools are now under state control, while the hostels for the school children remain under Army care. The Bapatla High School in Andhra Pradesh with 1,000 students and the Trivandrum High School in Kerala with accommodation for 1,722 students, and other similar, but somewhat smaller, Salvation Army schools maintain a high standard of instruction and discipline.

During the International Year of the Child (1979) a new school building at Valliyoor, South Eastern India Territory, known as the Noble Memorial Middle School, was erected in memory of Colonel (Dr) William Noble and his wife Etna. This school will give opportunity of further education for children in the Army's 10 primary schools in the Rhadapuram and Valliyoor district, many of whom would otherwise only be able to study up to the fifth standard. The money to build the school has been contributed by family and friends of William and Etna Noble and by the USA Southern Territory. Tamil Nadu's chief educational officer, Thiru T. Krishnamurthi, declared the building open.

Vacation Bible schools are held in every territory with the purpose of 'creating in each student a love for God and His word and a sense of responsibility to love and serve mankind'. A number of children attending these vacation Bible schools are from non-Christian backgrounds. A vigorous programme is carried out in all territories to train the children to take their stand as loyal citizens of their country, with love to God and love to their neighbour. Youth rallies, young people's councils, scouts and guides and corps cadet brigades (training for young Salvationists) are all part of that programme.

'Keep on supplying halls,' said William Booth. Hardly a month goes by without some reference in editions of *The War Cry* to new halls having been erected. Some are built in memory of officers who have gone to their reward. The hall at Allivagaram Corps in the Madras and Andhra Territory tells its own story. On the foundation stone is written:

> To the Glory of God and for the salvation of the people, this hall has been erected to commemorate the service of Staff-Captain Anantham (Steven) who died in a train in west Godavari while on active service for the Master.

The cost of the building was met by his widow living in retirement in Australia.

Many halls throughout the sub-continent bear the name of Booth-Tucker in memory of the founder of the Army's work in India. In Sri Lanka a hall was recently opened at Gonapinawella, the village home of Arnolis Weerasooriya, early pioneer and Booth-Tucker's right-hand man. Weerasooriya's sole surviving sister declared the hall open and a nephew, the Rev Arnold Painter, spoke with feeling of the need for the Army's evangelical and practical service in present-day Sri Lanka. The Territorial Commander of Sri Lanka is Colonel P. William Perera, like Weerasooriya, a Singhalese.

Building of new halls is part of a development plan leading up to the centenary of Salvation Army service in India. Some are built through local enterprise; in Mizoram a hall was built entirely by the efforts of the comrades of the Dinther Society assisted by gifts from the Aizawl Corps and other friends.

Things have changed from the time when Private Nelson, the Armenian convert, was appointed Barracks Master by Booth-Tucker and commissioned to erect a meeting hall in Bombay. 'A very simple structure measuring 70 by 40 feet (to accommodate 800-900 people) consisting of a tiled roof supported by posts and surrounded by boarding.' The total cost was 800 rupees (£60). More ambitious is the $3,000,000 scheme for the redeveloping of the headquarters site in Colombo, including a 10-storey commercial building, social services centre, meeting hall and headquarters, of which the foundation stone was laid by General Arnold Brown in January 1979.

The fifth point in William Booth's 1895 memorandum emphasizes the need for 'the establishment of corps in all large cities'. Even allowing that this was written in the arbitrary fashion of Victorian times, it was, on the face of it, a tall order for a country the size and complexity of India. Or did the Founder perhaps have mainly the state capitals in mind? In that context, it can be said that the Army has come a long way, for today it is represented if not in all, at least in nearly all regional capitals of the entire sub-continent. As for India itself, the national capital calls for special comment.

Historically, Delhi is best known as the capital of the great Mogul empire, though its founding goes back before that to the first century AD. In the context of the British Raj in India, Delhi's importance was greatly enhanced when, in January 1912, it became the nation's capital in place of Calcutta.

The previous month saw Fakir Singh and Dutini (Commissioner and Mrs Booth-Tucker) on the way home to England because of the latter's health. They boarded ship in Bombay and were about to sail when they witnessed the arrival of King George V and Queen Mary *en route* to Delhi for the Coronation Durbar, at which the king was to declare the transfer of the capital. Booth-Tucker recorded for *The War Cry*:

> It was a cause of sincere regret that neither of us could attend the Delhi Durbar, to which we had received a very cordial invitation from Sir John Hewett, President of the Durbar Committee. However, it is a great satisfaction that the Army will be well represented.

One gathers that at that time there was no permanent establishment of the Movement in Delhi. Indeed, this important city receives but scant mention in records of the Army's first 33 years in India and relatively little even after that until recent times. It was not until 1915 that a serious attempt was made to establish permanent work in Delhi, as the December issue of *The War Cry* of that year records with intriguing artlessness:

> Delhi, the new capital of India, would certainly not be complete without the presence of The Salvation Army, so it was decided to commence operations here, and although it started work only eight months ago it has become a well-known factor in the city and under the supervision of Adjutant Khushal (Wyatt) it has been able to make itself popular in that it has helped to reduce the begging element with the opening of the industrial home.

Perhaps hopes were not altogether realized. Certainly very little seems to be recorded regarding Delhi during this period, and we must go on for some years. Eventually New Delhi saw the establishment of a naval and military home. This became well known, and did excellent service for many years.

'An interesting event of the year (1939)', says *The War Cry* for January 1940, 'has been the opening of a Hindustani corps in Delhi for Salvationists accompanying their employers to that city for the colder months of the year. About half of the comrades attached to the corps are soldiers of the Simla Hindustani Corps, who return there for the Simla season.'

Those were the days when the entire British administration in Delhi used to pack up every summer and move lock, stock and barrel up to the hills. Hence the 'Simla season' which lasted for about six months of the year. Simla was known colloquially as the summer capital. Salvationist employees (mostly servants) moved between Simla and Delhi with their masters.

It was not until August 1948—a year after the partition of India and Pakistan—that a territorial headquarters was first established in Delhi, for the new Northern India Territory, the former territory of that name becoming the Pakistan Territory, with headquarters at Lahore. Both territories were realigned in accordance with the frontier between the new countries of India and Pakistan. This was at a time when only limited funds were available, resulting in the new administrative centre being located in unprepossessing premises in Rohtak Road, Old Delhi. For better or for worse, this arrangement was to survive only four years, for in 1952 further administrative changes came about. The Delhi headquarters closed and the Northern and Eastern Territories amalgamated with headquarters at Calcutta. Incidentally, this arrangement made the new North-Eastern Territory geographically the largest in India, stretching from the Lushai Hills Division in the east up to the Punjab in the north-west, with territorial headquarters at the far end of the 1,000-mile stretch and covering 12 different language areas—Assamese, Bengali, English, Hindi, Mizo, Nepali, Oriya, Punjabi, Santali, Urdu, Manipuri and Paiti.

With headquarters closed down, it is worthy of note that, alone, the small Hindi-language corps in Delhi valiantly maintained the Army image and evangelical outreach in this great city until the Year 1977, when, as recorded elsewhere, the International Audit Office was transferred to New Delhi in September, thus strengthening the Army presence in the capital.

The growing importance of New Delhi in the national and international context strengthened the judgement in the minds of many present-day Army leaders that it should be the administrative centre for northern India. But apart from that consideration, long experience showed that Calcutta was too far removed from the biggest concentration of the work to make it a viable administrative centre for the Punjab and Uttar Pradesh where, over the years, a sound evangelical work has been maintained, in more recent times under the leadership of officers such as Lieut.-Colonel Zorawar Singh, and three having the name Ghulam Masih (Slave of Christ)—Lieut.-Colonel Ghulam Masih (son of Maggar), Lieut.-Colonel Ghulam Masih (son of Mahla), and Lieut.-Colonel Ghulam Masih (son of Prem).

Thus, further changes were made in 1980, Calcutta becoming command headquarters for the Eastern Command with Lieut.-Colonel Kapliana as Officer Commanding, and Delhi once again a territorial centre for the re-named Northern India Territory

187

with Colonel Jaikumar Makanji, Territorial Commander, until his retirement later in the year when Colonel Douglas Kiff took over leadership.

In March 1980 New Delhi was the venue for a territorial commanders' conference, presided over by Commissioner Edwin Marion, International Secretary. Delegates were able to be present for the official opening of the new territorial headquarters, in rented premises on Green Park Extension. All Salvationists in any way connected with India would prayerfully endorse the sentiments expressed in General Arnold Brown's message read at the opening:

> The establishing of an effective Salvation Army presence in the capital city of New Delhi has been one of my hopes since my earliest days as Chief of the Staff. It is therefore with great joy that I learn of the official opening of the new headquarters on Saturday 29 March, and I would ask you to convey not only my greetings to all those associated with this venture, but to challenge them to ensure that it succeeds, to the glory of God and to the development of the Army's work not only in the Northern India Territory but throughout the sub-continent.

'To work out a social scheme to benefit the poor,' was William Booth's last charge. In Booth-Tucker's day industries were started to enable the poor to increase their earnings—loom factories and cotton and silk weaving schools were set up—the landless were given opportunity to acquire land on easy terms—the women were taught handicrafts to make it possible for them to earn while remaining at home looking after the family.

The farmers in the Army's land colonies now own their own land and have prospered, while hand-loom weaving is no longer a paying proposition. Conditions have changed, but 'the poor are always with us' and need help.

In a drought-stricken area in the South-Eastern India Territory, Colonel N. J. Samuel launched a novel scheme in 1978 to help the poor villagers. One hundred families were given a goat each on the condition that the goat may not be sold and that its first female offspring be given back for redistribution to another needy family, thus making the scheme self-propagating.

It is interesting to look back to the days of Dayasagar (Henry Burfoot) who in 1886 advocated the keeping of goats. 'You see,' said Dayasagar, 'the reason why I keep a goat is that I can have a cup of tea at any time of the day or night with milk in it, because you can milk a goat any time you like.' But an even more important reason was because a goat costs next to nothing to keep, 'being on self-support like its master', he said jokingly.

To the poor villagers in south India this simple, practical scheme meant milk for undernourished children, and as time went by an increased income as the goats multiplied. A widow raised enough money to pay for her daughter's wedding from the herd of goats which were the progeny of her first goat given free. Another family used the money from the sale of goat's milk to pay for the education of the children.

Under a 'Get your Goat' drive, money has been donated from local service clubs and friends abroad, thus developing the scheme in many more areas. The project has been carried through with the co-operation of local government.

A new development in recent years is the pattern of the Army's medical programme to suit the changing times. Various causes have brought about this change. The increasing high cost of maintaining privately-owned hospitals and the rapid development of government and other health services being one. In 1958 one of the Army's larger general hospitals, the Thomas Emery Hospital in Moradabad, Uttar Pradesh, had to be closed down. But there are other positive reasons for the change. The large majority of people still live in the villages, many in areas without medical facilities. To help such people the Army has set up medical clinics. In a statement made by the minister for health in India, national and international voluntary organizations were urged to co-operate actively in the country's endeavour to provide primary health care for its rural masses.

In Kerala, under Colonel Robert Bath's energetic leadership, six rural medical centres were added to the already existing three during 1978-1980. Dr Mrs Major George Scott is medical consultant for the territory.

Eight medical centres are operating in Pakistan, some in remote areas. The emphasis is on health care, the aim is to develop healthy communities through preventive measures and education.

When General and Mrs Clarence Wiseman visited Gujarat on their tour of the South Asian territories in 1976, both they and the territorial leaders, Colonel and Mrs David Durman, were received at Raj Bhavan by the Governor of Gujarat. His Excellency Shri K. K. Vishvanathan showed interest in the work of the Army and was pleased to know of present plans for social outreach in Gujarat State.

At the time Harry Andrews (pioneer of The Salvation Army's medical mission) first came to Anand in Gujarat and the Emery Hospital was built in 1904, the road from the railway station leading past the hospital was just a sandy track, and so it remained for many, many years. From an insignificant village, Anand has grown to a prosperous town and the road past the hospital is a sandy track no longer, but a broad boulevard with bourgainvillaea in brilliant colours.

The Army has kept pace with the town's development. To the already existing institutions of hospital, training college, corps, boys' and girls' boarding schools and babies' home has been added a home for orthopaedic handicapped children. An impressive-looking building, financed by the Christoffel Blinden Mission, adding dignity to the district.

Joyland, for so the place is called, was declared open in November 1978 by Mr W. Stein, of the German organization Overseas Services, after which the then Territorial Commander, Colonel Maurice Griffiths, dedicated the building to the glory of God. On weekdays the children join in morning prayers before being transported to the Salvation Army primary school. Doctors and staff of the Emery Hospital provide the necessary medical care. In off-school hours the youngsters are engaged in games and various handicrafts. Whatever their religious background may be, they all enjoy the services in the Booth-Tucker Hall and the weekly joy hour. To see the children's eager faces as they sing with zest, 'We shall overcome' is a moving experience.

The social scheme which William Booth envisaged now comprises:

 2 schools for the blind
 1 school for the deaf
 2 hostels for blind working men
 5 women's and children's homes
36 children's homes
 6 young women's hostels

```
 1  eventide home
 1  home for elderly men
 2  homes for destitutes
 1  industrial home
 4  social services centres
 3  farm colonies
 1  home for physically handicapped children
 4  vocational training centres for the physically handicapped
 6  general hospitals
 2  leprosy hospitals
20  rural medical centres and clinics
```

All in all—excluding hospitals—no less than 3,295 children and adults are under The Salvation Army's daily care in the five countries under review.

Invariably the question arises—what of the future? The future is secure as long as Salvationists continue to serve in love, for our work will in the final issue be judged on whether we are 'By love compelled'.

When Salvationists from all over the sub-continent and beyond gather in Bombay to celebrate the centenary on 19 September 1982, songs of praise will ring through the air in the words: 'O tell to earth's remotest bound, God is love!' and Christians everywhere will re-echo the truth—God is Love.

Bibliography

The Discovery of India	Jawaharlal Nehru	Meridian Books Ltd, 1945
Gandhi, His Life and Message for the World	Louis Fischer	The New American Library, 1954
The Crisis of India	Ronald Segal	Penguin Books Ltd, 1965
A Short History of India and Pakistan	T. Walter Wallbank	The New American Library, 1963
Gitanjali	Rabindranath Tagore	Macmillan & Co Ltd, 1959
Friends not Masters	Mohammad Ayub Khan	Oxford University Press, 1967
Something Beautiful for God	Malcolm Muggeridge	William Collins, 1971
Kulu	Penelope Chetwode	John Murray, 1972
Muktifauj	Frederick Booth-Tucker	SP & S, Ltd, Marshall Bros
A Missionary's Memories	Henry Bullard	SP & S, Ltd
Booth-Tucker Sadhu and Saint	R. A. Mackenzie	Hodder and Stoughton
Booth-Tucker, William Booth's First Gentleman	Harry Williams	Hodder and Stoughton, 1980
The Undauntables	Matilda Hatcher	Hodder and Stoughton, 1933
The Mud Bank	Mildred Mackenzie	M. E. Mackenzie, 1959
It Began with Andrews	Miriam Richards	SP & S, Ltd, 1971
I Missionärens Spår (In the Steps of the Missionary)	Erland Richter	The Salvation Army, Stockholm, 1916
He had no Revolver	Frederick Coutts	SP & S, Ltd
In Good Company	Frederick Coutts	SP & S, Ltd, 1980
Indian Pilgrim	Rosalie M. Wheaton	SP & S, Ltd
Kawl Khuma	Rosalie M. Wheaton	SP & S, Ltd
Capturing Crims for Christ	H. Pimm Smith	SP & S, Ltd
My India	Jim Corbett	Oxford University Press, 1952

Sergeant-Major in the Andamans	Edwin H. Sheard	SP & S, Ltd
Dr Beer Returns	John Atkinson	SP & S, Ltd
Clara Case, Nurani	A. Rendle Short and S. Carvosso Gauntlett	SP & S Ltd
They Ran to Him	John C. Waite	SP & S, Ltd
East is East	Solveig Smith	SP & S, Ltd
Doctor in a Hurry	Leslie C. Rusher	Unpublished
The Call of the Jackals (A study on criminal work)	W. Bramwell Baird	Unpublished
The History of SA in Kerala (Travancore)	Joseph Chacko	Unpublished

Private papers of Henry Bullard, Herbert Mitchell, Muriel Booth-Tucker, Leslie J. Russell, Rose Flood and Herbert S. Hodgson.

The Staff Review, All the World, The Year Book, The Indian *War Cry,* Hospital Reports, the VTCs 10-year report, *The Musician* and other reports.

Synopsis of Chapters

Leaders for all India

Commissioner Frederick Booth-Tucker (Fakir Singh), 1883-1891
Colonel Lucy Booth-Hellberg (Ruhani), 1891-1896
Colonel Henry Bullard (Jai Singh), 1896-1898
Commissioner Edward Higgins Snr, 1898-1905
Colonel Joseph Hammond (Jang Singh), 1905-1907
Commissioner Frederick Booth-Tucker (Fakir Singh), 1907-1919

Territorial Commanders and Officers Commanding

1896	Colonel Grundy (Ishwar Das), Northern
	Colonel Paynter (Jai Bhai), Central
	Colonel Musa Bhai, Southern
1899	Lieut.-Colonel Clara Case (Nurani), Central, South 1905
	Brigadier Catherine Bannister (Yuddha Bai), Punjab
	Major John Hipsey (Yesu Das), Northern
	Brigadier William Stevens (Yesu Ratnam), South, 1917
	Major Arthur Blowers (Sukh Singh), Madras, Nagercoil 1903, Ceylon and South 1920
	Major John Hunter (Bahadur), Maharashstra
	Brigadier William Johnston (Jeya Kodi), Ceylon
1905	Brigadier Jivanandham, Marharashstra
	Lieut.-Colonel Frederick (Tej Singh), Punjab
	Brigadier Charles Knott (Weera Singh), Ceylon
1907	Brigadier Gustaf Hjelm (Himmat Singh), Ceylon
1908	Commissioner Arthur Blowers (Sukh Singh), Western, South and Ceylon 1919
1909	Lieut.-Colonel William S. Measures (Guru Singh), Ceylon
1912	Brigadier Van der Werken (Dayalee), Maharashstra
	Lieut.-Colonel Charles Duce (Iman Singh), Northern
	Brigadier James Melling (Deleri Singh), United Provinces
1915	Colonel Mary Tait, Ceylon
1917	Brigadier Fleury Clayden (Satguna), Ceylon
1919	Commissioner George Punter French (Ajeet Singh), Western
1920	Commissioner Henry Bullard (Jai Singh), Northern
1921	Colonel Harry G. Millner, Ceylon
	Lieut.-Commissioner Edgar Hoe (Hira Singh), Northern
	Lieut.-Commissioner Julius Horskins (Jivanand), Western
1923	Lieut.-Colonel Herbert Colledge (Prakram Singh), Ceylon, Madras and Telugu 1929, Western 1937
	Lieut.-Commissioner James Toft (Jai Kumar), Northern
	Colonel Stanley Ewens (Jaya Veera), Eastern, Western 1928
1924	Colonel Narayana Muthiah, Madras and Telugu, Northern 1929
	Mrs Lieut.-Colonel Annie Trounce (Priya), Southern (Lieut.-Commissioner)
1926	Colonel Charles Baugh (Himmat Singh), Northern
1928	Lieut.-Colonel William Hancock (Ko Ko Gyi), Burma
	Lieut.-Colonel Edward J. Coles, Ceylon
	Colonel Charles Mackenzie (Anandham), Eastern, Southern 1936
1929	Lieut.-Colonel John S. Bladin, Ceylon
1930	Lieut.-Colonel Gilbert Carter, Ceylon

1931	Colonel Alfred Barnett (Gnana Dasen), Western

1931   Colonel Alfred Barnett (Gnana Dasen), Western
1933   Major Arthur Hughes (Vidya Sagar), Burma, Pakistan 1948 (Lieut.-Colonel)
1934   Lieut.-Colonel Henry G. Bowyer, Ceylon
1936   Colonel Kate Stewart (Jeyavathie), Eastern
        Lieut.-Colonel William Pennick (Jai Singh), Madras and Telugu, Northern 1938
1938   Lieut.-Colonel Edwin Maslin (Daya Ratnam), Madras and Telugu
        Lieut.-Colonel Frank Mortimer (Yesu Prakash), Ceylon
1939   Lieut.-Colonel Alex Cunningham (Bharosa), Eastern, Southern 1945
1940   Brigadier Edward Walker (Jang Singh), Madras and Telugu
        Brigadier Joseph Lownes, Burma
1942   Brigadier Clayson Thomas, Burma
1944   Lieut.-Colonel William E. Carter (Gulab Singh), Northern, Eastern 1948
        Colonel Archibald Moffat (Sena Singh), Western
1945   Brigadier Victor Thompson (Jaya Theebam), Eastern, Ceylon 1949
        Lieut.-Colonel Janet Allan (Devoli), Madras and Telugu, Western 1951, Southern 1954 (Commissioner)
        Lieut.-Commissioner Herbert Hodgson (Vijai Singh), Northern, Western 1948
1946   Colonel Emma Davies, Ceylon, Madras and Telugu 1950
1947   Lieut.-Colonel Roy L. Rust (Vetha Dasen), Eastern
        Lieut.-Colonel Ivar Palmer (Muktanand), Madras and Telugu, Northern 1948, North-Eastern 1952, Southern 1957 (Commissioner)
        Colonel Edwin Sheard (Fauj Singh), Southern
1948   Colonel S. Manuel, Madras and Telugu, Southern 1950 (Lieut.-Commissioner)
1952   Lieut.-Colonel Muriel Booth-Tucker, Madras and Telugu
        Colonel Charles E. Green, Pakistan
1953   Lieut.-Commissioner Theo. Holbrook, Western
1954   Lieut.-Colonel Carl O. Richards, Pakistan
        Colonel M. Gwendoline Taylor, Ceylon, Pakistan 1960 (Lieut.-Commissioner)
1955   Brigadier W. Wycliffe Sharp, Burma
1957   Lieut.-Commissioner Joseph Dahya, North-Eastern, Southern, 1962, Western 1969 (Commissioner)
        Colonel E. Stanley Hannam, Madras and Telugu, Western 1960 (Lieut.-Commissioner)
1958   Lieut.-Colonel John Stobart, Ceylon
1960   Colonel Donald A. Sanjivi, Southern
        Colonel Lawrence V. L. Fletcher, Madras and Andhra, Burma 1951, North-Eastern 1962 (Lieut.-Commissioner)
        Brigadier Edwin Robertson, Burma (Lieut.-Colonel)
        Colonel Mrs Violet M. Stobart, Ceylon
1961   Colonel John W. Blake, Pakistan
1962   Colonel Arthur Long, Madras and Andhra, North-Eastern 1965 (Lieut.-Commissioner)
        Lieut.-Colonel Burton Pedlar, Ceylon, Ceylon 1966, Pakistan 1973

1963	Lieut.-Commissioner Catherine Jarvis, Ceylon, Sri Lanka 1972 (acting)

1963   Lieut.-Commissioner Catherine Jarvis, Ceylon, Sri Lanka 1972
      (acting)
1965   Lieut.-Commissioner Samuel Gnanaseelan, Madras and Andhra
      (Commissioner)
1966   Colonel Henry J. Warren, Western
      Colonel Don A. Smith, Pakistan
      Major Ba Sein, Burma (senior officer)
1969   Colonel Fazal Masih, North-Eastern (Lieut.-Commissioner)
      Colonel B. L. Benjamin, Pakistan (Lieut.-Commissioner)
      Colonel Harry Williams, Southern
1970   Lieut.-Colonel William Fleming, Sri Lanka
      Major Saratha Perieswami, Burma (liaison officer)
      Colonel V. Joseph Chelliah, South-Eastern
      Colonel James Kennedy, South-Western, Madras and Andhra
      1973
1973   Lieut.-Colonel P. E. George, South-Western (Commissioner)
      Commissioner Gladys Calliss, Sri Lanka
1974   Lieut.-Colonel Gordon Bevan, North-Eastern
      Colonel David Durman, Western
      Colonel Maurice Griffiths, South-Eastern, Western 1977
1975   Colonel Mannam Samuel, Madras and Andhra, Western 1980
1976   Colonel Gulzar Masih, Pakistan
      Colonel Jaikumas Makanji, North-Eastern
1977   Colonel Narayana J. Samuel, South-Eastern, Madras and Andhra
      1980
      Colonel Ernest Yendell, Pakistan
      Colonel Eva Burrows, Sri Lanka
      Lieut.-Colonel Kapliana, Eastern India Command
      Colonel Robert Bath, South-Western
1979   Colonel Arthur Holland, Pakistan (Commissioner)
      Colonel P. William Perera, Sri Lanka
1980   Colonel Douglas Kiff, Northern
      Colonel Inez M. Newberry, South-Eastern

South Asia territories and commands as at 1 October 1981

Burma Command
  Headquarters: 176-178 Anawrahta Street (Bigandet),
      East Rangoon; Tel: 16760.
  Liaison Officer: Major Saratha Perieswami.

Eastern India Command
  Headquarters: 37 Lenin Saranee, Calcutta 700 013;
      Tel: 24-3910
  Officer Commanding: Lieut.-Colonel Kapliana.

Madras and Andhra (India) Territory
  Headquarters: 15 Ritherdon Road, Vepery,
      Madras 600 007; Tel: 33148.
  Territorial Commander: Colonel Narayana J. Samuel.

Northern India Territory
  Headquarters: Rana Place, H-14 Green Park
      Extension, New Delhi 110 016;
      Tel: 662394.
  Territorial Commander: Colonel Douglas Kiff.

South-Eastern India Territory
  Headquarters: High Ground Road, Maharaja Nagar PO,
      Tirunelveli 627 011,
      Tirunelveli District, Tamil Nadu;
      Tel: 2682.
  Territorial Commander: Colonel Inez M. Newberry.

South-Western India Territory
  Headquarters: Kowdiar, Trivandrum 695 003,
      Kerala State; Tel: 60626.
  Territorial Commander: Colonel Mannam Samuel.

Western India Territory
  Headquarters: Sheik Hafizuddin Marg, Byculla,
      Bombay 400 008; Tel: 394705.
  Territorial Commander: Colonel Varampettan Sughanantham.

Pakistan
  Headquarters: 35 Shara-e-Fatima Jinnah,
      Lahore 4; Tel: 53422.
  Territorial Commander: Commissioner Arthur Holland.

Sri Lanka
  Headquarters: PO Box 193, 2 Union Place,
      Colombo 2; Tel: 24660.
  Territorial Commander: Colonel P. William Perera.